A confident life
in an age of change

For Janet,
Eileen and Megan,
'that you may know . . .' (1 John 5:13)

A confident life
in an age of change

Gavin J. McGrath

Inter-Varsity Press

INTER-VARSITY PRESS
38 De Montfort Street, Leicester LE1 7GP, England

Unless otherwise stated, Scripture quotations in this publication are from the Holy Bible, New International Version. Copyright © 1973, 1978, 1984 International Bible Society. Published in Great Britain by Hodder and Stoughton Limited.

First published 1995

ISBN 0-85111-141-6

Set in Palatino

Typeset in Great Britain by Parker Typesetting Service, Leicester

Printed in Great Britain by Cox & Wyman Ltd, Reading

Inter-Varsity Press is the book-publishing division of the Universities and Colleges Christian Fellowship (formerly the Inter-Varsity Fellowship), a student movement linking Christian Unions in universities and colleges throughout the United Kingdom and the Republic of Ireland, and a member movement of the International Fellowship of Evangelical Students. For information about local and national activities write to UCCF, 38 De Montfort Street, Leicester LE1 7GP.

Contents

Foreword

The end of the twentieth century is a tough time to know what to believe. It is especially difficult to apprehend the truth not only just amongst contending contradictory claims to truth. There is also a growing sense that, where important issues matter, there is no truth. Gavin McGrath knows this situation well, not just from contending with it for himself, but in hearing firsthand the stories of others as they have come to him for counsel.

The sources of our doubt are both the intensely personal and the culturally characteristic. Personally, we are beset with a sense of guilt for disobedience to what we sense is right. We wonder why we and others suffer pain in ordinary life as well as in troubling tragic events. Culturally, the postmodern rejection of rationality, objective morality and our identity as significant human beings undercuts the very foundations of our civilization. We long for a place to stand.

Gavin McGrath shows clearly why we can live our Christian lives with confidence that our faith is not misplaced. His answer takes us through the central motifs of Christian doctrine: biblical revelation, the creation and fall, the glory of Christ and the trustworthiness of God especially as manifested in Jesus.

Two aspects of Gavin McGrath's account are especially helpful. The first is his explanation of the role of biblical revelation and why it is trustworthy. Second is his insistence that the foundation of our confidence does not rest with us. Rather it rests with God himself. He reveals himself to us as we engage in worship, community with other Christians, Bible study, prayer and meditation. It is not *our faith* that holds us firm; it is the *object of our faith* who himself engages us. This means that confidence is not so much an intellectual certainty that certain propositions about God and us are true, as it is a *lived experience*, an encounter with God, his people and his world.

Gavin McGrath explains a host of reasons why our faith in God need not be an irrational leap in the dark. I was struck, for example, by the coherence and explanatory power of the biblical worldview as he explains it. It really does make sense out of the confused chaos of our lives. But Gavin McGrath's main goal, and his main contribution to a healthy Christian life of faith, is to demonstrate why we can live a confident Christian life and to show us how to do so.

Since placing my faith in Christ almost fifty years ago, I have never been a heavy doubter. Still this book has helped me understand much better why consistent confidence is the natural child of Christian faith.

James W. Sire

Preface

I doubt, therefore, I write. Allow me to explain. The Swiss writer, Paul Tournier, in *The Meaning of Persons*, wrote, 'For me, to write is to converse with my readers, known and unknown. It is to raise with them questions which are raised for me in my own contact with life.' While writing this work, I began to understand what he meant. I do not parade my struggles as a noble virtue; at the same time, I cannot deny their reality and influence. I have tried to be both honest and objective. You, the reader, must judge. Two further prefatory comments are necessary.

First, this book is *theological*. By this I refer to what we can know about the one true God: the creator God and Father of the Lord Jesus Christ, who dwells in his people by his Spirit. I am concerned with how knowing and relating to this God influences our confidence. I begin here, rather than with the psychological or sociological significance of confidence. I deal with ideas of people (both past and present) and how these ideas relate to biblical passages and the Bible's general themes (as I understand them). I hope I move from exegesis (though it may not be given explicitly) to doctrine. Theological doctrine and how doctrine relates to contemporary ideas shape this book. Most of us in today's Christian communities are theologically confused, for reasons I explain. Many of our experiential problems follow from this. It seems to me we have become weary of thinking, evaluating and pondering on a *theological* level.

Admittedly, some readers, picking up a book on *confidence*, might wish for emphasis on human temperament and psychology and their relationship to confidence. Others, especially those in pastoral counselling ministries, would probably wish for step-by-step guidelines to specific pastoral problems. There are many excellent and available books that offer help along both lines; I would only be duplicating their work. Instead, I try to offer a theological framework in which we can think through, pray over and work on particular issues. My sense is that we need this framework just as much as we need others to help us manage some of life's problems from the vantage points of psychology or pastoral methodology. My small contribution is in pointing to this theological framework.

I hasten to add, however, that this book does not come close to a full theological study. I hope those wanting to go further in their thinking will look to the references and comments in the notes. It will also become apparent that few of the good ideas in this book are mine: I am deeply indebted to thinkers of the past, especially John Calvin and John Owen (on whom my PhD research was based). Equally, I owe considerable credit to the thinking and ministry of the late Francis Schaeffer, whom I wish I had met. Though they would not necessarily agree with all my conclusions, I am also grateful to the important work by Harold Netland, Diogenes Allen, John Stott, James Sire, Jim Packer, Os Guinness, and Tom Wright. When I use the word *theological*, I have in mind their writings and the (albeit differing) models they present.

The second comment I wish to make is this. If I have been rightly theological then I trust this book is truly *experiential*. I unashamedly follow the lead of the Reformers of the sixteenth and seventeenth centuries and the later English Puritans. As Richard Baxter (1615–1691) once wrote, 'Divinity is a practical science.' All the material in this book was originally worked out in real-life situations by a pastor-teacher, addressing Christians and those who, by their own admission, would not call themself Christian. I was furthermore fortunate to present parts of this work to groups in the Netherlands, Finland, the USA and Bulgaria. There are real faces to the material in this book.

I hope, therefore, that my writing will help people in their evangelism (which includes biblical apologetics) and pastoral care of contemporary men and women. I would like to think that some readers will see the theological framework I point to and say, 'Well, that's nothing new, but I now see better how much there is to share with people.' The benefits come when, with this framework, readers appreciate the symbiotic relationship between theology and experience. Problems in one affect the other. When we are clear and honest in one and striving to be truthful in the other, then come growth, maturity and wisdom. It is with this conviction that I offer this small book.

As is customary and right in a preface, I want to thank various people. Special acknowledgment must go to Colin Duriez of Inter-Varsity Press. His kindness, encouragement and editorial skill enabled me in this work. I also greatly appreciate the careful reading of an earlier version of the manuscript by John Horder and Jock McGregor. All errors and infelicities, however, are entirely my responsibility.

I wish to thank the members of Christ Church, Fulwood, Sheffield. Through the years they heard bits and pieces of what appears in this work. Their care and support remain a valued part of my life. Particular thanks go to Dr Robert L. Webb, now living and teaching in Canada, who encouraged me in this project from the beginning. His critical reading of the manuscript was a great help; but he does not share my errors or faulty conclusions. Nick Kirkpatrick-Wilson graciously and generously helped me regarding the intricacies of personal computing. Fiona Lockwood read each chapter and offered thoughtful reactions. My thanks also go to the hundreds of university students, who, over the years, have crowded into our home on Sunday nights. Their questions, their responses to various lectures, and their lives, influenced this book more than they know or appreciate.

Finally, I want to express gratitude to my family. My daughters, Eileen and Megan, lived through the days of irony, struggle and final accomplishment. Eileen's question, 'Daddy, *why* are you writing a book?' has been a salutary interrogative. More than anyone else, my wife, Janet, deserves heartfelt acknowledgment. Her own burden to meet, help and speak to contemporary people encourages me enormously. Ultimately, her daily reminder of him who is greater than my doubts is one of his gifts that I might know and experience legitimate confidence in these changing days. To him, I owe everything. *Soli Deo gloria.*

Introduction:
The search for confidence

A legitimate goal, desired by all

A new look at an old problem

Contemporary western culture may be no worse than previous cultures, but as we come to the end of the century and millennium, things are not quite right. True, there have been some important social advances, benefiting us all. We need not plunge into a pool of despair. Yet how could our modern life, with all the advantages and advancements, be so threatening to so many today? It is only one era of a long history of human existence. It seems, however, that something hard and fast is knocking our grip on life.

Must I give examples? Wars with frightening technology persist, showing that some modern technological developments lead to both blessings and curses – depending on which side you are on in the conflict. Famines in Africa reveal both the fragility of some economies and the greed of the richer nations. Political instability in various parts of the world eclipses optimism elsewhere. Marriages break down, leaving wounded men and women and bewildered children. 'Crack' and other forms of cocaine are the means for many young people, even children, to buy the material goods that catch their eye. Our western society seems exhausted and broken.

Nevertheless, in the midst of this troubled modern life are people who love, care, create, think and live. Again, not everything in life should cause doubts or misgivings. New symphonies are written, plays performed, paintings painted, and babies born. While some people catch the attention of the media, most are not necessarily glamorous or remarkable. Yet ordinary people live life bravely, especially in the face of uncertainties.

One group particularly intrigues me. Why? They are different from others. What distinguishes them is their belief in a creator

12

God, known supremely in Jesus Christ. They are Christians. Christians live in this world, where there are uncertainties and problems. Life for Christians has its variations, which both invigorate and challenge. Life is not something to avoid but to live. Jesus stressed the complexity of a disciple's life. But, I ask more and more, does being a Christian give a true and real handle on life? Does Christianity fit with the way life really is?

I move in the direction of these questions because, from time to time, life gets just a bit too raw, even for Christians. Questions emerge.

'God, how can I be sure I really do trust and believe in you? Was it just a contrived experience? Are you simply a projection of my own needs?'

'Lord, I've sinned again the very same way I've been doing all these years. Have I gone too far? Is there a limit to your forgiveness and love?'

'Jesus, are you truth? My friends are not even interested in truth!'

Admittedly, there are particular assumptions in these questions. Yet one thing is intriguing. They are asked not by the faithless, but by the faithful. They are looking for something. They want assurance. I can say this because I am a Christian, a follower of Jesus, God's King. As a Christian living in this present age I wrestle with particular questions.

The problem is not just 'Am I a Christian? Am I saved?' It is more striking, 'Can I be sure what I believe is even true? Is Christianity really the best option, considering the other available choices today? Am I experiencing the truth?' A lot is at stake when it comes to the worldview (a way of perceiving, understanding and interpreting all of existence) we accept. As Diogenes Allen, in *Christian Belief in a Postmodern World*, puts it:

> The needs religion fills are relevant to an assessment of its truth, as we shall see, but were it merely a matter of finding religion to be helpful, then a religious commitment would not be essentially different from a personal preference. We would rightly say that some people prefer to be Christian rather than something else or nothing at all merely as a matter of taste. But when something is said to be true, we have a different situation, especially when it is said of a religion.

Christian, as well as other religious claims, are so serious and so demanding personally that adherence to them cannot be properly described as merely a matter of personal taste.[1]

Allen's valid point is that we all – whether we are Christians or not – need an awareness of the way things really are. Our lives matter. For those of us who are contemporary Christians, we deal with many of the same challenges, opportunities, joys and problems that people of other faiths and no faith at all have to face. The Christian, however, faces a particular concern. In the midst of life's diverse issues, at the centre of all of them is a common requirement. Can we live in our contemporary world, confident that biblical Christianity and our experience as Christians are truth? This relates to people who have been Christians for many years, and those relatively new to the Christian faith.

The issues are so diverse and wide-ranging that I believe we must go further than a search for personal assurance. Assurance is vital. But as I argue in this book, our assurance must lead to a confidence that Christianity is really truth. It is the best-fitting worldview. This confidence is more than an intellectual conclusion or an emotional feeling. It is both, and yet much more.

What is this confidence and what does it mean? I define Christian confidence as *a consequence of my faith in Jesus Christ, brought about over time by the Holy Spirit, experienced in my heart and realized in my mind, that God's promises in the gospel are true and personally applicable to me as a believer.*[2] Here we see the close association between personal assurance and that which extends further: a conviction that the basis for personal assurance is the universal truthfulness of the gospel. In other words, a Christian can legitimately say, 'By God's grace and Holy Spirit I know that my Christian experience is true, even with my inconsistencies and problems. And the reason I can say this is that what the gospel of Christ tells me is true, the way things really are.' There is a subjective side to confidence and an objective reality to confidence. This confidence is God-given, essential and universally relevant to God's people throughout history. To be a Christian involves confidence.

Let us go further to illustrate this point.

Christian confidence *relates to the whole of a Christian's life*. What

14

do I mean? The good news is that *true* Christian confidence, in contrast to foolish arrogance or stoic self-denial, is all-embracing. It touches upon every aspect and dimension of a believer's relationship with the Lord. No matter what we experience in the Christian life, the importance of confidence arises. It is part and parcel of the whole of Christian living.

Think of it this way. In a healthy marriage a husband and wife sense a confidence in the love they receive from each other. We could ask them, 'Are you sure your spouse loves you?'

'Yes,' they answer.

'But how do you know for sure?'

If they thought about it, their confidence in each other's love is almost indistinguishable from how they talk with each other, how they share household responsibilities, the gifts they exchange on birthdays, and the physical intimacy they enjoy. Confidence in marriage is not something a spouse can pick up and hold like the family car keys. It is part of the couple's day-to-day living. Their confidence impinges on the entirety of their relationship.

Similarly, the Christian's life in relationship with the Lord is always greater than the sum of its parts. The Christian life is a relationship between God and a person as a member of God's larger family. This is what the Bible calls a covenant relationship. Individual theological doctrines can describe the qualities and dynamics of this relationship. These doctrines are far from dry and abstract, but explain and highlight the relationship between God and his people. Nonetheless, the confidence we will consider is more than a single theological doctrine or a particular philosophical idea; it is central to a *personal relationship* between the one true God and humanity.[3]

To search for confidence is not to lack faith

'But,' someone in our church fellowship says, 'every believing Christian *ought not* to question the truthfulness of the gospel. To question is to make too much out of a person's problems, it is all too introspective – one of the marks of today's generation.' This objection may have its merit, but for one point. Searching for confidence and desiring confidence is not just a present-day problem. It is not simply that today's Christians are weaker or spiritually lazier than previous generations. We may well be, but this is not the immediate point. Even the faithful look for the confidence defined above.

From the days of the patriarch Abraham, who waited for God's promise, to Moses, the leader of the Hebrews during their exile from Egypt and years of wandering in the wilderness, to the passionate cries of the psalmists, to the prophet Jeremiah, who struggled in an apostate culture, to John the Baptist, who wondered about the ministry of Jesus of Nazareth, to Jesus, who himself in the Garden of Gethsemane faced the horrific implications of his own imminent death, to the early apostolic church, with all their trials, the Scriptures illustrate the very real, painful and complex search for confidence. Also, some of the best-known Christian writers have wrestled with the question of confidence. We think of Augustine's *Confessions*, Martin Luther's hope found at last in the letter to the Romans, John Bunyan's labyrinth-like spiritual journey in his autobiography, *Grace Abounding to the Chief of Sinners*, and John Wesley's liberating experience at a meeting in Aldersgate Street. These are familiar examples of the search for what I call confidence.

I also think of those who will never publish their journals or write their memoirs. There was the man who came to me with all the passion his agnosticism could muster, but weeks later tearfully pleaded to know, 'Could Jesus Christ really accept me?' An elderly man who knew and trusted the promises of the gospel of Jesus Christ, yet facing death from cancer, worried about his (as he put it to me) 'weak and unemotional' love for God. The university student with whom I spoke one afternoon was not the first to ask me if the quality of her lifestyle could nullify her profession of faith made years before. There have been others who struggled with confusion about guidance or the pain of suffering, wondering if such confusion and discomfort indicated God's displeasure with them. Those on the frontlines of contemporary evangelism who encounter the doubts, bewilderment and hostility of our postmodern culture occasionally wonder, 'If the gospel is so powerful, why are there not greater results?' People ask these questions when a close friend, family member or spouse seems, for the moment anyway, uninterested and resistant to the gospel.

So let us be clear about one thing right from the start: to search for confidence is not to lack faith. Individuals' personalities, situations and intellectual abilities differ, but those who recognize the need for confidence have not necessarily lost their faith. It is an astonishing paradox, but their faith in the one true God may well be strong, growing and rich. It just may not feel like it all the time.

God's people have always wanted *true* confidence. Certainly one generation's problems may be different from another's. For example, living during the great eighteenth-century spiritual revivals in England and New England must have been different in some significant ways from the experience of believers in Stalin's Soviet Union. Yet there are subtle, but real, parallels. Can God be trusted? Is the gospel truth? Who really rules in world affairs? There are some aspects of living by faith in the one true triune God that transcend every culture and point in history. Contexts differ, but because people are people there are some significant constants.

In fact, throughout this book I will draw upon the insights of previous generations in order to help contemporary Christians. Sometimes we need, as it were, to stand on their shoulders to see over the particular hurdles facing us at the close of the twentieth century. The need for confidence is universal and transcultural. Christians have always wanted confidence.

A confident life is not a problem-free life

Throughout this book we will see that confidence does not exclude struggles. At this early point in my argument it may seem like a contradiction, but as a Christian grows in confidence she or he may experience all sorts of challenges. This is a fact of life for a follower of Jesus. We need to understand that Christian confidence, as I define it throughout this book, is not the same thing as 'the victorious life' or the 'triumphant life' – both occasionally offered in some quarters of today's church.

No, on the contrary; some of the most confident Christians I know have been in tough and trying circumstances: single parents, former prisoners in Communist countries, victims of abuse, cancer patients, and unemployed people. We do not have to have these experiences to know Christian confidence. On the other hand, these situations do not automatically keep us from experiencing true confidence.

Undoubtedly, unnecessary and unhelpful fear, introspection, or wrong behaviour can develop as a person struggles for confidence.

There are times when these problems should be confronted. Rebuking unhelpful thinking, emotions or behaviour, however, can sometimes cause more problems. Searching for confidence is not faithlessness; it may be honest doubt.[4] It is important to ask questions about what we believe. Our experience of life often forces us to do so. Other people, who may not share our faith in Christ, do too, and their questions and criticisms are not insignificant. There are times and circumstances which are not at all clear-cut. I think it is quite legitimate to read the Psalms and wisdom literature (especially Job) and the prayer concerns of Paul in his letters and see that doubt is not altogether a mark of total faithlessness. Doubt that humbly seeks for understanding and correction is frequently the sign of greater growth and learning. If nothing else, it certainly is part of the believer's struggle in this world. We should consider what the Reformer John Calvin (1509–1564) wrote:

> Surely, while we teach that faith ought to be certain and assured, we cannot imagine any certainty that is not tinged with doubt, or any assurance that is not assailed by some anxiety. On the other hand, we say that believers are in perpetual conflict with their own unbelief. Far, indeed, are we from putting their consciences in any peaceful repose, undisturbed by any tumult at all. Yet, once again, we deny that, in whatever way they are afflicted, they fall away and depart from the certain assurance received from God's mercy.[5]

Despite the problems of introspection and self-concern, searching for confidence among today's Christians is important and legitimate. It is the pursuit of the faithful.

Seeing the grand interrelationship: the theological framework and our personal experience

A Christian's confidence ultimately depends upon who God is and what he promises and accomplishes. This implies that our confidence is not immediately based on us. Yet we must quickly acknowledge that our personalities, temperaments and circumstances have a great influence. Still, the point to stress is that who we are is not as paramount as who God is and what he does.

This is what (I sense) is easily forgotten or misunderstood in our contemporary Christian circles. Even in good pastoral counselling and ministry this essential theological truth can either be assumed too quickly (and without careful consideration) or forgotten due to the complexities of temperament, situation or behavioural consequences. This is why I want us to think *theologically* in our pastoral care and counselling. Many of our problems over a lack of confidence are because of the theological confusion of *today*.

We need to see the interrelationship between many truths: who God is and how this God makes himself known (revelation), the profound significance of the person of Jesus of Nazareth (incarnation), Christ's self-offering on the cross (atonement), the pardon and peace that God offers in the gospel (justification), the very real and hopeful promise that God can change us (sanctification), the continued care and concern that the risen Lord Jesus has for his church (mediation), and the ultimate confidence that time and history are moving towards a final point, namely, the return in history of Jesus the Lord (eschatology). Each deserves a book, but we are principally concerned with how each contributes to Christian confidence. These truths compose the theological framework in which we know and experience Christian confidence today.

I stress *today* for another reason. While confidence inextricably relates to the doctrinal whole, the need for confidence is very much an *experiential* reality. People may know the truth but feel and live in contradictory ways. They can understand right doctrine but find in their day-to-day life situations, choices and people that throw their thinking into a bundle of inconsistencies and inadequacies. Perhaps this is a pastoral warning for those of us prone to excessive abstractions or obtuse theological arguments. Confidence will not come from just intellectual persuasion of doctrinal formulae.

This book is for people trying to *live* by faith *now*, at the close of the twentieth century. It does little good to sit in our theological armchairs and offer a clever understanding of confidence if it does not help us to live in our contemporary culture. If we cannot offer a valid, relevant and beneficial confidence for Christians living in our changing age, then we are, sadly, no more helpful than the band that played on the *Titanic*.

So chapters 1 and 2 describe the context in which we live today. I focus on two aspects to highlight the demand for Christian confidence. Chapter 1 examines some personal experiences that a Christian may face, illustrating how important is the need for the right kind of confidence. Perhaps some readers will recognize the necessity for confidence and then hope that I will move on to provide a step-by-step guide to experiencing confidence. This is not only difficult, it is, in my opinion, doomed to failure. In the first instance it can easily overlook the fact that people are individuals. Furthermore, these guides or books of pastoral methods run the risk of being simplistic. In what way?

We must appreciate how some important changes in the way people think and evaluate life make the quest for confidence today so challenging. This aspect, I believe, is often missing in well-meaning counsel. Chapter 2, therefore, presents the contemporary, *postmodern*, intellectual and philosophical changes, or shifts, that contribute to the experiential problems identified in chapter 1. Both chapters are essential to the context in which Christian confidence must take place. I will argue that only by appreciating both these aspects will we develop the specific implications and benefits of Christian confidence in today's world. In chapter 3, and the following chapters, we look at essential theological truths in relation to confidence. Here I present what I called in the Preface the theological framework in which we can work through pastoral problems. Some of our problems and questions may not have easily identified answers, but seeing the framework helps us press on and not give up in despair. In this respect, we conclude in chapter 9 with how we experience Christian confidence – in all its fullness as well as its impartiality. Our complete confidence waits for the day when the Lord Jesus returns and accomplishes the totality of his purpose and plan. Supremely, Christian confidence in our present age depends upon our hope and patient longing for the coming age.

I hope all readers will think hard about the people they know, and themselves too, who try to live by faith today. I am convinced it is possible to receive helpful and significant confidence. I base this entirely on the God who is, who acts, who speaks, who is knowable and who gives us truth that we may know and have a confident life, even in an age of change.

1

The face in the mirror

Problems in our personal life

The experiential side of life

The American humorist and author Garrison Keillor stated it
perfectly: 'Life is complicated and not for the timid. It's an
experience that when it's done, it will take us a while to get over
it.'[1] His words underline what we often *feel*; and what we feel is
part and parcel of our experience. Life is never theoretical, it is
always actual.

Consequently, Christian confidence in an age of change has to
interact with the personal *experience* of the Christian. Our daily
experience matters as much as the powerful influence of our
culture. We need assistance with living as disciples. Of course,
experience alone does not determine the truth of Christianity. Our
experience does not authenticate God's truths. Yet, because God
calls us into a reconciled *relationship* with him, through Jesus
Christ, we can never sufficiently speak of Christian confidence in
abstract theoretical terms alone. The struggle for confidence is not
simply the result of our failure to understand various passages of
the Bible or postmodernity's philosophical challenge. Our problems never occur in an existential vacuum. The questions we ask
today exist in real-life actualities, in other words, the 'stuff' of life.
Christian living is never theoretical, it is always actual.

What does this look like? In this chapter we look at the
relationship between our struggles and our confidence in God's
promises. Doctrine and existential problems intersect; their
convergence is where we live by faith moment by moment. Six
particular issues arise: guilt; the acts of obedience in Christian
discipleship; pain and suffering; guidance; frustration; and the fear
of 'falling away'. We will pay close attention to the ways in which
these problems lead to tension in the relationship between the

doctrinal and the experiential. Christian confidence in an age of change has to correspond to this interconnection.

1. Guilt

Probably the most frustrating problem for Christians is guilt. This is ironic, for an essential aspect of biblical Christianity is the complete satisfaction and reconciliation between God and the believer through Christ's merit and death on the cross.[2] Guilt is answered and satisfied. When a man or woman understands and accepts this refreshing gospel hope, his or her life is radically transformed. This marvellous truth is the bedrock of their existence. The problem, however, is day-to-day living. Richard Lovelace, in his book *Dynamics of Spiritual Life*, writes:

> Only a fraction of the present body of professing
> Christians are solidly appropriating the justifying work
> of Christ in their lives. Many have so light an
> apprehension of God's holiness and of the extent and
> guilt of their sin that consciously they see little need for
> justification, although below the surface of their lives
> they are deeply guilt-ridden and insecure.[3]

Lovelace expresses theologically what many believers experience. But what does he mean in practice? We can highlight at least three experiential paradoxes.

First, there is the riddle of how to deal with our guilt feelings. It is helpful to draw a distinction between guilt feelings and true or moral guilt. We may feel guilty when, in fact, there is no objective or substantiated validity to these feelings. A person's guilt feelings may be the result of another's manipulative suggestions, say, a parent's, spouse's, friend's or child's. These suggestions may have very little to do with fact. Exaggeration and misunderstanding, rather than accuracy, might account for the guilt feelings. For example, consider Jane (not her real name).

In her childhood, Jane was rarely praised or encouraged by her parents. They loved her and wanted the best for her. Unfortunately (for all concerned), they demanded the best from her. If she brought home a painting from school, her parents were more concerned with how her work related to the other children's. As she grew up, and, like most adolescents, went through

THE FACE IN THE MIRROR

'awkward' stages, severe words were spoken when she accidentally spilt her glass of milk or when she forgot to put the top back on the toothpaste or if she ate her meals too quickly. When she began dating boys, her parents displayed an over-protective attitude, but they were more critical of her personal values than of the boys she dated. She took on a way of evaluating herself which was overly analytical and even judgmental. Jane was quite an achiever in school. By the time I met her, however, she was constantly fearful and insecure. She told me she felt 'not good enough. I feel guilty, sometimes not really knowing why'. Jane thought this was a theological problem. Indeed, it was causing problems for her as she considered the gospel. I gently suggested, however, that her problems had less to do with theology than with poor self-esteem and unnecessary guilt. The gospel can meet her where she is, and answer her problems. At the same time, unconditional love and acceptance, of which the gospel speaks, is what she needs in the light of her damaging guilt feelings.

In other circumstances, there is real guilt. By 'real' I mean what is objective, external and not imaginary. For example, in *Schindler's List*, Steven Spielberg's film portrayal of Nazi attrocities committed against Polish Jews, the camp commandant does not display any remorse for his actions. He gave evidence of no guilt feelings. Nonetheless, despite orders given to him from his superiors, he incurred true, objective guilt. He is an extreme example, but there are lesser cases too. If I exceed the speed limit (knowingly or even unknowingly) I incur real guilt because there are laws prescribing speed limits and the consequences of exceeding those limits. We might think this a trivial matter, until someone hits us or runs into our child! Then there is moral outrage. When we watch movies like *Schindler's List* or hear of random crime or tragic accidents, we are emotionally upset. We are (or should be) morally disturbed. We say things like, 'But it's not right, it's wrong.' Why?

There is ultimate, true and real morality because God is moral. This supremely explains why we are upset over injustices. There is good reason for us to be disturbed. Moreover, when we act, think, speak and live in ways that are contrary to true and valid morality, we are guilty. We may not necessarily *feel* guilty or be even aware of our guilt, yet the validity remains. Thus, a distinction between guilt feelings and true guilt is philosophically and psychologically helpful, but only up to a point.

The difficulty is that our experience is rarely this clear-cut. Life's complexity makes guilt problematic. There are times and situations when guilt feelings are invalid and unhelpful; for a variety of complicated reasons, we have them anyway. Think back to my friend Jane. At other times guilt feelings may show what Christians call 'conviction'. This is an inner appreciation caused by the Holy Spirit and the Word of God (the Bible) that our behaviour or attitude concerning a particular issue is wrong. I recall a businessman, responding to a sermon, telling me how he *knew* God confronted him about the ethics of a particular investment he made. He was convinced he had to take decisive steps to get out of this investment. In his case (and I had to take his word for it), things looked clear. There were many other business people who heard the same sermon, but may not have felt the same in response. Not all in life is clear-cut. Yet, how do we tell the difference? In the mess and jumble of normal living it is not always easy to diagnose our problem with dispassionate clarity.

The second relevant paradox about forgiveness in Christ and our experience in Christ involves the aim and motivation of our life *precisely as Christians*. As followers of Jesus Christ, we live with the knowledge that we ought not to live contrary to God's will. We trust that God pardons our past, present and future. Furthermore, we know we are progressively changing through the work of the Holy Spirit to become more Christlike. Appropriately, a new way of choosing, responding and living shapes our life. We are not to live as we used to live. This is the 'ought not' of our existence. To state it the other way around, we are not only freed *from* sin and emptiness, we are free *for* holiness. These are important truths and wonderful promises.

Yet here too guilt casts its shadow. It is quite common for Christians to exclaim, 'If God is changing me, then why am I still messing things up?!' Many a Christian who struggles with homosexual attractions, and out of repentance seeks to stay celibate, is pained by the continued temptations, even more by the occasional glance at certain glossy magazines or videos. We can think of other examples: proud, angry outbursts, jealousy, clever verbal put-downs or shoplifting.

Do followers of Jesus Christ really do such things? Some do;

many do not. *All* Christians, however, do what they ought not. This is not the culpability incurred through ignorance, social conformity or omission. Such problems are in an altogether different category, though equally serious. Actual, deliberate and wilful acts create a real and unavoidable experiential tension.

We continue to struggle with wrong habits, thought patterns and attitudes. Have we tried rationalizing the problems away? ('Well, I'm not perfect and, after all, perhaps I'm being just a bit too legalistic.') Have we asked the Lord for change? ('Maybe if this well-known Christian in the healing ministry laid hands on me . . .')? Did either alternative really and effectively work? Of course, there are those claiming the victorious life. There has always been, and probably always will be, the tendency among some towards antinomianism (the Christian life has nothing to do with obeying moral laws) or the search for an additional experience (second-blessing holiness).

Even if these positions are not immediately evident, some well-intentioned Christians will draw a tidy theological distinction between temptation and the actual sin: 'It is no sin to be tempted. Jesus was tempted, wasn't he? It's what you do with the temptation.' There is a degree of truth here but also a subtle problem. Strictly speaking, it is not sinful to be tempted. Nevertheless, consider the attraction and appeal of temptation itself. Personally, more often than I care to admit, I struggle with specific temptations because of particular weaknesses in my character and temperament. Each of us has our Achilles' heel, or vulnerabilities: often the result of our previous foolishness and acts of wilful disobedience. The distinction between sin and temptation may be theologically accurate, but in practice it is a moot point.

We might encounter another line of advice: 'You are free, you don't need to do what you are doing!' I heard a Christian psychologist tell a group of Christian men that they could overcome heterosexual fantasies and lust. They could work at thinking about other, more positive, things. Think instead of cross-country skiing or a game of tennis or, even, memorize certain portions of the Bible. It's just as 'easy' as that.

There is a considerable measure of truth in this counsel, and thinking about what is positive and pure can help. Thinking and meditating on the truths of Scripture are important and valuable ways of living an obedient life. Christians need not sin. No external constraining force compels us to sin. Temptations never nullify our volitional capabilities. Nevertheless, certain techniques can lead to fascinating mental gymnastics but help very little. It is possible to minimize the painful reality of our existence in a fallen world. Though redeemed, we still struggle with a continued measure of the fall's reality (see Rom. 7:14–26 and Gal. 5:16–26) around us and in us.[4] Moreover, we can too easily cheat – thinking we have conquered a problem when instead the problem (be it lust, pride, envy or anger) creeps into another part of our day-to-day living.

A third aspect of a Christian's experiential struggle with guilt concerns, paradoxically, the Bible. Imagine the woman (or man) whose marriage has failed. Her spouse left her for a younger woman, one whom he thinks is more exciting and more affirming. Of course, she concludes, what her husband did is wrong. Nonetheless, she cannot help but wonder if she gave into his demands for divorce too quickly. Was she wrong? Her friends tell her 'No'. Yet on Wednesday night, in a home-group Bible study, her group happens to reach a critical point in their study of Malachi 2. In the midst of the denunciation of Israel's rebellion, a particular rebuke comes: ' "I hate divorce," says the LORD God of Israel, "and I hate a man's covering himself with violence as well as with his garment," says the LORD Almighty. So guard yourself in your spirit, and do not break faith' (2:16). Despite the leader's best efforts and the other participants' assurances, she is desolate. Would she have been better off, she thinks, not reading the Bible?

On the one hand, God's Word arrests the Christian in his or her impropriety. Consider the example of the businessman I mentioned earlier, who spoke to me after hearing a sermon. This is the work of God's grace and mercy, and we should thank the Lord for it. Even in judgment there is the positive call to repentance. On the other hand, a Christian's self-perceived guilt may be compounded by reading certain passages in Scripture, like the woman in her home-group Bible study.

We only have to read Matthew 5:48; 7:15–23; John 15:2, 6; 1 Timothy 1:19b–20; Hebrews 6:4–8; 10:26–31; 2 Peter 3:17–18, along with the story of the Israelites in the wilderness wanderings (Ex. 32; Nu. 12, 14, and 16), the fall of Samson (Jdg. 16) and the tragic failure of Saul (1 Sa. 15), to close the Bible wincing. When we read of the awesomeness of hell and final judgment, we are confronted with a serious problem. Either we ignore those passages, and deny their more immediate and obvious meanings, or we take them seriously.[5] Later in this chapter we will consider the issue of 'falling away'. At the moment, the issue is the way in which these biblical passages can increase a person's struggles with guilt.

To be sure, one person can take these verses out of context just as easily as another can reduce them to nothingness. Equally, what may be in question is the individual's self-perceived guilt. Self-perception can be both hypercritical and excessively lenient. Appropriately, we would want to insist, 'Balance these passages with others!' Yes, indeed; but the *experiential* question can remain large and daunting: 'Am I claiming the Bible's promises and benefits presumptuously and improperly?'

Guilt relates to self-awareness but also to Christian confidence. Over 300 years ago, John Owen (1616–1683), in his book *The Nature, Power, Deceit and Prevalency of the Remainders of Indwelling Sin in Believers* (1668), wisely suggested: 'The man that understands the evil of his own heart, how vile it is, is the only useful, fruitful, and solidly believing and obedient person.'[6] Obviously more needs to be considered. As Owen implied, we need to understand ourselves accurately. The problems of guilt and the continued struggle with sin are powerfully disruptive. If we are to offer a legitimate confidence, it must deal with these issues.

2. The acts of obedience in Christian discipleship

We become Christians by grace through faith in Jesus Christ. We repent from sin. Our lives are not only marked by forgiveness; they are also characterized by discipleship. The New Testament writers tell us not only what a disciple is, but what a disciple does. It is like two sides of the same coin.

There is a complication. A Christian knows that faith expresses itself in obedience. Obedience is the outworking of faith. Taking it a step further, faith is more often than not expressed in duties. Duties are particular acts that correspond to and promote our fellowship with the Lord. Believers look to prayer, studying Scripture, giving of time and money for Christian service, worship, sharing our faith, standing up for issues of justice and performing our vocation to the best of our ability. In these activities faith is expressed in obedience and obedience is the corollary of faith. The two are distinguishable but inseparable.

Dietrich Bonhoeffer, the German theologian murdered by the Nazis, wrote: 'Faith is only real when there is obedience, never without it, and faith only becomes faith in the act of obedience.'[7] Bonhoeffer is a stirring challenge to us. That, however, is actually the rub: *us*. Here is another precise theological statement that becomes profoundly complicated in practice. In our lives we try to separate faith and obedience. Nonetheless, they are inextricably related.

How do we avoid legalism at one end of the spectrum, paroxysms of guilt in the middle and presumptuous laziness at the other end? Do we measure our walk with Christ by our performance of duties? If not, dare we suggest that reading Scripture, prayer, sharing our faith, caring for others who are the victims of oppression and injustice are irrelevant or secondary? What we can say is duties are perplexing. Consider the following.

Many of us who have grown up as Christians in a particular style of spirituality learned that without a daily time of Bible reading and prayer our lives would be less than healthy. This is good advice. Ordering our day to spend time with the Lord is quite important. Nevertheless, a problem arises when we see 'quiet times' in excessively mechanical terms: if we miss a quiet time in the morning, the rest of our day will be a failure. It is possible to approach our quiet times with an almost medieval superstition, as if a half hour were like a lucky rabbit's foot.

When certain life pressures, however, complicate our day-to-day routine, guilt and anxiety develop. A Christian leader once told some friends and me, 'When the Reformer Martin Luther faced so many pressures and demands, he actually increased his time in prayer!' There is helpful counsel here, but it can crush an already stressed individual. A young mother, waking at various hours of the night to nurse a young baby, finds it difficult to have a disciplined devotional life. Sitting beside the hospital bed of a dying husband may involve powerful times of prayer and Bible reading but also the anguish of devotional irregularity.

Similarly, we know the crucial need to share the gospel with our family and friends. We pray and look for natural and right opportunities to share the gospel. Yet there is antagonism, indifference and ridicule of the good news. We accept it from some, but, if it is from loved ones, our theology battles with our heart. We run the gauntlet of conflicting emotions and thoughts. If we remain silent and hope that our lifestyle speaks more loudly than our words, what happens when our temper, laziness or forgetfulness emerge? If it is a matter of time, then how do we evaluate the situation if our parent or spouse is facing terminal cancer?

Perhaps some readers may wonder about the following example, but it is a real one in my work among university students. She has fallen in love with a non-Christian guy. They are thinking about marriage. Her anguish and concern are over-whelming, as she sits in my office. As we look at the biblical texts which, *she* knows, are rightly relevant, the conclusion hits her with full force. 'But it will hurt him so badly,' she explains. I agree, and point out that it will hurt her too. She admits she already knew that marrying someone not interested in Jesus Christ is fraught with problems. It would be terribly unwise. The cost of disciple-ship for her is very high, extremely demanding, because her boyfriend is caring, compassionate and genuinely nice. As she leaves my office, I cannot help but wonder what decision she will make. She needs confidence that obedience to Christ is intelligent and worthwhile, because living in today's age of change tells her the opposite.

Confidence must relate to these experiential complications. They raise questions about God's promises. Because we live in an age when many of us have difficulties with self-discipline, live a frenetic lifestyle, and there are a plethora of manipulators around, we should pay closer attention to Christian duties. Simultaneously, because we are inconsistent and falter due to complexities, our experience of Christian duties intersects with our need for true Christian confidence.

3. Pain and suffering

In his very helpful book on suffering, *How Long, O Lord?*, Don Carson reminds us that pain and suffering are very real. While we think of examples like war, natural disasters or gratuitous violence, just living brings us pain and suffering. He writes:

> The truth of the matter is that all we have to do is live
> long enough, and we will suffer. Our loved ones will
> die; we ourselves will be afflicted with some dis-
> ease or other. Midlife often brings its own pressures –

disappointments, sense of failure, decreasing physical strength, infidelity. Parents frequently go through enormous heartache in rearing their children . . . Live long enough and the infirmities of old age eventually catch up with you, compounded by the fact that all your friends have gone and left you alone.[8]

Suffering, pain, grief or psychological trauma are real and part of life. Yet I am convinced there is something more, and to which Christian confidence must relate.

Because God is who he is, pain and suffering are enigmatic. If there were no moral order, because the universe was empty of a personal God who would define morality, then pain would cease to pose its *ultimate* problem. People would acknowledge the physical problems of pain and suffering; they would have to do so even if humanity were reduced to merely a mechanistic or lower-animal level. Men and women bleed, cry and break. This is not, however (and we must express it carefully), the most demanding issue.

The fundamental problem of pain and suffering is *why* they occur. The question involves the relationship between good and bad, justice and injustice. Reconciling what is so painful and ugly with the God whom Christians know in Jesus Christ is the dilemma. If God is taken out of the equation, then the question ceases to have its ultimate significance. Because God is as he is, the quandary is real.

Suppose I arbitrarily beat my child in the course of her upbringing. I offered no explanation or justification; the beatings just occurred. Her context, the family, could initially provide no other framework in which she could evaluate her experience. 'This is my father and this is what he does.' She would, obviously, feel the physical pain. Yet in what sense could she think that these beatings were unfair and even evil? These moral terms, not just the evil physical abuse, introduce a whole other set of issues. She might well reach an intuitive conclusion that my behaviour was inappropriate, but inappropriate to what or whom? Only when she met other children and learned about their family life and other human relationships would she eventually conclude that the beatings she received were not only socially deviant; they were contrary to the very nature of what a *personal relationship* between a father and daughter should be. She would learn that beatings are not consistent with love, parenthood and relationships. Her question would be, 'Why would he do this?'

This horrifically illustrates the question 'why?' at the heart of our struggle with pain and suffering. At the most fundamental level pain and suffering do not make obvious sense in relationship to the revealed character of God. If he or she is consistent, the atheist cannot be too concerned with this question. The agnostic will struggle with it, indeed with anger or great, defiant courage; but in rejecting the framework of biblical revelation he or she will have to find an alternative way of resolving the dilemma. By contrast, while not at all indifferent to pain and human suffering, Sogyal Rinpoche, in his bestselling book *The Tibetan Book of Living and Dying*, quotes the Dalai Lama:

> Your suffering is due to your own karma, and you have to bear the fruit of that karma anyway in this life or another, unless you can find some way of purifying it. In that case, it is considered to be better to experience the karma in this life of a human where you have more abilities to bear it in a better way, than, for example, an animal who is helpless and can suffer even more because of that.[9]

Rinpoche's Buddhist counsel is attractive to many westerners, who have for too long either trivialized suffering and death, or faced them with anxiety and fear. Nonetheless, this advice (at least in his book) does not ask larger questions about suffering – namely, *why?* Instead, we are urged to move through these experiences with spiritual sensitivity and awareness, following our *karma*. My observations, therefore, are that those who view life through a Judeo-Christian world view will feel and think through the problem of pain and suffering with the greatest discomfort.

But read me clearly. We cannot minimize any human's suffering! Christians *do not* suffer more than others. Because of the character of the God with whom believers are in a personal relationship, however, pain and suffering hurt. At the level of raw human experience, pain and suffering stand seemingly in profane contrast to the revealed character of God.

How do we reconcile suffering with the God we can know? Is

one or the other illusory? If both are real, how can they co-exist? Are these questions too esoteric and philosophical? I do not think so. Read the book of Job and, significantly, the gospel accounts of Jesus in the Garden of Gethsemane; these questions are very real. Listen sensitively and closely to your friends and loved ones in the midst of suffering.

Christian confidence must relate to the question *'why?'* to be real. This question stands in correlation to the character of God. The best books which deal with the question of suffering acknowledge this approach.[10] Related issues such as healing, prayer and bereavement touch the question *'why?'* The common answers – the fallenness of the world, the free choice of human agents and the hope of Romans 8:28 – while true, go only so far. In the light of divine providence and sovereignty we logically ask, *why*? Experientially we cry out the question. Can we really have any true confidence?

4. Guidance

A missionary spoke of her first shopping trip to a supermarket after being in a two-thirds-world country for several years. The sheer quantity and diversity of available items were mind boggling. She froze with indecision.

Christians today have a great variety in life from which to choose. There are educational choices, career choices, partner choices, and consumer choices greater than those of previous generations. The world of information expands and the diversity of options increases. Consequently, the problem of choosing becomes more acute; and choice is involved in guidance. Yet multiple choice is not the only issue. Who God is, and how he relates to the decisions and choices we face are equally fundamental.

How does a believer understand God's guidance? Does God just leave us to our personal choices or does he direct us in ways pleasing to himself? Is it actually a mixture of both? Taking it one step further, how do we evaluate our personal choices and desires? Can we trust ourselves? Fundamentally (assuming that God does guide), the question is: how may we discern this leading? Here the problem of multiplicity dovetails with two basic problems. The first concerns the significance of choice, the second our perception of God's leading. These are not disconnected, but distinguishing them helps us to identify the relevance of guidance to confidence. Both relate to the believer's personal relationship with the Lord and God's promises about this relationship. It also relates to our understanding about our humanity.

Why is choice significant? It is intrinsic to what we mean when we say that humanity is personal, or more precisely humanity is with *personality*. Human personality is not defined solely in terms of choice, but one way in which personality expresses itself is in choice. Without choice there is a deterministic or mechanistic system. We are either programmed or forced to do what we do. In either of these systems there is no personality. At the very least, we may say that if there is no personality, humanity becomes non-humanity. Humans are radically fallen, however, but not non-human.[11] Choice is significant because it reflects the endowed dignity of every human being.

Yet we struggle with the problem of guidance and are prone to fall into the extremes. One we may call the pit of Wrong Choice (determinism). The other we will call the pit of Divine Indifference (neo-deism). Walking between the two does not feel very comfortable either. Let us consider the first danger, the pit of Wrong Choice.

Some Christians wrestle with the notion that God has a personal will for their lives which they need to discover. It is an external will in the decrees of God, which awaits their discovery so that they can please him. In this sense, 'finding God's will' becomes a tortuous process involving self-denial and abrogation, countless attempts to find a clue hidden by the Lord in Scripture or else an irrationality. They dread making a wrong choice and missing God's best. Like a game-show contestant, they do not know which door to choose. This is the pit of Wrong Choice. What does it feel like in this pit?

A Christian considers a variety of legitimate choices (a choice of universities or careers or even members of the opposite sex to marry) with the idea that God has a 'perfect will' for him or her, sometimes called the 'individual will of God'. Yet what if he or she chooses wrongly due to ignorance or sin? Is he or she resigned to knowing that God can relate to them only according to his 'secondary will'?[12] The believer lives in terror of second best. Life is threatening enough without this dread.

This is not an abstract problem. People do struggle with this, especially if some of their choices subsequently prove to be bad mistakes. A high level of anxiety develops. We must acknowledge this experiential battle. It is about confidence. God tells us in his Word that he can and will guide and lead us. But does he lead us only when we are humbled enough? Does he force us to jump over decision-making hurdles to prove our character? What happens if we make a poor choice? The pit of Wrong Choice is too easy a trap.

The second pit is what we can call the pit of Divine Indifference. We can fall into the pit of Divine Indifference in an attempt to compensate for the dangers of the pit of Wrong Choice or determinism. We rightly see the crippling implications of a determinism that minimizes personal choice. In contrast, we emphasize a wonderful and liberating freedom. We are free to choose according to God's moral guidelines. No hidden blueprint for our lives exists other than the moral framework of Scripture. We can fall into the pit of Divine Indifference when we reason that since a decision is made within the broad moral parameters suggested by biblical revelation, what we choose is a matter of indifference to God.[13]

Undoubtedly, there is some truth here. When taken too far, however, this ultimately strikes at the nature of the *personal relationship* between God and us. For example, if I am considering an invitation to another job, I face responsibility. I must evalute the offer on many levels. Am I free to move? How would this new position affect my wife's desires and present activities? What would this new place mean for my children – their education and friendships? I also have a freedom. I can choose, and, provided I have been responsible and sensitive to others and prayerful, I need not fear that I might miss 'God's perfect plan'.

Nevertheless, I could take this line of thought to an extreme and box myself into a 'closed universe'. I mean that when I pray, for example, I may begin to assume that I am asking for wisdom, discernment and integrity for a matter that is not *specifically* significant to my overall relationship with the Lord. 'What does it matter where I minister, as long as I am faithful and dedicated and as long as the school system is adequate?'

Some readers may wonder how anyone could be so tied up in knots. Yet this danger exists. We are in an agonizing dilemma: does God care about us *personally*? Our lives are made up not of generalities, but of specifics. We do not fall in love generally or consider a move to another location generally. The specific choices are part and parcel of our lives. How can there be an indifference or benign ambivalence on God's part, even concerning so-called mundane matters? This is the dangerous pit of Divine Indifference.

Here are profound implications for the way we pray, read the Bible and go about our daily living. It is a matter of confidence. It relates to how the individual believer understands and receives the promises of God. Guidance relates to our relationship with the Lord and has tremendous ramifications. The two pits described are caricatures of real problems. Both extremes are harmful. Walking the narrow path between the two is hard. Circumstances at times push us to the edge of either pit. Confidence abates.

Whatever else we might say about guidance, it at least takes place within the context of a love relationship. The pastoral implications are significant. Therefore, we must have something to say about this to contemporary Christians. With a variety of options before us, Christians need a confidence that God is actively and personally concerned about them.

5. Frustration.

One characteristic of our present western culture is impatience. In many ways our impatience is proportional to the many aids and conveniences in our life. When our dishwashers, coffee-makers and microwaves do not work, we find washing dishes at the sink, boiling a kettle and warming up the conventional oven a nuisance. Impatience is reflected in other ways. Waiting is hard for many of us.

Do we not find waiting in shops, restaurants, traffic hold-ups and queues quite difficult? The audible complaints and displays of temper we encounter in such situations suggest that others have similar problems. We struggle with impatience; and if our impatience is unresolved we become frustrated. Many of us are in a hurry. We want our relationships, our adventures, our intellectual growth, our financial benefits *now*. One billboard had a catchy line in its advertisement: 'Remember when you used to save for what you wanted?' Many today would have to answer, 'No!'

Impatience and its consequential frustration exist in the Christian life. Eugene Peterson is correct:

One aspect of [the] *world* that I have been able to identify as harmful to Christians is the assumption that anything worthwhile can be acquired at once. We assume that if something can be done at all, it can be done quickly and efficiently. Our attention spans have been conditioned by thirty-second commercials. Our sense of reality has been flattened by thirty-page abridgments.[14]

Impatience with our life in Christ touches upon particular issues that show us how interconnected many of our problems are.

Some people struggle with a relentless perfectionism. They are driven. Where they get this perfectionism from is hard to say. In part, it may be due to their own character and experience. Perhaps the social mindset of their Christian community contributes. Whatever the sources, when these individuals examine their lives and conclude that they are marked with laziness, failure, imperfection and joylessness, trouble follows. They give more time, money and effort. They attend this seminar and that festival for teaching and spiritual refreshment. Life feels like a treadmill. They are more exhausted, and come close to spiritual and emotional burnout. What is so poignant is that they want to honour the Lord, but their perfectionism blinds them. Even in their present, imperfect, condition they can please God. Only through a life-long growth and struggle, however, finally raised from death, do they achieve the glory for which they so lovingly long. Waiting moment by moment is hard.

Times of suffering, confusion, depression, conflict and spiritual dryness can cause real problems. They are difficult in themselves. Quite understandably, we want to finish these difficult times to get on to what we consider the more normal points in our life. When we experience testing or difficulty, either because we live in a fallen world or because we are followers of Christ, we commonly see these disturbing moments as abnormal. Panic or despair follows; or we spiritualize them away. Furthermore, we try to relate these periods to what we understand to be the whole of our life. They demand an *immediate* resolution.

It is like the parent listening to her child practising scales on the piano. Each time the child played a scale she left out the final note. The parent cringed inwardly; the note demanded inclusion, and the scale completion. So after the child left the piano, the parent walked into the room, struck the right key and felt enormously relieved. There, it is complete. It is whole!

We want the same in our experience. Our day-to-day experiences affect our confidence. When they are good, joyful and clear-cut, we have little difficulty. Yet unanswered prayer, conflicts within our church fellowship, dry and dull times in worship or the effects of growing old, often confuse our perspective. There is a tension between the *facts* of our Christian life and our *feelings*.

Either we distrust our emotions as indicators of our spiritual condition or we search for the latest spiritual highs, to serve as a narcotic or analgesic. Life would be so much easier if we always lived with clear-cut consistency. But our lives are complicated and coloured in varying shades. The result is frustration, and some believers become upset and confused.

Christian confidence pertains to this problem of frustration. We will have to consider how the promises of God relate to the frustrating experiences of today's believers. These situations involve divine providence, sanctification and the perseverance of God's people. We will see how an appropriate confidence can help us view our lives more holistically and with greater patience as we live moment by moment.

6. Fear of 'falling away'

He was a good friend to the pastor. They both enjoyed going out cross-country skiing or sitting out on the lake enjoying a summer's day of fishing. As their friendship deepened the man confessed to the minister his problem with alcohol. In fact, it was quite a problem. Moreover, his drinking involved both violent behaviour and paying to have sex with prostitutes. The pastor was deeply concerned for his friend. His friend meant something to the pastor, and not only because they shared a love of the outdoors. The young minister's friend was a leading member of the church. He professed a faith in Jesus Christ.

As time passed, problems increased. Drinking and prostitution were accompanied by physical threats to his wife and children. The man stopped attending church. He saw the pastor, but even this relationship went sour. As news travelled through the small town, word soon got out that the man was denouncing the church, his pastor and, above all, the gospel. Eventually, he left his wife for another woman. He continued to deny the lordship of Christ and the claims of biblical Christianity. He denied his faith in Jesus Christ.

Is this man unique? Sadly, he is not. Why do some people do this? Is there an eventual change of heart and return to what was once held most dear? Yes and no, along with 'We just don't know'. While the man I described is an extreme example, a believer might feel that he or she could fall away from the faith. It may not be for identical reasons. That believer may have his or her own problems – in fact, those identified in this chapter come immediately to mind. This is not an altogether irrational concern.

Jesus clearly taught there will be varying responses to the message of the kingdom (Mt. 13:18–23; Mk. 4:13–20; and Lk. 8:11–15).

> When anyone hears the message about the kingdom and does not understand it, the evil one comes and snatches away what was sown in his heart. This is the seed sown along the path. The one who received the seed that fell on rocky places is the man who hears the word and at once receives it with joy. But since he has no root, he lasts only a short time. When trouble or persecution comes because of the word, he quickly falls away. The one who received the seed that fell among the thorns is the man who hears the word, but the worries of this life and the deceitfulness of wealth choke it, making it unfruitful. But the one who received the seed that fell on good soil is the man who hears the word and understands it. He produces a crop, yielding a hundred, sixty or thirty times what was sown (Mt. 13:19-23).

Jesus warned his disciples in another place, 'I am the true vine, and my Father is the gardener. He cuts off every branch in me that bears no fruit, while every branch that does bear fruit he prunes so that it will be even more fruitful' (Jn. 15:1-2).

The author of the letter to the Hebrews repeatedly warned his readers about falling away from the gospel of Christ. The whole letter deals with the sufficiency and supremacy of Christ in comparison with an earlier Jewish temple ceremonial spirituality. The letter is full of glorious promises of assurance. Nonetheless, the warnings run through the author's entire counsel. 'We must pay more careful attention, therefore, to what we have heard, so that we do not drift away' (Heb. 2:1). Few believers treat dismissively the puzzling challenge in chapter 6:

> It is impossible for those who have once been enlightened, who have tasted the heavenly gift, who have shared in the Holy Spirit, who have tasted the goodness of the word of God and the powers of the coming age, if they fall away, to be brought back to repentance, because to their loss they are crucifying the Son of God all over again and subjecting him to public disgrace (Heb. 6:4-6).

Because of guilt, temperament, psychological make-up, or misunderstanding, some Christians wonder if they have committed the unpardonable sin (see Mk. 3:28 and possibly 1 Jn. 5:16).[15] Furthermore, we may see and know individuals who started in the Christian faith but who subsequently stopped attending church and meeting with other Christians. Many a pastor knows the anguish of watching an individual turn back to a lifestyle totally inconsistent with New Testament teaching. Within the last few years, we have seen the blatant and tragic failings of notable Christian leaders. The shock-waves are still felt in some circles. When we examine Scripture, we see many possible examples in the New Testament: Judas (Mk. 14:44-46 and parallels); Ananias and Sapphira (Acts 5:1-11) and perhaps Hymenaeus and Alexander (1 Tim. 1:20). There are some Christians who are frightened.

We know our hearts, too. Our inconsistencies and failures stand in front of hidden tensions. The Reformers used to speak of our concupiscence, a strong, lustful desire. Yet as Martin Luther (1483-1546) observed, our problem is more than sexual. 'I do not deny therefore but that concupiscence of the flesh comprehendeth carnal lust, but not that only. For concupiscence comprehendeth all other corrupt affections, wherewith the very faithful are infected, some more some less; as pride, hatred, covetousness, impatiency, and such-like.'[16]

Something in us resonates with temptation and disobedience. We find sin nagging at us, drawing us away from what we know and whom we love. Sin insists. The desire to sin lurks like a cancer, and we are never in remission. Experience tells us, if we are honest, that unless we are careful an increasing desire for an actual sin develops. The warnings and cautions of Scripture and the Holy Spirit are ignored. Despite the experience of deriving only momentary pleasure and satisfaction from sin, we could easily continue in specific disobedience.

Can we go too far? Is there a quantifiable limit to the Lord's patience and grace? Does God give us strength and support only as long as we are working hard to obey? Would our Saviour ever allow us to reach the point of giving up? Could we arrive at a moment when we actually say, 'Stuff it all! I'm tired of the battle!'?

The ultimate issue is a day of final accountability and judgment. In chapter 8 we will consider this reality more fully. The point is that to take the Bible seriously we must take hell seriously. Divine judgment is minimized not only by those who find it archaic and incredible, but also by many Christians who themselves find it impossible to believe that someone could really be 'lost'. Yet we cannot help but see the themes of hell and divine judgment running through the New Testament. It is quite true that generations of Christians in past centuries, frightened no doubt by horrifying paintings and extreme verbal pictures from preachers, feared what would happen to them at death. Our postmodern culture has dismissed these notions. Nonetheless, biblical Christians do not easily dismiss altogether the New Testament teaching.

At one time or another every believer wrestles with some sort of concern about 'falling away'. It is sheer arrogance and avoidance behaviour to think otherwise. Think of Peter's brash words in Mark 14:29 (cf. Lk. 22:33) and Jesus' response. Paul warned the Corinthians, 'So, if you think you are standing firm, be careful that you don't fall!' (1 Cor. 10:12). The apostle even watched himself carefully, so that he 'will not be disqualified for the prize' (1 Cor. 9:27).

Yet there are the equally wonderful assurances in God's Word (see Is. 43:13; Jude 24; 1 Jn.1:8 – 2:2). Jesus promises, 'And this is the will of him who sent me, that I shall lose none of all that he has given me, but raise them up at the last day. For my Father's will is that everyone who looks to the Son and believes in him shall have eternal life, and I will raise him up at the last day' (Jn. 6:39–40). Do these promises, however, carry certain qualifications?

Our explanation of confidence must be relevant. There are individuals who need to receive sane and understanding counsel when they look inwards and are discomforted. The anxiety and sensitivity of many Christians never arise in a single dimension. We must neither minimize their concern (for Scripture actually takes the issue seriously) nor reduce the issue to an encouragement just to 'trust' the Lord.

A key called Promise

Confidence is not just a theoretical term, for life is never vicarious. Life is not like watching professional sportsmen or sportswomen – we pay, they play. We are all involved in life. A Christian's life intimately involves a relationship with God in Jesus Christ. This means that a Christian's personal experience raises the question of confidence. Whether it be guilt, duties, pain, guidance, frustration or fear (or a combination of any of these), an individual's experience is real and significant.

As we have seen in this chapter, many issues and questions stand out. True confidence involves these. So consider once more how we define confidence: *a consequence of my faith in Jesus Christ, brought about over time by the Holy Spirit, experienced in my heart and realized in my mind, that God's promises in the gospel are true and personally applicable to me a believer.*[17] In this chapter we raised experiential issues which can cause a contemporary believer difficulties. He or she could have problems knowing and feeling 'that God's promises in the gospel are true *and personally applicable to me as a believer*'.

There is, however, a vital qualification. How we handle issues will depend upon our individual temperament and the Christian teaching and support we receive. Some individuals experience situations more intensely than other believers. Equally, we may go through a period of suffering, for example, and sense a powerful assurance and confidence. When this occurs, the Christian is filled, in the truest sense of the word, with joy; or, as Paul expressed it, with 'the peace of God, which transcends all understanding' (Phil. 4:7). It would be a great exaggeration to claim that every time a Christian faces temptation or guilt he or she plunges into despair.

41

We do not have to fall apart and give up.

There are many things to cause Christians to lose confidence. But we cannot stop here and surrender. There is good news for us. We can well relate to Christian in John Bunyan's allegory *The Pilgrim's Progress* (1678), trapped in Doubting Castle. The problems identified in this chapter could entrap us just as the Giant and his wife imprisoned Christian and Hopeful. Bunyan, however, saw that confidence offered them a means of escape:

> Now, a little before it was day, good Christian, as one half amazed, brake out into this passionate speech: 'What a fool,' quoth he, 'am I to lie in a stinking dungeon, when I may as well walk at liberty! I have a key in my bosom called Promise, that will, I am persuaded, open any lock in Doubting Castle.' Then said Hopeful, 'That is good news, good brother: pluck it out of thy bosom, and try.'[18]

We may not always come up with neat and tidy answers concerning confidence, but we must appreciate one fundamental truth. God wants us to be assured of his personal love and care for us. Our most serious failure is not lack of confidence; it is thinking that there is no such thing as Christian confidence in our present age. We may not find *exhaustive* reasons for being confident but God offers us appropriate and sufficient help.

He wants us to *know*. The author of 1 John wrote: 'I write these things to you who believe in the name of the Son of God so that you may know that you have eternal life' (1 Jn. 5:12). Even in the face of questions raised by living today, we can have a true confidence. Our Lord provides this for us in the ways he cares for us. To these God-given means of confidence we turn – yet not before we reveal some of the philosophical and intellectual problems of our postmodern culture. As I will argue, we will not be able to know Christian confidence in the midst of these experiential problems without understanding how much the way our contemporary society views truth, knowledge, morality and what it means to be human. Our experiential struggles never occur within some sort of Christian vacuum. They develop and take place *today*, in an age of change.

Questions for reflection and discussion

1. Throughout this chapter a link is made between experience and the 'beliefs' of a Christian. Do you think experience and feelings are changed by knowing the facts of belief? Why or why not?

2. Are there other situations and experiences in which a Christian's confidence actually grows stronger and clearer?

3. How much do you think a person's temperament or personality influences his or her sense of confidence? Why is it that some people never seem to struggle?

The shifting sands

Living in a changing age

Contemplating the invisible in the obvious

Talk with people born in the early part of this century. The many changes they have witnessed in lifestyles, technology, political systems and entertainment are staggering. More change and development have occurred this century than in most previous centuries. As for the last fifty years, we live in an age when things are not what they used to be; and change matters.

Today's changes are tomorrow's givens. What was earlier novel and surprising is later assumed and normative. O. B. Hardison, Jr, in *Disappearing Through the Skylight: Culture and Technology in the Twentieth Century*, makes an astute point:

> There is another fact about cultural innovations. If an innovation is basic, simply because it *is* so, a generation after it has been introduced, it becomes part of the world as given – part of the shape of consciousness, you might say, rather than the content of consciousness. Television seems to the generation of the 1940s to be an amazing triumph of human ingenuity and pregnant with social implications. Its influence on modern culture has been every bit as great as those who witnessed its birth imagined. But now that it has been assimilated, it is taken for granted, which means that, in a sense, it has become obvious and invisible at the same time. Anyone who discusses modern culture has to do a great deal of contemplating of the invisible in the obvious.[1]

To speak of Christian confidence today we must contemplate 'the invisible in the obvious'. Too many ways of thinking and acting are too easily assumed. We fall into the trap of thinking that people have always, more or less, viewed the world as we do today. Consequently, we fail to see the contours of our culture for what they are. Throughout this book, I accept that many of our problems relating to a lack of confidence are similar to those experienced by earlier generations of Christians. Nevertheless, our struggle for confidence involves some contemporary, up-to-date twists and turns. The confusing issues and experiences we face are closely associated with the times in which we live. In other words, the problem is not just us, it is us *as we live in and are associated with today's world*.

We are all affected. It is like passive cigarette smoking: we may not personally accept most secular assumptions, yet many around us do and the presumptions affect us too. Consequently, some ways we choose, think and act may not be biblical. Still, we may think they are, and read the Bible accordingly. Clearly, it is difficult, if impossible, to leave completely the influence of our culture's worldview. In this sense, for the gospel's sake, we must appreciate the obvious and invisible of our culture.

To consider the issue of confidence helpfully, we have to realize the context in which we live. Our teaching and counselling about confidence must relate to our contemporary intellectual and moral problems. To resolve this discomfort partially, we need to understand some general ways in which our society thinks, chooses and acts. This book cannot possibly present a detailed analysis; some very helpful resources are available.[2] Nevertheless, it is vital to consider the following crucial observations about modernity and postmodernism.

The collapse of a superstructure: living in modernity's rubble

For close to 350 years western culture has stood on a foundation built in the Renaissance (roughly, the fourteenth, fifteenth, and sixteenth centuries) and the Enlightenment (most noticeable from the eighteenth century). Increasingly, scholars argue Renaissance and Enlightenment thinking rejected the influence of Christian tradition and biblical faith and accepted a confidence in human reason and human independence.

Generalizations are fraught with difficulties, but we may argue that over the past 350 years human autonomy, human reason and human positivism have been held as the noble virtues. Humanity is independent and can cope very well on its own. As one commentator, David Harvey, observes, the Enlightenment 'took Alexander Pope's injunction, "the proper study of mankind is man," with great seriousness'.[3] Yet the Enlightenment (and should we call it that at all?) led thinkers into scepticism, and from scepticism to despair. As John Carroll in his book *Humanism: The Wreck of Western Culture* points out, 'humanism was doomed from the start . . . it carried within its own seed the elements of its destruction'.[4] Renaissance and Enlightenment humanism eventually resulted in modernism and modernity.

It is important to define these terms. In a way, we come close to a helpful understanding when we see that *modern* relates to 'now'. It is a measure of time, especially a time of change. The time to which *modern* refers, however, is longer than just the 1990s. *Modern*, in this sense looks back to the eighteenth century. Thomas C. Oden argues that the words *modern* and *modernity* have three distinct strata of meanings.[5]

First is the intellectual and cultural dominance of a period in western history which goes as far back as the French Revolution. Oden points to the significant characteristics as moral relativism, an insistence that everything can be reduced to its simple mechanical or biological make-up, narcissistic hedonism, and the autonomy of the individual.

Second is the development occurring in the nineteenth and early twentieth centuries of a mentality that assumes that 'today's' ways of knowing are superior to 'yesterday's' ways of knowing. Essentially, it is a mentality, especially among the intellectual élite, which rejects previous generation's values, assumptions and beliefs. This way of thinking notably dismisses, even despises, premodern thinking.

Third, and quite ironic, is the gradual deterioration of a confidence in human reason and autonomy as well as a loss of confidence in the self-evident superiority of contemporary perception. We see this all around us today. It is, in a way, modernity at last turning upon itself and seeing its own failure. This development, according to Oden, probably began sometime in the 1960s.

Thus, modernism not only has gone through its mid-life crisis; today it senses its own senility and impotence. Like Bonnie and Clyde, the 1920s gangsters, or Butch Cassidy and the Sundance Kid, Hollywood's memorable western outlaws, modernism looks upon its past actions, rampages, adventures and plundering, yet has nothing to show for it today.

Diogenes Allen, in his valuable work *Christian Belief in a Postmodern World*, explains in a further way the breakdown of modernism. His observations are particularly relevant to our study. Allen notices, first, a change in the areas of philosophy and cosmology. For centuries it was assumed by philosophers and cosmologists that the existence of God was a needless hypothesis.[6] According to Allen, however, recent studies about the origins and meaning of the universe no longer unquestioningly presuppose Enlightenment axioms. A radical shift, or revision, is taking place. Not everyone in these fields accepts Christianity. 'All they can say is that the order and existence of the universe pose real questions that they cannot answer and recognize that God is the sort of reality that would answer them.'[7]

Secondly, Allen claims that with the breakdown of the modern mentality there is 'the failure to find a basis for morality and society'.[8] The social breakdown and appalling rise in crime, seen all over the world, are disturbing facts of contemporary living. Unquestionably, people a century earlier were frightened. In England, just for example, we think of the popular writings of Charles Dickens, who protested at his society's moral wrongs. Dickens, however, assumed that his generation worked with an agreed moral framework. Yet the inability of today's politicians and social theoreticians to find both fitting explanations and suitable solutions is alarming. Political persuasion or party platform is not the issue. Fundamentally, the problem today is the lack of a coherent, reasonable and humane philosophical basis for morality.

Thirdly, Allen points to a collapse of confidence in science and technology as bringers of positive progress.[9] Social improvement is no longer inevitable. Success through education and technological wizardry is not guaranteed. Coinciding with this loss of confidence is, fourthly, a reconsideration of the Enlightenment belief in knowledge as inherently good. Some contemporary exploration and scientific enquiry give cause for concern. Allen suggests the worries many have regarding, for example, genetic engineering. This field of medical research could be beneficial in some ways, but it has its ominous implications too.[10]

We are living in an enormous and significant period of change and transition. Modernity and modernism, as ways of seeing reality, are failing conspicuously. It may be a slow and drawn-out end, but we are witnessing the death throes. The horrors of two World Wars, Stalinist socialism, the environmental disasters caused by western industry and expansion, and a fundamental loss of utopian idealism have resulted in chilling pessimism. But there is something deeper, or less obvious.

Barry Smart argues that modernism thought it could order and structure society into a better way through reason and rationality. It hoped for order and improvability, but was blind to the inverse reality of disorder. He writes, 'Modernity simultaneously creates the promise and the possibility, perhaps even a fleeting experience of satisfaction, but it is driven by an endless pursuit of innovation or change which creates restlessness, discontent, and dissatisfaction, and in consequence diminishes the experience and meaning of existence.'[11] Smart's further observation strikes at the root. Modernity, in turn, has become 'the focus of increasing critical reflection in the course of the twentieth century. The benefits and securities assumed to be a corollary of the development of modernity have become matters of doubt, the possibility of their realization, if not their desirability, the subject of question and criticism as faith in the doctrine of progress has been dissipated.'[12]

We must not, however, be too quick to write modernity's obituaries. Modernism is still around; it is hard to let go of something so familiar. As a way of thinking and evaluating, it is like an old habit. It is a worldview with which we have all grown up in the late twentieth century. If this analogy works, it can help us better to appreciate the particulars of what is called *postmodernism*.

Yet, in saying this, postmodernism is not easily defined. This is because postmodernism is both a reaction and an extension. The expression '*post*modern' could well reveal the difficulty of definition. Whatever we see in modernism, postmodernism is, to use Matei Calinescu's expression, one of its faces.[13] The point is that it is the increasingly dominating face of our days, an age of change.

Postmodernism: the illusive description of our changing age

In his book *Reality Isn't What It Used To Be*, Walter Truett Anderson passes on a joke, which remarkably illustrates postmodernism's underlying structure:

> Three baseball umpires are sitting around over a beer, and one says, 'There's balls and there's strikes, and I call 'em the way they are.' Another says, 'There's balls and there's strikes, and I call 'em the way I see 'em.' The third says, 'There's balls and there's strikes, and they ain't *nothin'* until I call 'em.'[14]

The first umpire is, essentially, a modernist. The second reflects a kind of relativistic, construct-your-own-worldview, perspective. It is the third umpire who best displays radical postmodernist assumptions.

It is a way of looking at everything, a particular worldview. As in the third umpire's expression, in postmodernism there is nothing fixed or determined; things are fluid or juxtaposed. This is why the umpire denied the existence of the balls and strikes. Balls and strikes, in this illustration, are creations, playthings, in the mind and communication of the postmodernist umpire. As we will see shortly, postmodernist thinking is similar concerning various aspects of life.

When, however, did the cultural evolutionary development reach this stage called postmodernism? Many cultural commentators refer to the climax of the anti-modernist protests that occurred in the 1960s. We think of the counterculture expressions in clothing, music, literature and lifestyle. In these years westerners followed Alan Watts' lead and looked towards Zen Buddhism, or attempted to find the transcendental through LSD as advocated by Timothy Leary and Richard Alpert.[15] Particularly, we recall the tumultuous days of worldwide student rioting in 1968. David Harvey writes, 'Though a failure, at least judged in its own terms, the movement of 1968 has to be viewed, however, as the cultural and political harbinger of the subsequent turn to postmodernism.'[16] Harvey's conclusion is expressed succinctly by Walter

Truett Anderson, 'The '60s were the true beginning of the postmodern era. The decade brought forth audacious critiques of the modern worldview, attacks on all belief systems.'[17] Here is where we come to the heart of postmodernism: not only a change, but a reconstruction of worldviews.

Whether seen in art, film, music, architecture, linguistic studies, philosophy or social theories, postmodernism is a worldview marked with illusive characteristics. As Nicholas Fox writes, 'Reality has been replaced with simulation, rationality by multi-vocality, monolithic organization by fragmentation, theory by play.'[18] There is no unified field of truth, no clear absolute point of reference for language, knowledge, morality or human experience.

In fact, postmodernist thinkers like Michel Foucault or Jean-François Lyotard attack what postmodernists call meta-narratives, meta-language, or meta-theory. These are theories that try to explain how everything is: think, for example, of Marx's ideas or Freudian psychology or, particularly, a religion. For postmodernism, no theory holds everything together. Instead, fragmentation, discontinuity and the chaotic form 'power-discourse' formations or 'language games'.[19] These can be defined simply as the ways individuals, groups or societies get on with their own particular way of interpreting and 'acting' in the world. There is nothing universally unifying. Every attempt to articulate a coherent representation of reality, it is argued, leads to oppression or illusion.[20]

Some readers may well wonder what our presentation of modernism and postmodernism has to do with Christian confidence. Again, however, I must stress the fact that our culture influences our struggle for confidence. Imagine watching a play at a theatre. In the interval we go out for a refreshment. Upon returning to our seats, and as the curtain rises, we immediately notice a completely different stage-setting, entirely different costumes, and entirely different character names. An extremely disconcerting feeling comes over us. What has happened? What does this all mean? Where is the play we were first watching?

A contemporary Christian could well feel the same, living in the 1990s. Things are changing, and this throws Christian confidence (as I defined it earlier) into question. But, to use my theatre illustration again, if we could only go back stage during the interval, we would see what has happened. Seeing what has happened, we can understand what the changes mean or imply. When we can do this, not only can we ask our own critical questions, we can explain things to the confused audience.

In the rest of this chapter let us go behind the postmodern curtain and see what is going on today. This may puzzle some readers, yet this task is not unfruitful. It will enable us to articulate a real and true Christian confidence in this age of change. Not only will this help us who are Christians, it will equip us with a clear and compassionate proclamation for our bewildered generation. For (as we now start to show) postmodernism only takes us into a lonely and desolate cul-de-sac. The gospel is the way to truth, freedom, and life.

Abandoned children in a postmodern world: the implications of postmodernism

Beneath postmodernism's cynicism is a hunger and an openness. No longer is there a clinging to Enlightenment patterns, humanism's boldness or modernity's assumptions. Western men and women are searching. Today, however, people are living like abandoned orphans when it comes to their moral, intellectual and spiritual conclusions. In the final analysis it is up to them. There are no guidelines, no outside resources. So, whether they realize it or not, many in our culture flip back to escapism, neo-romanticism, fantasy and irrationality. It is the way people get on with life. Some, out of boredom and despair, escape through drugs and alcohol. This fundamental go-it-alone attitude among people leads to particular views of reality. Especially, it questions the possibility of knowing truth. We can identify five character-istics of the postmodern perspective. As we identify these characteristics we will inevitably anticipate, in response, particular aspects of our theological framework.

Make it up as you go along

There is a crucial, paradoxical twist to postmodernism. It seeks to make sense of the world and human experience, but, by its own assumptions, cannot make sense of anything. There is an ineluctable human desire to create, to communicate, and to live among those who advocate postmodernist views. Nonetheless, these very same desires and human longings are suspect. Because coherence is wrong, and disjunction is ideal, a tension exists in postmodernism. Consider the following opinion of the architect and postmodernist theorist Robert Venturi:

> I like elements which are hybrid rather than 'pure,' 'compromising' rather than 'straightforward,' ambiguous rather than 'articulated' ... inconsistent and equivocal rather than direct and clear. I am for messy vitality over obvious unity.[21]

Whether it is in art, music, architecture, literature, philosophy, social theories or theology, nothing is straightforward. There are countless levels of expression and ambiguity. But this is acceptable in a postmodern world, even if there is a massive and terrible set of contradictions.

Think of David Lynch's film, *Blue Velvet* (1986). In this bizarre film, not for the faint-hearted, Lynch masterfully overlays a set of contradictory stories. On the surface, his characters live in a peaceful American town. Yet underneath all the stereotypes is the hidden and complex world of the characters' sexual desires, including sado-masochistic fantasies. *Blue Velvet* is a postmodernist film in as much as it avoids any attempt to harmonize, or explain, these two stories. The viewer feels these two worlds pulling things apart, making the film almost fall apart. This, however, is exactly the point. Apparently, Lynch wants us to feel this tension, because this is the way things are in all of life: disharmony, tensions and ambiguity.

Michel Foucault expressed this specific aspect of postmodernism. He referred to what he called 'heterotopia'. Reality consists of various worlds, in fragmentary fashions. Life is like a story, a play. There is no unifying whole, but rather each character's actions, thoughts and position in time–space reality. Yet they do not know, really, which world they live in, and neither do we. Are we observers, or are we too part of the drama?[22]

There is a denial of objectivity and knowableness. We can observe this postmodern theme in hermeneutics and literary studies. Hermeneutics is not interpretation, it is the way we interpret a text when we read. In other words, hermeneutics is to interpretation as a pair of spectacles are to reading. Over the past forty to fifty years, a major set of revolutions has occurred. Like a David Lynch film, in which things are not what they seem, postmodernist ways of reading a text tell us that language and writing and reading are not what they appear. 'And when people begin to question the ability of written works to contain or communicate reality, they are asking questions about reality itself.'[23]

Two significant developments in literary criticism are deconstructionism and reader-response theory.[24] Deconstructionism, notably put forth by Jacques Derrida, who builds on the work of Martin Heidegger, is not so much a theory as a philosophical explanation about reading. Deconstructionism tells us that there is effectively no clear or straightforward meaning in a text. This is because the author brings to the writing various conscious and unconscious levels. So too the reader. Meaning is virtually impossible because a text deconstructs, it falls apart into various worlds of implication.

Yet this is no real problem, according to various 'reader-response' theories. Each of us brings our own previous reading experiences to a text. Because in a text there are multiple levels of presentation (some unknown to both the author and to us as readers), interpretation is at a personal, subjective, level.

Not every aspect of these theories is wrong. Deconstructionism and reader-response do point to certain ways in which we read a text. Whether these theories fully and correctly interpret *all* that we do when we read or when we write is debatable. Moreover, such postmodernist interpretations decry any universal explanation (meta-narrative) but, are in fact, just one more offering! They tell us we cannot really know anything for sure. But how can we know this?

Postmodernism dismisses challenges to or critiques of its conclusions. Postmodernity embraces as axiomatic the belief that reality is what each of us makes it out to be. Nonetheless, in this book we will constantly ask whether this feature of its worldview holds water. We do not do this out of an appreciation for Enlightenment thinking or modernist conviction. Instead, we will ask what 'tools' they suggest we use to construct our own view of reality. These tools or assumptions become evident as we look at further characteristics of postmodernism.

Truth is true only because 'it works for me'

Contemporary people think there is nothing outside a person by which he or she can measure personal existence. At least, they are not sure. Peter Berger was quite helpful when he suggested that men and women in the West no longer have any 'plausibility structure'. Berger meant that western society no longer accepts ideas and practices that can help to determine the plausibility of beliefs within any given society.[25] Lesslie Newbigin takes Berger's observation one step further. 'It is not that there is no socially accepted plausibility structure and thus we make our own choices. This *is* the ruling plausibility structure, and we make our choices within its parameters.'[26] What difference does this make?

Today people often appeal to truth on a pragmatic or functional basis. It works, or it helps, or it makes life better. All they can say is, 'This present moral or philosophical position is true only because at present we are all almost agreed. Besides, it is proving to please 51% of the population. It works for most of the people.'

Our contemporary scene is one in which people view truth as resting 'somewhere in the middle'. Knowledge of truth is found between two extremes, and the way to resolve problems is to seek a degree of compromise. No longer do we use categories of truth and non-truth. Moral, philosophical and theological absolutes are denied or subsumed into a desire for collegiality and the process of 'searching together'.

Yet is there not something wrong here? A position is true only because it works or makes a person happy, is this enough? Happiness, or usefulness, is incredibly hard to define. Besides, some truths may not make me happy, but they are still correct. The logical and fundamental question ought to be asked, 'Where is any valid external point of reference? Is the subjective "I" or "we" the sole determiner?' In other words, where or to whom can we go for a way to test out claims of truth?

Given the contemporary cultural thinking-patterns, however, these questions are rejected. Michel Foucault confidently declared, 'Critical analysis of the truth, of both our forms of thought and our selves, serves to alert us to the absence of epistemological and existential guarantees, and to detach the power of truth from the forms of hegemony, social, economic and cultural, within which it operates at the present time'.[27] It takes a moment or two to follow his complicated argument. Walter Truett Anderson puts it more succinctly, 'The old epistemology that equated human beliefs with cosmic reality is now a minority report. Ancient and not-so-ancient systems of eternal truth lie in ruins everywhere around us. The mainstream of social reality has shifted.'[28] Practically, this leads to relativism.

The mix-and-match style of relativism

Relativism says that there are no real or absolute truths. Truth is relative to the individual and to the time and place in which he or she lives. Relativism also associates with pluralism. In our culture there are many different philosophies and religions. All make truth claims. We need only listen to some discussions among university students to hear this. Whether the question is abortion, sexuality, politics, relationships or a popular television programme, we will discern a passionate insistence on the unassailable claim that truth is not the sole possession of any one group. Sometimes the debate is so intense that a person will exclaim, 'How dare you push your opinion on others!'

In his controversial book *The Closing of the American Mind*, Allan Bloom pointed to the axiomatic relativism of today's American students. This is not confined to philosophy or sociology departments. Furthermore, the consequence, argued Bloom, is far from being merely intellectual; it is actually a moral position held by students in all disciplines that influences the choices and values they accept in life:

> The danger they have been taught to fear from absolutism is not error but intolerance. Relativism is necessary to openness; and this is the virtue, the only virtue, which all primary education for more than fifty years has dedicated itself to inculcating.[29]

I once attended a conference at which the principal speaker proclaimed with great confidence, 'The only absolute is that there are no absolutes!' Most of those attending were delighted. Why? Because they are caring and compassionate men and women. They fear bigotry and intolerance, for rigidly held opinions have often resulted in injustice and violence. Yet was not the speaker's statement a contradiction?

To say there are no absolutes certainly sounds like an absolute philosophical statement. It comes with humility and tolerance (rare commodities), but the statement is like the Emperor's new clothes: there is not much here. Ironically, relativism's dismissal of any claim for truth threatens pluralism. Relativism subtly undermines the notion of tolerance. Tolerance at least acknowledges the diversity within a pluralistic society. Relativism essentially waters everything down to meaninglessness.[30]

Relativists presuppose a detachment. They insist that truth is in no one idea or philosophy. This sounds open-minded and tolerant. Paradoxically, their view is a claim for a particular truth: their own! How do they know they are correct? How can they prove their argument? In other words, if there are 'many roads up the mountain', how do relativists know this? Can a person break free from his or her own path enough to see the whole mountain?[31] These are fundamental and logical questions that every person must ask. We do not have to take everything at face value, though others doubt all.

Cleaning up the past with historical revisionism

Historical scepticism compounds the problem. What passes for knowledge and so-called 'facts' at one point in human history only prove in the end to be mere wisps. David Harvey observes, 'Eschewing the idea of progress, postmodernism abandons all sense of historical continuity and memory, while simultaneously developing an incredible ability to plunder history and absorb whatever it finds there as some aspect of the present.'[32] There are no long-lasting heroes, there are no ultimate virtues and there is nothing really out there in the universe. Only the 'now' and 'I' matter. This may be fearsome autonomy but this is the world as men and women perceive it.

'So', advise some voices, 'it is best to jettison the hindrances of earlier views of what is right and wrong. Time passes, and what is appropriate for one generation is not always so for subsequent generations.' The old social order is gone, a new way of societal organization is desired. What was considered true yesterday is rejected today.

In some ways this is not a bad process. In other ways, however, it can lead to scepticism. We might think there is no truth other than what is agreed upon by social contract and agreement. Truth is relative only to any given point of a society's development. In years to come, truth will be revised.

There are some popular and seemingly innocuous examples. In 1992 books, documentaries and films were made about Christopher Columbus' famous voyage in 1492. For years most people looked upon Columbus as a hero, the man who bravely set sail for India and discovered instead the New World. In 1992, due to the influence of both political correctness and historical revisionism, Columbus was understood as an exploiter and manipulator. He may have been; but at the popular level of entertainment, no allowance exists for accurate investigation. Entertainment provides *instant* revisionism.

Kevin Costner stars in three films which display a revised image. The old ideas and views are rejected. Costner's *Dances With Wolves* paints a different picture of native North Americans. According to this film, the Sioux were innocent and environmentally friendly people, until, that is, white Europeans invaded their land. Costner's film is fascinating. The film quite rightly points to evils inflicted upon native Americans by white men. Nevertheless, it presents to a generation of young film-goers a distortion and a biased view of history. In his highly controversial book, *Hollywood vs. America*, film critic Michael Medved is stinging. 'That social and political message, of course, involved a gigantic distortion of the American past and an absurdly idealized view of Indian society.'[33]

This is also the case with the film *J F K*. Oliver Stone's film about the assassination of President John F. Kennedy is based entirely on an unsubstantiated conspiracy theory. Yet the film-watchers are given no mental distance or time to stop and ask, 'Is this account the way things really happened?' Instead, many people walk away with a new way of looking at things, a perspective they question only slightly.

In the same way, Costner's *Robin Hood: Prince of Thieves* revises more than the legend of Robin Hood. The twist to this film is its subtle attack on Christianity and Christians in favour of the Saracen Muslim. Is it such an innocuous film? Should we be so concerned? Yes; for it illustrates that what takes place at the grassroots level is not detached from the lofty philosophical rhetoric of the intellectuals. We may not all understand philosophers; we can understand Costner and others.

Radical historical revisionism and excessive political correctness work to change the view we have of the past. It is not so much an attempt to sift through historical prejudice in order to arrive at a more knowledgeable interpretation as an effort to change the way people think. This revision and rejection explain why some of our contemporaries are highly sceptical about the claims of biblical Christianity. They question history and doubt the Christian's argument that, for example, the New Testament Gospels are historically trustworthy.

Moral and religious truth is non-objective

With the predominance of scepticism and the uncertainty of absolute truth and a doubt about history, it is not surprising to notice the way in which many western thinkers view moral and religious beliefs. Moral and religious truths are thought to be non-objective. There is a great deal of inconsistency. When they discuss their own understandings, they are certain. In response to others, however, they exercise a high level of either scepticism or agnosticism. A. N. Wilson, in his book *Jesus*, insists:

> Once, when I visited the Garden Tomb in Jerusalem, there was a party of American tourists. Their tour leader was informing them that 'the Resurrection of Jesus Christ is the best-attested fact in human history'. This would not have been Paul's claim for whom it was a matter of faith. Nor for the author of the Fourth Gospel, who believed that there was blessedness in not having seen, while having believed.[34]

Wilson writes as if his interpretation of Paul and John's gospel are unquestionable. They are most definitely not; and Tom Wright's response, *Who Was Jesus?*, reveals Wilson's errors.[35] Yet notice the thrust of Wilson's view of faith and historical objectivity. 'We have reached the point in our narrative where we must abandon our efforts to pursue "what really happened". Subjectivity is the only criterion of Gospel truth.'[36]

Today, religious claims are classified in a different category from, say, scientific theories. Spirituality, it is claimed, has more to do with the non-rational and the intuitive. We meet this kind of thinking in Eastern spiritualities and in New Age spiritualities. In

The Tibetan Book of Living and Dying, Sogyal Rinpoche assures the reader that the book's insights are true. He does so, however, by challenging traditional western ways of thinking:

> My students often ask me: How do we know what these bardos are, and from where does the astonishing precision of the bardo teachings and their uncannily clear knowledge of each stage of dying, of death, and of rebirth come from? The answer may seem initially difficult to understand for many readers, because the notion of the mind the West now has is an extremely narrow one.

He concludes:

> The source of the bardo teachings is the enlightened mind, the completely awake Buddha mind, as experienced, explained, and transmitted by a long line of masters that stretches back to the Primordial Buddha.[37]

Unfortunately, even some contemporary Christian theologians equate the non-objective and the non-rational with the truths of Christianity. So, for example, to ask if Jesus' tomb was empty on the third day is to ask entirely the wrong question. The valid question is, what does it mean that the first followers believed the tomb was empty? We are told not to pursue any so-called objective facts of history. None exist. Religious truths transcend the objective. It is the faithless, we are told, who require objective proofs. Faith, so the argument goes, looks beyond proofs.[38]

This characteristic begins to explain why so many today question any claim of Christian certainty or confidence in knowing. I refer to the epistemological doubt, expressed in relation to the gospel proclamation. Many a university student has told me that 'seeing is believing' and 'relationship experience is the touchstone of knowledge'. People in the here and now are real and verifiable; God, however, is in an altogether different category. There are no real and objective verifiers of faith, so the thinking runs. Accordingly, some Christians have tentatively expressed their confidence in the truthfulness of the gospel. It is, for the moment, the best option. Were something 'better' to come around, then they would reconsider. This way of thinking, to which we will respond repeatedly throughout this book, is compounded by a process that is taking place today. It is not a postmodern phenomenon, for it began centuries ago. Nevertheless, the five postmodern characteristics identified above are accentuated by this process.

The body-blow of secularization

If we begin with our 'self' because there is no sense of knowable truths, little wonder that traditional religion is dismissed in a particular way in the West. Religion no longer makes *practical* sense to many people in our culture. It is not that spiritualities or religious theories are unpopular! They are more popular in the 1990s, possibly, than in the previous decade. The issue is not religious interest or spiritual searching. The frame of reference is different. It is important to remember the flow of ideas mentioned in the previous pages. This flow helps us see a corollary. It is a process within culture called *secularization*.

Os Guinness defines secularization as 'the process through which, starting from the centre and moving outward, successive sectors of society and culture have been freed from the decisive influence of religious ideas and institutions'.[39] In other words, as time passes, religion is less relevant to specific issues and practices in culture. Hans Küng puts it this way:

> . . . more or less all the important spheres of human life
> – learning, economy, politics, law, state, culture, educa-
> tion, medicine, welfare – have been withdrawn from the
> influence of the Churches, of theology and religion, and
> placed under the direct responsibility and control of
> man, who has himself thus become 'secular'.[40]

I can illustrate it like this. In our home we have a print of an etching made in 1645 by Wenceslaus Hollar of the city of London as seen from Bankside. There are interesting features of the period before the Great Fire of London in 1660. One notable aspect of the etching is that Hollar used famous churches as points of reference. My opinion is that he did so not just because church spires were dominant architectural features of his day, but because spires reflected a still prevailing theistic worldview. In other words, the intellectual framework of his day was shaped by the church. Secularization, however, changes the contemporary view.

If we saw an annotated photograph of London today, the orientations would not be churches. This is due not simply to architectural development. Men and women do not view the church as their cultural reference point. Why should they? Christianity's relevance is just not clear in a world of the microchip, fax machine and McDonald's. Less and less in western culture is influenced by biblical Christianity.

Intriguingly, the process of secularization continues unabated, even among those who would still insist that they enjoy religion. This is the paradox, even with the apparent postmodern interest in spiritualities. Most people do not claim to be secularists. They probably express some sort of 'faith' in a god or a higher being. Very few know how much they have accepted the progress of secularization. The problem is that their religion touches very little of their life, other than some small part of their existence. With each passing decade, traditional religion, and specifically biblical Christianity, feels so irrelevant to people. This process makes contemporary people even more vulnerable to the effects of secularization.

Of course, in recent years the transcendent and the mystical are apparently back in vogue, hence the interest in New Age philosophy and spiritualities. At the very least, the New Age movements reflect a dissatisfaction with the empty secular humanism of the sixties and seventies. Many thoughtful and sensitive men and women appreciate that they are more than material beings. These people recognize that they have a spiritual nature.[41] Significantly, the New Age movements are the counter-culture come of age, addressing the situation of the eighties and nineties.

The New Age movements are responding to the void created by a secular humanism. Secular humanism, with its pronounced atheism and reductionism (the view that humanity is reducible to chemical and physical description), offers humanity little real hope. It can deny humanity's spiritual longings, but these prove to be inevitable. Men and women are desperate for hope, and they still possess mystical and spiritual longings which secular humanism cannot satisfy. There is an insatiable human spiritual longing.

This longing may well provide biblical Christians with new opportunities to present the gospel. With the slow end of Enlightenment confidence, postmodernism's shift could be a promising time for evangelism. Yet this is not altogether clear-cut, and I would argue that postmodernism carries with it some enormous obstacles. Nonetheless, as Alister McGrath suggests, 'the claustrophobic and restrictive straitjacket placed upon western Christianity by rationalism has gone. In the space of two decades, there has been a major cultural shift in western society, which opens up new opportunities for the churches'.[42]

Intriguingly, Barry Smart writes:

> Refusing to accept the relativising consequences of modernity, the fundamentalist turn evident in each of the three monotheisms of Christianity, Judaism, and Islam has promoted resistance to modern forms of life. Whether the religious movements which were thought to have been left behind by modernity have become the *avantgarde* of postmodernity is open to question. Less controversial is their contribution to the debate over the limits and limitations of modernity and the associated possible emergence of a mood or condition of post-modernity. The resurrection of the 'sacred' as a sphere of experience pertinent to modern forms of life, as a counter to the nihilism of the modern world and the 'vision of reason that brought this world into being', certainly constitutes a part of what has been described as the postmodern condition.[43]

There could possibly be something to this argument, but we must accept it with the utmost caution. An interest in the mystical, sacred or spiritual does not mean worship of the one true God. With an openness to the gospel, there is also an openness to the occult and to contemporary forms of idolatry. Similarly, postmodern spirituality, within a postmodern constructivist worldview, may not necessarily resist the process of secularization.

We still grope for answers beyond ourselves

At the heart of our crisis is a way of understanding truth and the knowledge and perception of truth. The scepticism of the last several centuries shapes the way we view culture, male–female relationships and the nature of biblical literature. Modernity was secular; there is no higher point of reference. It was, and is, a way of thinking, choosing and living that seeks the novel and rejects past assumptions about knowledge, truth, morals and values.

As Paul Tournier points out,

> The modern soul is hesitant. The evolution of society since the Renaissance has shattered the traditional framework and now man is bewildered, tossed to and fro by contradictory doctrines. The world tells him that feeling, faith, and philosophical truth are unimportant. And this same man cherishes at the bottom of his heart a justified intuition that these problems are nevertheless important. His thirst for love, his spiritual loneliness, his fear of death, the riddle of evil, the mystery of God – he no longer speaks of these things; he represses them, but they still haunt him . . . Modern man suffers from repression of conscience.[44]

There is still a longing, or at least a search, for handles on life that are greater than our own existence. Essentially, men and women are frightened to be alone in such an enormous universe. Thus humanity gropes in the dark for hope beyond itself.

Humanity appreciates that it needs to explain the universe in terms beyond itself. In attempting to explain the 'why?' of existence, however, we are unable to come up with liveable answers. Men and women face a dilemma: either we despair of groping in the dark for hope or we can trick ourselves into thinking that we have found the answers. What we see in our present generation are people tricking themselves. In other words, men and women sense that the conclusions of their own thinking lead to despair and so compensate (whence the trick) by a contradiction or inconsistency.

This leads many of our contemporaries to live lives of boredom and frustration. Escapism is a common pursuit in western life of the 1990s. As modern reality increasingly discomforts and disillusions, postmodern people can switch to new and different worlds through virtual reality. High technology offers entertainment and ways to escape. An article in *Time* magazine quoted a German student's view on the music–video satellite channel, MTV. '"MTV is an illusory world," he says. "It is a flight of the imagination that fulfils a need for fairy tales."'[45] Do we see what this tells us? We do not see many people bravely wrestling with life to find answers; we see people bored and listless.

There are some men and women, however, whose personal integrity will not allow them to settle for meaninglessness. They question. They search to explain why humanity exists in the universe. The question 'Why does the universe exist?' demands answers too. Stephen W. Hawking in *A Brief History of Time* thinks that these questions are fundamental to understanding reality:

> We find ourselves in a bewildering world. We want to make sense of what we see around us and to ask: What is the nature of the universe? What is our place in it and where did it and we come from? Why is it the way it is?[46]

Hawking searches for a unified theory of the universe and asks 'What breathes fire into the equations and makes a universe for them to describe?'[47] He searches as do many of his contemporaries.

Men and women, like Hawking, search because they are human. They love, they create beautiful things, they have personality and they worship. Humans can try to forget or suppress their humanity (and we have only to visit some depressing parts of cities or read the evening newspaper to detect this), but they remain human. Being human matters, and, consequently, we must look beyond the postmodernist dead-end and see a further way.

Seeing the whole: knowing the task before us

A Christian friend asked why we need to understand the past 300 years of intellectual history. He agreed with me that our culture is in trouble. 'But there's no point explaining why we got lost. Tell us how to find our way!' he insisted. My friend said he could not care less about the past. He wanted practical, step-by-step, advice now.

His views are not unique. Many Christians today miss the point. The trends and patterns outlined above have affected and continue to affect the way we *all* think and communicate. In other words, the debates and considerations of philosophers influence the ordinary man and woman in the street without their even realizing it. Relativism, pluralism, modernism and postmodernism are in the very air we breathe. We may not use these terms in our everyday speech, but they influence our accent.

This must not and cannot continue. Our terms and styles must vary, but the desired end must surely be the same: to enable Christians to cope with the thought patterns, assumptions and whispers of our culture in a way that is neither blind nor defensive. I may liken it to my desire for my two daughters to play outside on a winter's day. I want them to have fun and enjoy the outside. At the same time, it is my responsibility to see that they dress to avoid catching colds (negatively) and can play outside tomorrow (positively). Similarly, our understanding of Christian confidence must be relevant to our world. A Christian today must find a way to live in the contemporary world without accepting some fallacies, while living a full, relevant and contributing life.

If we are going to help people gain Christian confidence, we must see them as individual men and women of today. So we cannot simply tell them to stop asking their questions and just believe. Simultaneously, their questions about truth, right and wrong, freedom, love, personality and justice have not arisen in a vacuum or in isolation; individuals bring with them many assumptions of our day. To help, we need to be aware of our mutual context and at times point it out to people.

Additionally, we cannot bring someone to the Bible without also responding to the fundamental question of the Bible's trustworthiness. We are unable to help our friends if we dismiss the implications of living in a pluralistic and multifaith society. Our task is to offer a reasonable and verifiable justification for accepting the gospel of Jesus Christ in contrast to something else.

Due to the shifting sands of this changing age, confidence is problematic. This is the reason Christians need a full and comprehensive understanding of confidence. Undoubtedly, there are many questions we cannot easily answer. We will call for a rational and sane, but nonetheless risky, step of faith by our contemporaries. Yet, this is not an irrational 'leap of faith'. There are good reasons for Christians to be confident in this age of change. We now begin the crucial task of explaining the confidence we can have.

Questions for reflection and discussion

1. What does it mean to see an individual as a man or a woman of today? Do you agree that more change and development have occurred this century than in most previous centuries? Doesn't each generation have basically the same problems and issues?

2. If language is a random arrangement of signs or symbols, what does this imply about our communication to friends, children and neighbours? At the same time, we do often misunderstand another's speech, gestures and writing. But how do we normally overcome these problems?

3. Which do you think makes the best sense: 'Seeing is Believing' or 'Believing is seeing'?

4. How would you answer the question, 'Are not all so-called truths simply ways of describing the same thing?'?

3

The majesty of revelation

We can know what we must know

Who moved the furniture?

If you were to visit my home, the furniture would matter to you. You could sit on the floor, if you so wished; then again, you would probably prefer a chair or the sofa. If I invited you to sit at the table for a meal, the table would contribute to your experience of the meal. To a large extent the furniture in a home dictates what takes place in the home.

The 'furniture' of our culture influences human existence. As furniture in a house defines and even restricts the activities in that house, so the intellectual, philosophical and moral conclusions of our generation influence the ways women and men approach important life issues. As we saw in the previous chapter, today's intellectual and philosophical furniture affects how people think about religious matters. Not surprisingly, the contemporary 'style' leads many people to reject the claims of Christianity. This is conspicuous in the ways they hear or read the Bible. They dismiss biblical Christianity as irrelevant, insignificant or inadequate.

Here is a key problem concerning Christian confidence in a changing age. Because non-Christians dismiss the Bible, their rejection can throw today's thoughtful Christian. This is especially so when the detractors' arguments sound persuasive, intellectually impressive and culturally up to date.

Furthermore, contemporary believers also struggle with the fact that within Christian groups believers differ on interpretations of key biblical texts. The so-called obvious meaning of the Bible starts to look less certain. Add to these problems the fact that the visual image has a stronger influence in our culture than the printed word, and it is not surprising to notice a decline in serious Bible reading and study in many churches. What is the result? Too easily the truthfulness of the Bible is underestimated. Three reasons stand out.

First, ironically, western people today are unaware of the origin of the intellectual and philosophical furniture around them. It is not their day-to-day concern. It is simply part of their life. Thus, as people dismiss the Bible, they do so for reasons they may not appreciate. People think they are rejecting biblical Christianity for self-evident reasons, yet do not ask if their reasons are as obvious as they think. To extend my analogy, contemporary people think that the 'furniture' around them has always been in 'the home', and judge the Bible accordingly. Today's style dominates. Accordingly, there is a scepticism about biblical Christianity as *truth*.

Secondly, there is ignorance of the Bible. It is not a 'story' with which people are familiar. Fewer and fewer young people know Bible stories and biblical characters. Furthermore, the kinds of stories in the Bible *seem* utterly different from today's films, videos and television programmes. It is important for Christians trying to share the gospel to recognize the initial confusion among many contemporaries: 'How could the Bible, of all things, tell me what I need to know about living today?'

Thirdly, Christians become confused as they hear and read others who challenge the truthfulness of the Bible. How do we know whether biblical Christianity is true when so many of our contemporaries feel that truth is nothing more than personal values and preferences? Moreover, all around us thoughtful people reject the claim that any one worldview has a monopoly on truth. The insidious problem is that soon our recognition of this popular denial can lead to our agreement with this denial. Today's pluralism, and the accompanying relativism, challenge Christian confidence. Contemporary ways of thinking question our confidence in the Bible.

These three reasons reveal the vital necessity of a theological framework to arrive at a legitimate Christian confidence. Without a framework that is true and comprehensive we are going to have problems. For if we think back to the experiential issues identified in chapter 1, and attempt to have a hopeful and sane set of guidelines or answers, we must deal with our total theological framework. We could go on to offer step-by-step pastoral solutions to these problems. We could work very hard to ensure that this counsel is biblical. But, unless we are looking to a valid theological framework, a huge question is before us: what do we mean by *biblical*?

Whether it be a Christian struggling with guilt, or another suffering from a dreadfully poor self-esteem, or a young couple confused about their sexual desires for each other, believers today must come to grips with the Bible's significance. Somewhere along this way we need to see, know and experience the truthfulness and rightness of the Bible. If we hope to reach a legitimate and authentic Christian confidence, we must consider how modernism and, increasingly, postmodernism disturb our understanding of biblical revelation. The furniture has been moved, and this is causing problems for so many of us.

In the present chapter we will see that there is a way of living in this world other than with the collection of contemporary furnishings. It is not an idiosyncratic preference for life in the past, like preferring Elizabethan furniture to contemporary Scandinavian design. A truly radical and alternative way of living is possible. There are truths we can and must know. These truths will begin to shape the necessary theological framework. We will consider what we mean by the term *biblical revelation*, and how that meaning relates to Christian confidence. Our aim is a confidence about the truthfulness and rightness of the gospel promises which we learn about in the Bible.

A matter of public truth

An important qualification, however, is necessary. When I use the words 'truthfulness' and 'rightness' of the Bible, I do so for a very important reason. Think back to our definition of confidence.[1] Confidence is knowing and realizing that the promises God makes in the gospel are *true.* How do we reach this degree of confidence, without a particular appreciation for the Bible? Without it, experiencing this distinguishing Christian confidence in an age of change is impossible.

Perceiving the truthfulness and rightness of the Bible is more than considering the Bible as a self-contained religious entity – a spiritual equivalent to the golf club's members' handbook, relevant only to the members of the club. Truthfulness and rightness should not be based on 'faith', as this term is understood by so many. Why not?

If we accept that the Bible is true and right solely because we believe it is, or our faith commitment leads us to this conclusion, we remove the foundation from underneath us. Undoubtedly, a person who has an active and genuine trust in Jesus Christ is going to read the Bible differently from another person who does not trust Jesus Christ. Apart from the Lord's supernatural influence upon our mind and heart, we will read Scripture with a spiritual, moral and intellectual blindness or dyslexia.[2] Yet if we make a person's faith the chief influence, the danger is soon apparent: biblical teachings could be limited to what people call 'spirituality' – something different from truth about morals, ethics and life for all humans. We are back to the analogy of a golf club's members' handbook. To put it bluntly, a person could say, 'Well, I'm not a Christian. I don't have faith in your God, so the Bible is utterly meaningless and irrelevant to me.'

Truthfulness and rightness mean seeing the Bible as the best and most accurate means of understanding the world, ourselves and, above all, the one true God. It stands true, whether a person acknowledges it or not. Faith is the valid response to the Bible's truthful proclamation – but the Bible is truth for all humanity, despite a person's response. This claim, of course, is controversial today!

Yet here is precisely where we must engage in critical and cautious thinking to shape a theological framework relevant to our contemporaries' doubts about the Bible. Since we too have our problems, what we have to say about the Bible also relates powerfully to our Christian confidence. I am convinced that Tom Wright puts his finger on the pulse:

> The reason why stories come into conflict with each other is that the worldviews, and the stories which characterize them, are in principle *normative*: that is, they claim to make sense of the whole of reality. Even the relativist, who believes that everybody's point of view on everything is equally valid even though apparently incompatible, is obedient to an underlying story about reality which comes into explicit conflict with most other stories, which speak of reality as in the

last analysis a seamless web, open in principle to experience, observation and discussion. It is ironic that many people in the modern world have regarded Christianity as a private worldview, a set of private stories. Some Christians have actually played right into this trap. But in principle the whole point of Christianity is that it offers a story which is the story of the whole world. It is public truth.[3]

It is crucial to see the Bible as 'public truth' to have a theological framework that will help us grow in confidence. For the five reasons I now offer, biblical Christians can know and proclaim the truthfulness and rightness of the gospel promises offered to us and explained for us in the Bible. We can know what we must know.

1. Truth is knowable, because he has made himself known

Over thirty years ago, one man made a remarkable journey. Gherman Titov, the Soviet cosmonaut and second man in space, reportedly announced upon his return to earth, 'I saw no God nor angels while in orbit.' Titov made not only a remarkable journey but an astonishing statement. His quip apparently assumed that if there were a God, we ought to be able to spot him in his back garden out in space.

A friend may well challenge us to prove the existence of God. In fact, we cannot. We may offer several answers, but these are not proofs in the sense that we can establish proof for a scientific theory. We may point to aspects of the universe around us or to particular qualities of our human character and experience as 'evidence' of God's existence. As humans, however, we do not prove God's existence. In this regard, Titov's alleged statement is astonishing: did he really think that orbiting the earth would solve our human questioning?

Where do we begin? Is there a proper way to speak of a knowable God? Here we touch the issue of objectivity and knowledge, a vast subject. Nonetheless, we can at least offer the following.

If there is a God, then logically and reasonably God must be greater than we. For the sake of argument, he, she or it cannot be human, otherwise it would be more accurate to identify God as simply one of us. Likewise, God cannot logically and reasonably be both God and an equal part of creation. Every child knows this when he or she asks, 'But who made God?' Taking things a bit further, if there is a God, and if he, she or it is not the result of our own psychological projections or imaginations, then God must be knowable principally through God's own initiative.

I repeatedly used the phrase 'logically and reasonably'; but this is not to say that human logic and reason prove God's existence. I am only pointing to an aspect of knowledge. We know someone because, in the first place, another person is there. In contrast, when my children were quite young they had imaginary playmates. There were occasions when I was invited to have tea with one or two of them! However vivid my children's imagination and play, these did not prove the existence of their playmates. These imaginary friends were not really knowable. There was never any real and verifiable communication. Communication (either verbal or non-verbal) is the means by which we start to know the existence of another person. Here is the vital point: because there is communication from the one true God, we can begin to know him.

God makes himself known. The 'how' of this revelation requires fuller definition and explanation, and we come to this shortly. What we are saying at this point is that truth is knowable because God's revelation is humanly intelligible. Humanity can receive revelation and understand this revelation. How humanity responds to this revelation (obediently or disobediently, in worship or not) will be considered. The immediate assertion is that God's revelation is not incongruent or irrelevant to men and women. God's revelation is not totally beyond us.

Take away the first claim, and God is silent. If there is a God, humanity knows God through its own discovery. It would be more logical to conclude that there is no God or that God is merely a human projection. Dismiss the second claim, and humanity possesses less dignity. God may reveal truth about himself, but humans are incapable of understanding his revelation. We are thus ignorant about the most important aspect of reality. Either way, if truth is not knowable, and not for the reasons mentioned, then there is no basis for Christian confidence. The knowableness of God, therefore, is fundamental to Christian confidence in our changing age. God's knowableness, however, is not predicated on the human ability to know. It is principally the result of God's kindness, mercy and sovereign intention. The next point amplifies my meaning.

2. God is knowable through his own initiative, not through human insight

God is. All discussion of the one true God really begins with God, not with humanity. As the Swiss theologian Emil Brunner wrote, 'There is a doctrine of God, in the legitimate sense of the words, only in as far as God Himself imparts it.'[4] Humanity knows God because he was, he is, he will ever be. There is no other legitimate starting-point. At the heart of revelation there is one who makes himself known.[5]

What does the word 'revelation' mean? A clear definition can help to avoid problems.[6] Revelation is communication from God to humanity. God communicates truth about himself and his relationship with his creation. Revelation is God's self-initiated and self-ordained disclosure; it is his own doing. J. I. Packer writes,

> Revelation is a divine activity: not, therefore, a human achievement. Revelation is not the same thing as discovery, or the dawning of insight, or the emerging of a bright idea. Revelation does not mean man finding God, but God finding man, God sharing His secrets with us, God showing us Himself. In revelation, God is the agent as well as the object. It is not just that men speak about God, or for God; God speaks for Himself, and talks to us in person. The New Testament message is that in Christ God has spoken a word for the world, a word to which all men in all ages are summoned to listen to and respond.[7]

Packer quite rightly underlines the personal nature of revelation. In one way, when we speak of God's self-revelation, we do not mean that God has physically shown himself, as in a blinding flash or cosmic display. Principally, God's revelation of himself has been through truths about himself. The distinction needs to be made.

Nonetheless, too sharp a distinction is unhelpful. The truths God makes known are, first, descriptive. God *really* is as he tells us, even through non-literal analogy, metaphor or simile. Secondly, revelation is not exhaustive, but what we are given truthfully tells us what God wants us to know about himself. These truths are not exhaustive (that is, total). We who are finite cannot possibly comprehend the infinite. Still, what we can know is sufficient and truthful.

Our knowledge of the one true God will grow, deepen and change in the sense that we will learn more about him. Yet this growth is not so much a matter of correction or updating as a development in intimacy. Consequently, revelation is purposeful. Truths about God are given to us so that we will turn away from our idolatry and autonomy and worship God in *relationship*. As Packer argues, revelation is always a summons.

Why do we stress this? Because God's revelation proceeds fundamentally from a divine origin, not from a human insight. The Bible is not simply the collective spiritual musings of nomadic, Jewish and Hellenistic cultures. It is not only the stories of the faith journeys of men and women. Of course, the Bible is earthed in particular human circumstances. In these human events, there is human interpretation of divine revelation. Sometimes Scripture expresses God's revelation through approved human activity; in other cases, the Bible tells us about God through condemnation or conspicuous silence regarding human behaviour. Furthermore, the Bible conveys a knowledge of God presented both incrementally (or progressively) and with an eye on the whole. In other words, we need the whole of the Bible's 'story', and its witness to Jesus, to understand the particulars of one part of the biblical narrative and revelation.

Nevertheless, the Bible is not the inherited spiritual meditations of one guru, the collected folk sayings of one tribe or the single momentary flash of a cosmic force. It is God made known through human language and reference. Scripture is his self-revelation.[8]

3. God is knowable through human language and reference

At this point the attentive reader can see the direction in which my line of argument is travelling. In the ancient biblical writings the one true God is knowable, supremely as these writings bear witness to the risen Lord Jesus Christ. Yet surely this is a problem. How can the infinite and transcendent be described by what is finite and immanent? Can human words adequately describe and convey the emotional power of a painting by Rembrandt or Monet? Can words and sentences correspond to the aesthetic, non-rational and experiential? If these examples highlight a communication problem, how much more do we have a problem describing God? Is not God ineffable, beyond descriptive words?

Allow me to give extra attention to this third important claim, for it is at this level that many challenges to the Bible arise and Christian confidence is troubled. We will concentrate on two crucial implications. First, though the natural world points to evidence of God's existence, we need the special revelation of the Bible. Secondly, though the Bible is human literature, which must be read as literature, it is possible for contemporary readers to obtain a sufficiently clear sense of meaning from the Bible. We can know what we must know.

(1) Though the natural world points to evidence of God's existence, we need the special revelation of the Bible.

Suppose a young person, not a professing Christian, takes a three-day hike with me in the Swiss Alps. He is taken aback by my opinion that the Bible gives me the best guide to knowing the one true God and to knowing myself. 'A book?' my friend asks. 'How can you limit this God in whom you say you believe to a printed page?'

'Well, I don't *limit* God to a book,' I reply. 'My chief point of reference is Jesus of Nazareth, God's king. I am saying that the Bible is the authoritative and trustworthy witness or reference to the one true God.'

'But surely,' continues my friend, 'we have a greater sense of this God's mystery or realness as we look at all these wonderful sights before us along this mountain path, as we feel the wind in our face and as we experience a certain kind of joy?'

Have we not heard similar objections from friends who not only are involved in New Age spiritualities but reject modernity's emphasis on technology and the material? Equally, in our changing age when more people are curious about the mystery of nature's 'wildness' or 'awesomeness', people are puzzled by our insistence on biblical literature as a testimony. How do we respond? Let me continue in Switzerland to make my point.

High in the Swiss Alps is the stunningly beautiful village of Mürren. Walking through the village and higher up to the Alpine meadows, hikers feel that they could reach out and touch the massive, impressive and forbidding Jungfrau. Towering over several villages, the snow-capped Jungfrau powerfully displays how small men and women are. Sitting in an Alpine meadow, gazing up to this mountain, the rugged awesomeness is almost palpable. At the same time, at the hiker's feet are delicate Alpine flowers. To look at the flowers and then at the majestic mountain leaves a person in wonder and amazement. There is grandeur, beauty and power.

In Mürren, a late twentieth-century man or a woman *knows* right there that humanity is not the measure of all; there is a greater, mysterious and awesome *otherness*. The poet William Wordsworth, after a visit to the French and Swiss Alps, put it this way,

> Tumult and peace, the darkness and the light –
> Were all like workings of one mind, the features
> Of the same face, blossoms upon one tree;
> Characters of the great Apocalypse,
> The types and symbols of Eternity,
> Of first, and last, and midst, and without end.'[9]

Like Wordsworth, my late-twentieth-century hiking companion is more inclined to look at nature than to a book to discover truths about the divine. It seems to make more sense. In one sense he is not wrong. Christians sometimes refer to what is called *natural revelation*.

Natural revelation is available to all humanity, particularly the evidence within creation and in the innate human sense of right and wrong which is expressed in various cultures throughout human history. We might point to the orderliness and grandeur of creation as natural revelation. Several psalms concur (Ps. 8, 19, 21). Some think that the apostle Paul appealed to a natural revelation in Acts 14:17–18, 17:26–28 and Romans 1:18–20. Apparently, Paul accepted a 'natural' religiosity.

Yet there are limits to natural revelation. It does not go far enough, or, more important, we do not go far enough with it. Psalms 8, 19 and 21 point to a kind of testimony in the created order. Nature's evidences are true and relate to what is real; yet nature is too great for humanity's intellect. More to the point, our hearts are turned inwards and we are reluctant to worship nature's creator.

The Bible stresses the insufficiency of natural revelation and the reprehensible ways in which humanity responds. We experience and know that we are more than material, more than what we see around us in nature. Yet we are at a loss to understand. The tension in natural revelation is its limited efficiency because of our sinfulness. The temptation to look 'downwards' at creation (ourselves, others or other created beings and objects) is too great. This is the apostle Paul's main argument in Romans 1:19–20, 'so that men are without excuse'. Similarly, in Acts 17:22–31, Paul challenges not so much the Athenians' innate sense of morality and religiosity as what they have done with this knowledge: idolatry and foolish thinking (17:29–30).

Any natural theology is flawed if it does not point beyond itself, the material, to the personal, God. This is where pantheistic religions, essentially monistic (in effect, saying that everything in reality is one, a single unity), cut any sense of personality out of the universe.

As Guinness points out:

> If pre-Christian Western deities failed because, although they were personal, they were finite (were the Greek gods behind the fates or the fates behind the gods?), the Eastern gods now fail because, although they are infinite (and so sufficient to carry philosophical unity as a universal), they are impersonal and thus offer no basis for the value of human personality.[10]

There is nature, but there is someone beyond and above nature. Here is the staggering claim of Proverbs 8:22-36, John 1:3–4, Acts 17:30–31, and Hebrews 1:1–3. Our humanity requires that we know the Personality above the created universe.

On our own, with natural revelation, we distort the evidence and move into idolatry. We need something further, something special. We must give greater attention to and trust in, what is called *special revelation*. Why? For the very reason that it is *special*. This brings us to the Bible. We are back, however, to the issue of the written page.

(2) Though the Bible is human literature, and must be read as human literature, it is possible for contemporary readers to obtain a sufficiently clear sense of meaning from the Bible.

He is one of the brightest young men I know. Before coming to university he became a Christian. While reading modern languages at Oxford, he began to experience a dilemma. As he read his Bible, he found that he was forced to read the Scriptures with an 'eye' or 'mindset' different from that with which he read his academic texts. He wanted to read the Bible with commitment and confidence. Faith was his reading 'key' into the biblical texts to find their meaning. In tutorials or lectures, however, he was expected to question whether any text had an obvious and agreed meaning.

He soon felt that he was in two literary worlds: the world of his contemporary literary studies and the world of his 'quiet time' Bible reading. His confidence in the Bible started to ebb. Furthermore, he heard various Christian leaders and preachers offer (some with considerable analytical detail) conflicting interpretations over such significant topics as women's ministries, healings, and congregational worship. He was left with the question, 'What does it mean to *read* the Bible and what does my reading *mean*?'

This young man is not alone in his struggle. Perhaps some of us may not understand what the problem is here; for others it is a daily battle. Nevertheless, all of us are affected to the extent that we seek to read the Bible to know what we must know. Whether we like it or not, we make certain assumptions: about the Bible, our ability to read an ancient text and our ability to apply what we read into our particular contexts. While there are various in-depth studies to help us, let us trace, in what follows, the general lines of our theological framework.

Human words, sentences, metaphors, similes, discourse and syntax are employed not only in a human attempt to describe God but in *God's personal communication to men and women.* To take one example, Moses encounters God, but not at Moses' initiation (Ex. 3:1ff.). The God of the universe makes himself known. 'When the LORD saw that he had gone over to look, God called to him from within the bush, "Moses! Moses!"' (Ex. 3:4). In this encounter, God self-discloses his name and character. God communicates in and through language symbols suitable to Moses' human comprehension, which are, simultaneously, truly and consistently appropriate to God's being. 'I am the God of your father, the God of Abraham, the God of Isaac and the God of Jacob' (Ex. 3:6). 'God said to

Moses, "I AM WHO I AM. This is what you are to say to the Israelites: I AM has sent me to you"' (Ex. 3:14). God fits his self-disclosure to human coordinates (words, sentence structures, names and language systems) that are understandable to his people at any one point in history. Otherwise, how could Moses understand and respond?

The expressions 'truly', 'consistently' and 'appropriate' mean that these language symbols in the biblical texts are not false or deficient means of divine revelation. What other than human symbols would God choose? If God's gracious intention is that humanity should comprehend and know him, then the medium through which the revelation comes is important.

This tells us that, at its very basic level, the Bible is not immediately ridiculous. It is the means by which men and women may know the one who is knowable, God. While it is human literature, with human syntax and linguistic structures, it is also the knowable God making himself known. Human language, human symbols, may be allowed to describe the divine because God so chooses.[11]

Human language, of course, cannot completely convey God's fullness. God is transcendent and infinite. All our languages are limited and set within a finite context, and they too are affected by human fallenness. We must not, however, accept the error of some contemporary thinking.[12] Human language and symbols in Scripture are valid and trustworthy referents precisely because God chooses to convey his revelation through them.

This becomes more crucial when we think about the Christian claim that the Word (Gk. *logos*) became flesh (Jn. 1:1, 14) in the historical person, Jesus of Nazareth. The Bible reveals what *really is*, but does so in and through human experience. God makes himself known in their life and situations. The incarnation (God the Son becoming the human Jesus of Nazareth) is the ultimate referent. In using the term 'referent' I mean that there is a meaningful association between *A* and that which identifies or describes *A*. For example, the sign tells me that the airport (what the sign refers to, the referent) is 5 km ahead. The sign is not the airport, but the sign is a trustworthy marker for me as I drive, aiming to meet a friend at the airport (the referent). How then do we know that human experience and language matter, and that it is a means by which the creator and redeemer God makes himself known? By Jesus, the Son of God.

Jesus Christ is revelation which is fully involved in human experience. He was not a 'pretend' human. He was really and fully human. His incarnation is, therefore, the supreme reference that tells us that God speaks to us in and through human experience, action and speech. The Bible tells us that truth is knowable through human language and reference because Truth himself became fully human and was a totally human referent in time-space history – speaking, acting and living. He is the point to revelation and the essence of revelation.

There is, however, another huge question before us. As readers, can we find legitimate meaning(s) when we read the Bible, in whole or in part? As I mentioned briefly in chapter 2, this is one of the large questions posed by particular themes in contemporary linguistics, hermeneutics and literary theories.

For example, when we read Jesus' parable of the good Samaritan (Lk. 10:25-37), may we say that this is a biblical injunction to use 'oil and wine' in a church's first-aid kit? If we think this is a silly interpretation, why? What makes a 'right' interpretation 'right'? If the parable were read by a group of people from the USA, Bulgaria and Thailand, would the nationals of each country read it differently from the others, precisely because they each come from a different society?

Consider the story of Gideon (Jdg. 6:1 – 8:35). If someone in our home-group insists that the meaning and significance of this story must be determined by where Gideon fits into the story of Israel's judges and how this period fits into God's overall covenant promises with the seed of Abraham, is he or she too academic? Suppose someone else 'hears' God telling him to ask for a sign concerning a choice between taking an overseas holiday or working at a two-week summer youth camp. Is this person too subjective? What is the meaning and significance of the story of Gideon? Can we reach a more or less common agreement? Or is each person meant to receive whatever he or she senses? Some Christians who take the Bible very seriously read it 'as the Spirit leads'. How do they differ from some academic advocates of postmodern reader-response hermeneutics who believe that a text has whatever meaning(s) the reader senses? Can we really say that 'we can know what we must know'?

These questions are not necessarily reserved for the academic élite. Think about the challenge we sometimes hear: 'You Christians can prove anything you want from the Bible!' What happens when we listen to a sermon or a small-group Bible study and begin to wonder if this accusation is indeed true?

In their very helpful book *Linguistics and Biblical Interpretation*, Peter Cotterell and Max Turner recommend a positive way through our possible confusion.[13] Through what they call *discourse analysis* we can reach a degree of *discourse meaning*. Essentially this implies that we analyse a discourse (any form of oral and written communication) in its structure before we reach a conclusion about its meaning. We can arrive at a meaning that we test or evaluate only after we analyse the discourse. In other words, we can explain the meaning of the parable of the good Samaritan only as we look at the structure and placement of this material in Luke's Gospel. Only then will we be in a position to shift the meaning to our personal situation(s).

How do we do this? We do this as we read a letter from a friend or an article in a magazine. In our analysis we look at a passage's immediate context (the words and sentences that make it up). We examine too how our passage relates to levels of context: for example, in one of Paul's letters, we appreciate that any one verse comes in a paragraph and the paragraph is part of the whole letter. In a somewhat similar way we look at (say) how the parable of the good Samaritan fits into Luke's Gospel and the book of Acts.

From this analysis we are better able to decide the *discourse meaning*.[14] To be sure, we run the risk here of letting our 'world' influence us. By 'world' we mean our own culture – its values, concerns and social structures. For example, it is hard to avoid the influence of our society's understanding of male and female relations as we read some sections of Paul's letter to the Corinthians. We need to be aware of this influence, and of the possibility that we approach the texts with some initial assumptions.

Cotterell and Turner however, stress the possibility that we can read a passage and see the sense, meaning and significance of the text before us. It is challenging, but possible to discover the author's meaning(s) for his readers. From this we can reasonably determine how this original meaning (or these original meanings) suggest a meaning (or meanings) for our day.

Is all this hard work? Yes. Does it necessarily deny the influence of the Holy Spirit, as we said earlier in this chapter? Not at all. Hard work by both preacher and reader is involved in the Spirit's help. We are to read, and read well. Is this to suggest that we must all be highly educated? Not necessarily. Yet the lack of confidence that many Christians have about the Bible is, in part, the consequence of the failure of pastors and leaders to help and teach them to read the Bible well. Here is where the book by Gordon Fee and Douglas Stuart, *How to Read the Bible for All its Worth*, is proving helpful.[15] I also recommend, for even more practical help, Anthony Bash's *Stepping Into Bible Study*.[16]

The fundamental basis for our confidence is a knowledge that men and women can read a text and reach a critical and realistic sense of the text's meaning. Any conclusion we make about a text's meaning and its significance for us will probably have to be tested and re-examined. For some of us, today's critical tools can be applied. Yet the bedrock of our confidence is a philosophical commitment that challenges some of today's desperate and hopeless assumptions about literature and reading.[17]

4. *The Bible tells us* who *God is*

God speaks to us, invites us and summons us to a new relationship with him. People are not called to know a theory or set of philosophical axioms. God makes himself known that we might worship him, relate to him, obey him and love him.

The clearest proof of this is Jesus. He, a human, speaking human words in a fully human context, is the goal of revelation and the supreme definition of revelation. In Matthew's gospel, Jesus declares, 'Come to me, all you who are weary and burdened, and I will give you rest. Take my yoke upon you and learn from me, for I am gentle and humble in heart, and you will find rest for your souls. For my yoke is easy and my burden is light' (Mt. 11:28-30).

Because Jesus is who he is, he gives the meaning and significance to the existential or experiential dynamic – the experience of entering into a good relationship with God. How does he do this? Each of the subsequent chapters in this book details this, but the immediate point here is that our relationship with the one true God is shaped by truth. God's revelation is, in one practical sense, his way for us to avoid error and confusion. Lest we worship the creation rather than the creator, God speaks to us. God tells us *who* he is, not just what he is; and there is a reason: that we respond. This is a theme running through the whole of the Bible, which Jesus' ministry confirms.

A notable example comes to mind. The prophet Elijah, battling against the pagan priests of Baal on Mount Carmel (1 Ki. 18:16–46), does not ask the people to choose between two equal deities. Instead, he confronts his people with their ignorance about the one true God. As the tension mounts, Elijah prays,

> O LORD, God of Abraham, Isaac and Israel, let it be known today that you are God in Israel and that I am your servant and have done all these things at your command. Answer me, O LORD, answer me, so these people will know that you, O LORD, are God, and that you are turning their hearts back again (1 Ki. 18:36–37).

When God speaks and acts it is always to enable people to *know him in relationship*. Elijah's prayer on Mount Carmel, like the ministry of all the Old Testament prophets, reflects a confidence in revelation. Men and women can know who God is; they can be freed from ignorance and wrong living through the Lord's merciful self-disclosure. Quite often, the Bible confronts God's people with the challenge, 'You should know better.'

Accordingly, Jesus' teaching continues this theme. His life and ministry provide not data but God's means to reconciliation, wholeness and salvation. This is noticeable in the way Jesus' words are linked with wisdom (see Mt. 7:24–29; 11:16–19, 25; 12:42; 13:54; 25:1–13; Lk. 10:21; 12:42). Wisdom is not a philosophical or simply a moral virtue. In the Old Testament, Wisdom is personified, especially in the book of Proverbs. Wisdom calls out to young men, to avoid adulterous entanglement (Pr. 8:1 – 9:18). She brings life and re-creation. When the New Testament writers spoke into their Jewish context and into a Hellenistic culture, gospel revelation as wisdom always remained *personal* (1 Cor. 1:18 – 2:16; Col. 1:9, 28; 2:2–3).

This personal relationship is a central aspect of Jesus' teaching. His revelation has the aim of establishing a good relationship between a believer and the triune God. In John's Gospel, Philip says, 'Lord, show us the Father and that will be enough for us' (Jn. 14:8). At this point in the Gospel, there have already been many 'signs'; there is enough for Philip to have 'seen'. Jesus' response to Philip reiterates a central theme in the fourth Gospel: believing is seeing; and both lead to relationship.

> Jesus answered: 'Don't you know me, Philip, even after I have been among you such a long time? Anyone who has seen me has seen the Father. How can you say, "Show us the Father?" Don't you believe that I am in the Father, and that the Father is in me? The words I say to you are not just my own. Rather, it is the Father, living in me, who is doing his work. Believe me when I say that I am in the Father and the Father is in me; or at least believe on the evidence of the miracles themselves. I tell you the truth, anyone who has faith in me will do what I have been doing. He will do even greater things than these, because I am going to the Father. And I will do whatever you ask in my name, so that the Son may bring glory to the Father. You may ask me for anything in my name, and I will do it' (Jn. 14:9–14).

Men and women can know God truly and really. Again, we must stress that our knowledge of God is of a particular kind and it is limited. Our knowledge of the Lord is not exhaustive, and it is often deficient due to our weaknesses and failures. Nevertheless, a deep-seated panic or nagging doubt about God's trustworthiness, faithfulness or power is never legitimate, given who he has told us he is. In particular circumstances we occasionally experience a degree of panic and doubt. Scripture implies that this is a common struggle. But the superior factor is the sufficiency of God's revelation (see Nu. 23:19; Rom. 3:4; Tit. 1:2; Heb. 6:18; Jas. 1:17; 1 Jn. 2:21). If we may put it this way, there will not come a time when we will be surprised and disappointed, as, for example, Dorothy, the Scarecrow, the Tin Man and the Lion were when they discovered that the great Wizard of Oz was nothing more than an old man behind a curtain. We can know what we must know about the one true God: Father, Son and Holy Spirit.

5. The Bible tells about the way things we know and experience really are

John Calvin insisted at the beginning of every edition of his

Institutes of the Christian Religion, 'Nearly all the wisdom we possess, that is to say, true and sound wisdom, consists of two parts: the knowledge of God and of ourselves.'[18] In the French version of 1560 he put it more forcibly: 'In knowing God, each of us also knows himself.'[19]

The Bible tells us not only about God but about ourselves and the world in which we live. It commands us to repent, to reject false worship and to begin true worship, to jettison falsehoods and to embrace wholesome truths; but it never asks us to be non-human and to live on planet Mars.

Here is a remarkable measure of the confidence we can have in the Word of God. While Christians point to archaeology, ancient non-biblical writings and the multiple extant manuscripts to prove the trustworthiness of Scripture, on their own these valid arguments do not answer people's objections and questions conclusively. They are helpful, but more is required.

If we look additionally in the direction Calvin suggests, we have another means of confidence. We may ask particular questions about the Bible, questions that relate to our humanity and the world in which we find ourselves. In this task we can be confident that we can at least know something about ourselves and our world. This is what Tom Wright calls the critical-realist epistemology.[20] By this he means that we can be realistic about what we can know – things really do exist and we can know them to some extent. Yet because our personalities, prejudices and limitations influence the way we know things, we have to be careful. In this respect we employ what Wright calls 'stories', with which we assess, correct or modify our understanding of ourselves and the world. Worldviews are 'stories'.[21]

I think Wright echoes Calvin, and that we can see how the biblical worldview, as a 'story', is a sufficient way of knowing what we need to know about ourselves, our world and our creator. I go so far as to argue that it is the best story or worldview. By 'best' I mean most accurate, most comprehensive, and most truthful. The basis of this confidence, however, is not a late-twentieth-century, contentless 'faith'.

In a helpful study on the justification of belief, David L. Wolfe declared, 'The believer is a critical adventurer, taking rationally responsible risks. If he or she takes a leap of faith, it should be a leap conditioned by criticism in its choice of alternatives and responsible for continued criticism after the leap.'[22] Building on his statement, I have found it most helpful to ask four questions about any worldview or 'story':

1. Does this describe the world we already know?
2. Does this describe the 'us' we already know?
3. Is this consistent with itself?
4. Is this liveable?

These questions may sound complicated, but it is essential to ask them of any worldview, including the major world religions. Harold Netland, in his book *Dissonant Voices*, does this superbly.[23] We need to ask the same questions about New Age spiritualities, hedonism and every other expression of our age. To be sure, our relativistic culture will not like this process, but even at this point we should ask the relativist if his or her worldview can answer these questions. The Christian and non-Christian *must* ask, 'How else can we accept and believe something unless it relates to what is fundamental to our human situation?'

I put it this way because, when I discuss these questions with university students, someone will ask usually why and how I think these questions are valid. The justification for asking these questions is our human predicament. As humans we live, feel, think, ponder and wonder. Human self-reflection is a hallmark of our species' history. Our humanity leads us to ask, 'Who am I? Who are we? How do we relate to what we see around us?' James Sire, in his important book on worldviews, *The Universe Next Door*, convincingly argues that these types of questions form the basis of every worldview.[24] So I do not think I am 'stacking the deck' when I invite non-Christians to ask these questions about their worldview. I insist that Christians should do the same. It is part of the process of considering if what we think we know is what we need to know.

For example, every worldview tries to describe reality. But we must ask, 'Is it consistent with itself? Is it liveable?' Consider some New Age expressions. Does the claim that 'all is one' (monism) match with the reality we see around us? Can we really accept that there is no material differentiation between one object and another, or between two people? Does it explain in a sensible way the reality I must face when I drive my car on the motorway or when I go for a walk with my daughters? These are justifiable questions, and what I also have to apply as I read the Bible. Will it tell me what I need to know? Can I consistently base my life on it?

For in contrast, say, to certain New Age emphases, the biblical worldview declares there is a created unity but also a metaphysical diversity. Genesis 1 – 2 come immediately to mind. There is unity in creation but also created diversity. Now before we read the Bible we already know and experience these truths. So as we examine the Bible, and ask, 'Does this describe the world we already know?' we not only read the Scriptures in a new way, we are also interacting with information not entirely alien to us. We learn things that, in a way, we already tentatively know. It is apparent to us that not all things are one. The New Age 'story' or worldview is not self-evidently real. To use Wright's idea of critical realism, New Age cosmology does not fit with what we can already know.

'But', someone insists, 'you say this only because you are so caught in your western culture. Your evaluation is biased!' Admittedly, this is a salutary warning. On the other hand, we must have some way of challenging and questioning. There needs to be some way of verifying the claims of differing worldviews. Does a radical change in thinking (what some in the New Age call a 'paradigm shift') really and completely explain the social problems of humans like us? In other words, is our problem really that we in the West think wrongly? Is our failure to accept monism simply due to our western intellectual traditions? If we are one with the whole of existence, then how is it that we perceive our own individualities? How is love explained? How can justice or injustice be explained according to the New Age worldview?

Yet when we turn to the Bible it not so much confirms our prejudices and presuppositions as defines and clarifies what it means to be human and how humanity relates to the created order. For example, the Bible also tells us what, in a way, we already know about ourselves: men and women have an intrinsic dignity. We are unique in the created order because we are made in the image of the one true God. To be sure, humanity is not to ignore the integrity of the created order, yet we are not on equal footing with a tree or with a squirrel up in that tree. It is not a question necessarily of superiority as much as of uniqueness and significance. We do not have to be Christians to sense and know that humanity is significant; we may even offer some explanation. The significance or distinctiveness of our humanity, however, is clarified and elaborated for us when we turn to the biblical worldview.

Of course the immediate question humans ask concerns our human dilemma. There is death. Whether through violence, war, disease or accident, death stalks us all. The tensions in family affairs, tribal relations, regional and national exchange and international relationships mirror the image of death. Something is not right. Harold Netland points out how every major world religion seeks to diagnose the human dilemma and offer a prescription.[25] When certain expressions of Hinduism or Buddhism tell us that our problem is ignorance or blindness concerning reality, how does this relate to the 'evening news'? Is the global solution a matter of 'enlightenment'? If Shintoism essentially tells us that there is nothing really morally wrong with humanity but that we suffer from defilement, how can we see this worked out in international affairs? Do these propositions really describe the 'us' we know?

Islam, Judaism and Christianity speak of human sin. Yet here too questions arise. What solution deals with our human dilemma, if sin is the explanation? Does this solution tell us about our humanity and does this solution tell us about the particular God or gods we can know? Does God, or do the gods, expect us to improve ourselves, look for pardon, blame others, rescue ourselves or something else? Where do love, justice and forgiveness come in this solution?

The Bible claims that our fundamental problem is captivity and rebellion. It is not our thinking that needs correction (although it too is profoundly affected) so much as our moral character. The Scriptures point to a loving and just answer in Jesus Christ. We already know what love and justice mean; the Bible explains and points to the definitive meaning and example. We begin to see how our creator rightly commands our worship.

At the heart of our problem is what the Bible defines as human rebellion. We may not like this idea, but, when we ask, 'Does this describe the "us" we know?' in honesty, we see sin's manifestations all around us. Perhaps we do not use the word 'sin', but we know something is not right. The Bible confirms our moral dilemma and trauma: it interprets them and defines them, also offering God's solution.

Equally, the biblical worldview argues that God is not within creation but is the creator. He is distinct from his creation; pantheism is quite mistaken. God is knowable not through looking into ourselves, but through receiving his revelation in the Old and New Testaments that reflects supremely the revelation in Jesus Christ. The one, true, creator God is not a force; God is personal, within the Trinity of Father, Son and Holy Spirit. God, however, is not in our image. He is infinite and transcendent. He is wholly other.

Admittedly, we do not necessarily know this about God on our own; and this has been the flow throughout this chapter. Nevertheless, critical realism assesses the claim that we are divine, part of a cosmic whole, and cannot but find this suggestion somewhat lacking. This is not merely a consequence of western philosophical traditions. Our devout Jewish and Muslim friends, whose traditions are not entirely western, would also have problems with New Age thinking.

To conclude, the biblical worldview, while quite supernatural, does not nullify what is reasonable and logical. Yes, there are many mysteries that our finite minds cannot begin to fathom but, as created beings in the image of God, we perceive and acknowledge that the fundamental realities are knowable and verifiable. This has been a theme running through this entire chapter on revelation. Take away our ability to know, and humanity is progressively dehumanized; however great the mystical experiences of Shirley MacLaine and others, we must be allowed to ask, 'OK, but how do you know that this is the truth?'

In a way, throughout the rest of this book these four questions, introduced above, stand in the background. To shift to another analogy, these four questions, and the biblical answers, begin to stake out the corners of our theological framework. While we may need to ask these questions often in our Christian living and learning (for this is what disciples of Christ do in the midst of contemporary ideas and life situations), we can still live a legitimately confident life. It is possible because it is biblical. We can know what we must know.

Hearing truth over the din of our culture's scream

'Did God really say ...?' has been the nagging question throughout human history (Gn. 3:1). Biblical Christianity always proclaims that God speaks authoritatively and transcends each generation. His Word is normative for every culture. The Bible makes this assumption, one that Jesus acknowledged and the apostles recognized. Apostolic faith stands on the sure trustworthiness of Scripture.

Christianity cannot be rightly understood and then 'accepted' without an acknowledgment of the Bible's trustworthiness. To become a Christian involves a conviction that what the Bible 'says' is universal truth. To be sure, being a Christian is more than acknowledging a book (a book that is a translation of ancient Hebrew and Greek writings into our mother tongue). Still, the process of becoming a Christian and living the Christian life includes a special conviction regarding the Bible.

God is not silent. He speaks and his people are commanded. The Bible does not provide us with exhaustive information. The point is that Scripture gives us totally sufficient knowledge. We learn about the creator and redeemer God. He tells us about ourselves and our life in the world. We know what we know because God is who he is.

We are not all-knowing and all-wise. Humility before God and before each other is mandatory. Yet we risk reckless folly when we accept our culture's scepticism and uncertainty about truth. Our culture may employ clever rhetoric but it is not always the mark of wisdom. Sadly, things at the end of this century do not appear promising. Nonetheless, there is a sane and life-giving alternative. In this alternative a Christian can be confident, even at the close of the twentieth century. Of course, we have only started to point out the theological framework in which we can see this confident life. We have yet to describe, explain and apply the characteristics of this life and confidence. To this task we now turn.

Questions for reflection and discussion

1. Can there be a Christianity that is not biblical? What does 'biblical' mean?

2. Isn't it sheer arrogance to say we know God?

3. Why is it important to see the Bible as the way God gives us to know him in a good relationship? Doesn't this run the risk of worshipping a book?

4. If the Bible is really God's Word, why didn't just one person write it – say, Jesus?

5. How would you begin to respond to the statement: 'Well, I'm not a Christian. I don't have faith in your God, so the Bible is utterly meaningless to me'?

The seriousness of the fall

Something is not right

Mapping the terrain of reality

Why are things in life the way they are? We take certain aspects of
life for granted, as given. Gravity keeps us on the planet. Seasons
come, followed by other seasons. In human affairs, children are
born, sons and daughters leave home. Countries go through
periods of economic recession, followed by degrees of recovery.
Political parties elect new leaders, modify policies and make new
promises. Even in a complex and changing life, some things come
with a degree of predictability and regularity. We call these things
normal.

Other parts of life are quite disturbing and shocking. They seem
not right, abnormal. Are they? What troubles us as we read of
gross injustices, both world-wide and in our own community?
Why do we feel that something is not right as we look at our
civilization as it comes to the end of this century? Are we simply
coming to another point in history, when, compared with a
hundred years ago, people are less confident about the future?

An interesting, amusing, but nonetheless telling article appeared
in a leading British newspaper:

> Here's the last word on Washington DC and its crime
> plague . . . Maharishi Mahesh Yogi, has abandoned a
> 10-year effort by his transcendental meditation sect to
> save the capital of the free world from itself. 'I would
> not advise anyone to stay in that pool of mud,' he says.
> He has had more than 1,000 followers collectively
> meditating to bring peace to DC streets, but to no avail:
> this year's murder rate (for a city of some 600,000) is set
> to top 1990's record of 483. The Maharishi's followers

will now move to the gentler surrounds of rural Iowa. One who is selling up and moving on has this message: 'Let's continue to do everything we can for Washington, but let's save our own nervous systems. The city awaits the apocalypse.'[1]

Whether it be Washington DC or Belfast or Sarajevo, there is an uncertainty. Of course, the curious thing is that this uncertainty does not hinder postmodernity's advance into the future. Gone are reasonably clear cultural markers with which to determine the course, but still we rush forwards in confused momentum.

Likewise, in our private lives, why are things the way they are? To fall in love, for example, is a wonderful experience. To go through the trials of a relationship breakdown is an altogether different thing. In the complexities of life there is often a richness, but also a sense that something is missing. What is it, and why is it missing? How do we explain the overwhelming sense of boredom and indifference in our culture? What all-encompassing statement will describe the psychological, spiritual and intellectual ennui that many late-twentieth-century men and women feel? We are amusing, entertaining and recreating ourselves into a torpor. Why? Why are things the way they are?

In his bestselling book *The Road Less Traveled*, M. Scott Peck writes of the essential need for a dedication to reality. As a psychiatrist, he is convinced that many of his patients view life and their problems through distorted perspectives. Sometimes it is not the patient's 'fault'. In other cases, the distortion is due to his or her sheer unwillingness to deal with reality. Health and well-being require a dedication to the truth. Peck writes:

> Superficially, this should be obvious. For truth is reality. That which is false is unreal. The more clearly we see the reality of the world, the better equipped we are to deal with the world. The less clearly we see the reality of the world – the more our minds are befuddled by falsehood, misperceptions and illusions – the less able we will be to determine correct courses of action and make wise decisions. Our view of reality is like a map with which to negotiate the terrain of life. If the map is true and accurate, we will generally know where we

are, and if we have decided where we want to go, we will generally know how to get there. If the map is false and inaccurate, we generally will be lost.[2]

We are concerned with reality. We must, for the experiences of reality are usually what plague and discomfort us. Of course, as I suggested in chapter 2, we can 'trick' ourselves through psychological denial, chemical or alcohol abuse and consumer escapism.[3] We could insist that an inconsistent worldview does not matter! Yet it is precisely here that our inconsistencies matter profoundly: we are forced to deal with the realities of life. To avoid (or try to escape from) some of them will lead to irresponsibility, insensitivity, injustice and, in extreme cases, insanity.

Simultaneously, followers of Christ need to be honest too. This is far more than an intellectual exercise. The difficulties or disharmony we sense makes us wonder if our trust in the Lord is insufficient, irrelevant, or, worse, futile. None of us would be so blunt, but this gnawing uncertainty exists. At times, we can ask, 'Which is real, faith in Jesus or the immediate, obvious and complicated circumstances?' There are times when the way things are and who God is do not meet in clear-cut association.

For example, a husband and wife are in great agony over their sixteen year old daughter's struggle with anorexia. The family are Christian and genuinely seek to do the Lord's will in these dreadful circumstances. After prayer, counselling and hours of family discussion, however, the daughter's health is deteriorating dangerously.

Well-meaning Christians told them that their own weak faith hinders her recovery. The mother and father were devastated. Later, they admitted to each other a subtle fear and anxiety. But are these necessarily the marks of faithlessness? They want their daughter to be well, and are scared. Yet as they wrestle with her suffering and pray for her, another growing uncertainty emerges. What they cannot figure out is how she ever entered into the downwards spiral of anorexia. Why would a lovely sixteen-year-old sink into the depths of self-destruction? What is it about the fragility of a human's self-esteem and assurance of being loved? Something is not right.

The confidence we are concerned with in this book seeks to respond to this 'something not right'. Christian confidence must

not avoid the realities of our contemporary life. The contrast will
come in the way or ways in which this confidence enables people
to get on in the realities of life. Our claim is that a confidence in the
trustworthiness and truthfulness of God's promises in Christ
enables us to make better sense of the way things are. We are
Christians through the saving work of a Redeemer who, in his
wisdom, not only brings us into an experience of his love but into
an encounter with reality, the way things are. Things become not
shadows, but clearer. This will disturb us, trouble us and pain us,
but we can still be confident.

We are again looking towards our theological framework in
which we may deal with our problems. If this framework is true
then we should be able to start understanding the ways things are,
but with a difference. We will not be content merely with a general
understanding; we will want to know how we can have and
experience a legitimate Christian confidence. Think back to the
parents of the sixteen-year-old girl. They desire much more than a
clinical description of anorexia. As they pray for her, they look to
comprehend her suffering with the promises of God. Here is the
nub of the problem: as we begin to know the way reality is, how
does what we can know about God relate to it?

Is the one true God indifferent to what we referred to earlier as
abnormal? Or is there anything abnormal to, say, anorexia? Are
things the way they are because God wants them *this particular*
way? Is the triune God involved in some power struggle with an
equally strong evil counter-force? In short, where do the goodness
of God, the sovereignty of God and the faithfulness of God
converge with the appearance of suffering, violence, pessimism?

In this chapter we continue to distinguish some of the lines of
our theological framework. We do so by looking closely at a
central theme in the Bible to see how our questions about the way
things are can be met within our framework. Building on the
arguments of the previous chapter and anticipating subsequent
chapters, we will consider the Bible's claim that the way things are
today is in part a result of human rebellion against the one true
God. The shorthand term is 'the fall'. We will look at this theme to
see how it can contribute to a legitimate confidence; because both
the realities of the fall and the fall's solution are central to our
understanding of who God is and who we are. Knowing both
enables us to live in this 'real' world with a true confidence. A

confident life in an age of change does not fly naïvely over the terrain of reality.

Not just a 'religious' story but a legitimate interface

But before we look at the particulars, a general point must be made. It cannot be assumed. Genesis 1 – 3 is not immediately straightforward, and not only for the non-Christian. A Christian can also have problems with this ancient narrative. It is not simply that she is studying contemporary cosmology theories. She could be in charge of a regional sales division for a cellular communications firm. She might be a primary school teacher with children from different ethnic origins and diverse religious backgrounds. She might be a neurosurgeon specializing in brain tumours. So much of her life is shaped by the pressures of the now.

Nevertheless, out of reverence and worship she turns to her Bible for words of hope and reassurance. The first several chapters of Genesis are *supposed* to be relevant. Yet she cannot avoid the conclusion that the opening chapters of her Bible and her contemporary world do not share a common grid. To use another metaphor, modernity speaks loudly even in the ears of the faithful.

One theologian insisted that 'even these pious and religious stories are not systematically didactic, nor are they theological, in intent'.[4] The influence and ideas of our contemporary society, which I highlighted in chapter 2, are evident. There is the feeling of a huge cultural gulf between the supposedly prescientific biblical culture and the late twentieth century. The popular influence of evolutionary thinking and the various strands of secular humanism leave many people bemused. How could there be a legitimate interface between this world and this ancient text?

Yet let us return to our Christian whom we introduced a moment ago. The truth is that her human experience does resonate with the Bible's account of the rebellion of Adam and Eve. Experientially, she knows that something is not right in the world. It is patently absurd to deny the daily evidence presented on television, radio or the written page. The Bible's account, therefore, may use non-contemporary vocabulary but it mirrors state-of-the-art diagnosis. The opening chapters of the Bible, and their greater interrelationship with the rest of the Scriptures, serve as gospel-modifiers. In other words, through the early chapters of Genesis she understands what the good news in Jesus Christ means. This good news also provides a clarifying and interpreting grid to the world she already knows and experiences. What is true for her is true for all of us.

This is why we stress that the story of Adam and Eve's rebellion is not simply a 'religious' story. By religious, I mean the way the word is used today in our modern and postmodern context. As we considered in chapter 2, many thinkers today place religious claims in a separate knowledge category from knowledge about the quantifiable, material and physical. Religion is non-objective and non-verifiable. Religion is rooted in the subjective, mystical and non-rational. At the close of the twentieth century those involved in metaphysics and linguistics will rarely employ biblical terms, phrases and ideas. This is because our way of thinking has accepted particular secular presuppositions. In this case, 'religious' stories, however emotive, are not practically and functionally significant for all people at all times.

If the first three chapters of Genesis were only religious, they would have little relevance. They would be a self-contained and self-limiting narrative, a mythic or tragic account of divine displeasure and the loss of human innocence. Genesis 1 – 3, however, functions less as a mirror of human experience than as a propositional explanation. Genesis 1 – 3, along with the rest of the Bible, tells us that 'this is why things are the way they are and the way they will change'.

Here is a description and interpretation of a crucial reality: why and how an originally complete context became distorted, leaving men and women in a less than ideal situation. They also speak of a hope to come. Francis Schaeffer argued,

> In some ways these chapters [Genesis 1 – 11] are the most important ones in the Bible, for they put man in his cosmic setting and show him his peculiar uniqueness. They explain man's wonder and yet his flaw. Without a proper understanding of these chapters we have no answer to the problems of metaphysics, morals or epistemology, and furthermore, the work of Christ becomes one more upper-storey 'religious' answer.[5]

Without the story of Adam and Eve we do not know enough, and this is what Schaeffer meant by an 'upper-storey' religious answer. It was his manner of describing the erroneous way in which thinkers separate objective, temporal and historical realities (the ground floor or first storey) from spiritual or religious beliefs (the upper storey). A late-twentieth-century person who makes this distinction can hold to an orthodox belief (a faith claim) while living in a real world where his or her orthodox belief has no significant relationship. In other words, we could say we believe *theologically* in a fall, but would not want to say that there has been an objective, real, historic, fall that explains the realities around us.

Does this interpretation really suggest a problem? Yes. The fall of humanity is precisely that: the fall of men and women. Attempts to understand and explain modern men and women that ignore or minimize the fall fail at the most fundamental level. No other explanation so adequately explains life, as both history and our own experience show. Most important, the gospel of Jesus Christ is unintelligible apart from comprehending the disobedi- ence of Adam and Eve. God's grace, mercy, and love are significant not only because of who God is, but also in the light of the fall and its effects on subsequent humanity. Life demands a commitment to reality, for reality is where we live and what affects us. If we are going to find a legitimate confidence, it must meet reality. In chapter 1 we presented a number of experiential problems faced by today's Christians. These reflect reality. Chapter 2 illustrated the ways in which today's thinking and philosophical assumptions are also part of the realities of our day. In the previous chapter I stressed the possibility of a knowledge of truth, because the one true God is knowable to us. It is possible to know what we must know. These are some of the initial elements of our theological framework. Now in this chapter we see how these preliminary aspects of our framework relate to the realities of 'why things are the way they are'. We have in mind not only the evils seen in our evening news programmes, but the fragility of a sixteen-year-old's self-esteem, the sense of personal loneliness in our modern age and the ever-present breakdowns in human relationships. As we consider the Bible's presentation of the fall of humankind, asking the four questions presented in the last chapter (Does this describe the world we already know? Does this describe the 'us' we already know? Is this consistent with itself? Is it liveable?), we have our eye on the realities of life. We have a valid and helpful interface.

Paradise lost: alienation and imperfection

Two 'particulars' or themes warrant our attention: alienation and imperfection. We know what alienation is. We all experience problems in relationships. Friendships run into problems for a host of reasons. Families suffer great pain when a marriage breaks up or a parent's rage and insecurity lead to harsh words. Alienation is not foreign to most of us. Imperfection is also familiar. We photograph a beautiful mountain scene, only to find that the process of developing cannot bring out the stunning colours we saw that day. In our marriages or friendships, despite our best intentions, we lose our temper or forget a birthday. Ideals are often not met, resulting in what is less than perfect.

The first chapters of Genesis present a vivid picture of alienation and imperfection, which the rest of the Scriptures magnify (*cf*. Ex. 32:1 – 33:6; 2 Sa. 11:1 – 12:25; Je. 2:1–13; Lk. 10:25–37; Rom. 5:12–19; Eph.2:1–3, 11–12). This story is all about a breakdown. Here are rebellion and guilt, expressed in highly poetic language with powerfully suggestive imagery. It is literature, and must be read and understood according to its style of literature, explaining and interpreting *real history*. By 'real', I mean that the narrative fits and coordinates with the way things are.[6] At points, this coordination employs ancient story touches (for example, a 'talking' serpent); yet the narrative is explanatory. This narrative is not an allegory; it does not simply mirror human affairs. When I use the word 'real', it explains the life we know because *of something that actually took place.*

The New Testament assumes this (Lk. 3:23ff.; Rom. 5:12-19; 1 Cor. 15:20,21). Before the events in Genesis 3, things were not the way life is now; and life now is not the way things were originally. This story tells us why the world we already know is messed up as it is. We are told that it is due to sin; and sin is really the way things are.

The message, however, is much fuller than a story of law breaking. Certainly, the New Testament points to sin as lawlessness (Rom. 2:27; 3:23; 1 Tim. 1:9; Jas. 2:9; 1 Jn. 3:4). But lawbreaking and lawlessness are tragic and illegitimate human elements of God's relationship with humanity. Genesis 3 is a thesis statement for the rest of the Bible, and illustrates what the rest of Scripture portrays. We see it all around us: there is alienation between a holy God and a humanity bent on insurrection.

Something once good becomes twisted and distorted. Genesis 3:8 affirms that God and the man and woman enjoyed a particularly special fellowship. It was originally wonderfully intimate. The question in verse 9, therefore, does not reveal divine ignorance but the first hint of alienation: 'Where are you?' Estrangement enters.

The tragic reality is heightened in verse 10, 'I was afraid because I was naked . . . so I hid.' Nakedness here is not primarily a matter of sexuality but a moral and relational issue. Verse 11 culminates with the question about the prohibited fruit. Alienation between God and humanity is severe. The fall of the first humans struck at intimacy.

This story possesses a heartfelt sense of tragedy. In verses 23–24 there is divine banishment and prohibition, the cherubim with a flaming sword flashing back and forth to guard the way to the tree of life. To borrow the phrase of the seventeenth-century poet John Milton (1608–1674), here is 'paradise lost'. Humanity has wanted to go back to paradise ever since. Genesis explains the alienation and imperfection we see and experience all around us.

At the same time, we need to avoid a particularly worrisome error. Alienation does not imply that God is less than God. He is not sulking in some corner of the universe. God is not a wounded partner. This is terribly important; for the rest of the Bible story is the unfolding of God's sovereign plan to bring back, through the second Adam, Jesus (Rom. 5:12-21), his redeemed humanity. God's being, character and purpose are not impaired because of his alienation from his creatures. God is still God.

God has not failed; he has not made a mistake. The reality we know, mirrored in Genesis 3 onwards, is not the way things have always been. There was a beginning when moral guilt, estrangement and alienation did not exist. This is why the Bible begins with Genesis 1 and 2 and not Genesis 3. Something has gone wrong; we live in subnormality. The wrong-doing is humanity's not God's.

What does this look like?

All God's creatures, great and small

Consider the wonderful and splendid position Adam and Eve originally had in the created order (Gn. 1:28–30; 2:15–17). This is not unhistorical myth. It is poetic language, set within a special narrative framework. Nonetheless, it describes a space–time event and reality. If this were not so, then Genesis fails to *explain* the serious sense of disharmony that humanity experiences in today's reality. We all know, experience and struggle with the implications of the fall described in Genesis.

Previous generations wrestled with the fear of the natural elements. Men and women still have this fear of earthquakes and other so-called natural disasters. In the West we recognize the problem of living in a material world where things break down, decay and corrode. This is not peculiar to western countries, for people living in the two-thirds world know and experience this too. There are of course many valid and verifiable materialistic explanations, but there is an ultimate framework as well, the fall. Imperfection is all around us. There is an alienation and imperfection between humanity and the rest of creation.

This explains why, for example, our society faces a crucial ecological crisis. We want to know, 'Why is our world so messed up?' What will explain why poisonous gases from a chemical plant at Bhopal, India, killed more than 2,000 people and blinded or injured some 200,000 more? How do we explain the grounding of the tanker Exxon Valdez that profoundly damaged the ecosystem of parts of the Alaskan coast? How may we account for the untold tragic global consequences of the oil fires in Iraq and Kuwait after the Gulf War?

Without reducing things to a simplistic level, the Genesis story provides an ultimate explanation: the fall of the human race, and the consequential curse.

> Cursed is the ground because of you;
>> through painful toil you will eat of it
>> all the days of your life.
> It will produce thorns and thistles for you,
>> and you will eat the plants of the field.
> By the sweat of your brow
>> you will eat your food

> until you return to the ground,
>   since from it you were taken;
> for dust you are
>   and to dust you will return.'
>
> (Gn. 3:17–19)

This is poetic language, but also descriptive.

Humanity's rebellion is radical and extensive. The consequence is imperfection, a fall from what was totally and comprehensively right, not some isolated spiritual dimension. The apostle Paul claimed, 'For the creation was subjected to frustration, not by its own choice, but by the will of the one who subjected it, in hope that the creation itself will be liberated from its bondage to decay and brought into the glorious freedom of the children of God' (Rom. 8:20–21). Human sinfulness must not be seen as confined to some remote, irrelevant spiritual aspect of life. The fall affects all of reality. Because of humanity's fall, creation is not right. 'We know that the whole creation has been groaning as in the pains of childbirth right up to the present time' (Rom. 8:22).[7] The rebellion of the first man and woman affected a much larger circle of creation.

The Bible is reflecting what many contemporary men and women think. Today we are quite aware of the fragility of our planet's ecosystem. Quite rightly, people are concerned for environmental issues. Surprisingly, for some people, the realities of our life in the 1990s match the interpretive grid of biblical revelation. Here is an important contact point in our discussion and activity among those who think that biblical Christianity does not fit the realities of our planetary crisis. There is an important interface. The fall does not excuse us from our environmental accountability and responsibility. The fall is abnormality or subnormality: in other words, the fallen world is not as the one true God originally planned. We are not to be careless or unaware.

There is more.

Alienation from our neighbours

In the West we are a highly individualistic culture compared to other parts of the world. Simultaneously, we increasingly sense we belong to a wider global community. Ponder the ways in which the electronic media bring home to us the problems of African famines, the plight of political refugees and the social aspirations of people longing for democratic freedoms. The world comes right into our living-room. We are members of a larger community.

This is not an altogether new idea. The Bible views humanity as a corporate whole; it rarely uses individualistic terms. The individual matters profoundly, but the greater emphasis is on the corporate social unit (the tribe, the nation, the church). Accordingly, Genesis also tells us about the problems of social alienation and imperfection. Derek Kidner helpfully explains, 'For all the emphasis which Genesis lays on the individual, with God calling men by name and seeking the outcasts, its model for human life is not that of the solitary mystic or the freelance, but of a social being who lives within a certain pattern of responsibilities.'[8] Why are there problems between people and nations?

Consider the biblical paradigm. The relationship between Adam and Eve took a decided turn for the worse. Lies and recriminations appear (Gn. 3:12). Where once there was beautiful intimacy (2:21-25), tension and imperfection occur between lovers. The impact of God's curse in Genesis 3:16 may be problematic but it is descriptive. There is certainly an imperfect relationship between male and female. Our society displays this imperfection: an imperfection that exceeds both feminist and arrogant male assumptions.[9] Here too the fall makes sense of the world and the 'us' we already know. We look on to Genesis 4:3-16 and are presented with the murder of Abel.

Although these are worldview stories, they are not limited 'religious' stories beyond us. Family breakdown and violence are all about us. The stories also illustrate a social and corporate breakdown. The rest of the Bible is startlingly clear: alienation affects the whole of humanity. There is alienation between one human and another, one group and another. Social disharmony and imperfection may have a myriad of causes and explanations. Yet, whether Freudian, Marxist or New Age, if explanations do not see the relevance of the fall and its consequential imperfection, they are inadequate. They describe but cannot explain.

Here is yet again a striking interface. Sin ultimately is defiance against God, but often its immediate profanity is against another human being. Not surprisingly, we read in the Bible God's call to society for corporate care and concern (see Ex. 20:12; Ps. 133; Is.

58:6–9; Jn. 13:12–17; Gal.2:10; Jas. 1:27). These commands state the importance of social responsibility. They also reveal the problem of alienation between neighbours. Yet there is a further and deeper problem.

Alienation with ourselves

The story of Narcissus could be an up-to-date account. Fascinated with his own image reflected in a pool of water, Narcissus became blinded and incapable of seeing anything. Ours is a very self-concerned culture. Peter C. Moore, in *Disarming the Secular Gods*, provides a helpful insight into narcissistic personality disorders:

> . . . grandiose sense of self-importance or uniqueness; focusing on how special one's problems are; preoccupation with fantasies of unlimited success, power, brilliance, beauty or ideal love; exhibitionistic need for constant attention and admiration; feelings of rage, inferiority, or emptiness in response to criticism or defeat; lack of empathy; sense of entitlement without assuming reciprocal responsibilities; tendency to take advantage of others and disregard their personal integrity.[10]

We try to 'find' ourselves through every conceivable means. But how successful are most of us? Judging from the workload of psychiatrists and counsellors, and the plethora of self-help books, people today are at odds with themselves. What explains this problem? Here too an appreciation of the fall can help. The fall has resulted in men and women being alienated from themselves at their most personal and intimate level: psychologically, intellectually and physically. Look more closely at Genesis 3:17ff. We see hints of humanity not only in disharmony with creation and between individuals, but alienated from itself. As the story unfolds, there is a terrible poignancy in chapter 5. 'Altogether, Adam lived 930 years, and then he died' (Gn. 5:5).

Consider what surprises us in this verse. We ask: how it is that one could have lived for such a long time? But surely what should strike us is that Adam *died*. We take death as a given, a normal part of human existence. Nothing could be further from the ideal!

Adam should *not* have died; death is part of the curse (*cf.* Gn. 2:16–17). While death strikes us all, it is a consequence of the fall. It reflects the imperfection in our world. Death also reveals the fundamental sense of alienation a man or a woman has with himself or herself.

Some readers of Genesis wonder if the consequence was as drastic as threatened. They claim that the curse never came about: Adam did not die then and there (*cf.* Gn. 2:17; 3:20ff.). But various levels of death are implied. Banishment is death, for separation from perfect intimacy with the Lord is death. Imperfection is death. Growing old and returning to dust is death. Adam experienced all these.

Physical death is part of our reality. It is also part of the present imperfection. While there are biblical accounts of healings and miracles, including references to people raised from the dead (two notable examples being the widow of Zarephath's son in 1 Ki. 17:17ff. and Lazarus in Jn. 11:17ff.), such occurrences in time and space did not ultimately reverse reality. These people eventually died, and they remain dead. Death is part of the imperfection we experience. Only one person has begun to reverse it: Jesus Christ. He is 'the firstfruits of those who have fallen asleep' (1 Cor. 15:20). Not until the final resurrection will death be totally defeated.

We also spend our lives in the shadow of death in a metaphorical sense. I do not mean that we all walk around with a morbid paranoia. Rather, we are at odds with ourselves. Other people hurt us and wound us, but many of our problems are self-induced. We are all sons of Adam and daughters of Eve.

Nevertheless, a problem to avoid is thinking that alienation and imperfection mean that humanity after the fall is rubbish. Humanity has not totally lost the image of God as described in Genesis 1:27. The image has been dirtied; humanity has fallen, has dropped from its original innocence and intimacy with God. Still, humans are humans and not beasts.

We read in Genesis 4:1 that Adam lay with his wife Eve. There is something here far more than a base animal sexuality. Fallen humans continue to love and care; we know this from the rest of Scripture. Humanity continued to worship God (Gn. 4:3ff., 26; 5:24). In the rest of the Bible flawed men and women create beauty, they communicate with one another and they use their minds to explore and wonder about the world around them. They are not

105

living and acting in paradise, but they are still humans in the image of their creator.

We must not have a negative view of humanity. We cannot allow certain philosophers and sociologists to reduce men and women to a bare minimum. Yes, men and women are creatures. Men and women are animals in one sense, but in a more important sense we are unique in the created order. We are made in God's image: so we love, we reason, we can hold abstract ideas in our minds, and we worship. We should not misunderstand the seriousness of the fall and so reduce humanity to a lower level than the Bible does. Humanity is fallen, and in this respect terrible; the severity of the fall and its consequences is frighteningly dreadful.

The fall means all

Another error to avoid is thinking that the fall suggests only a potential for wrong-doing rather than an actual and real propensity for disobedience. The fall resulted in *all* humanity sharing in the alienation. The Bible teaches a corporate inclusion of all humanity in the race of Adam. Paul argues this in Romans 5:12-21 and in a different context in 1 Corinthians 15:22. He saw all humanity born in the first Adam. Paul's point is that this corporate origin in Adam explains subsequent sin and death.

Only by our inclusion in the first Adam does Paul refer to the redemption of humanity in the second Adam, Jesus Christ. There cannot be the second without the first. Through faith a person comes into union with the second Adam and receives the consequence not of disobedience (death) but of obedience (right-eousness and life). We will have more to say about this in later chapters.

Scripture teaches a universal alienation (see Gn. 8:21; 1 Ki. 8:46; Ps. 51:5; Ps. 130:3; Jb. 4:17; 14:4; 15:4; 25:4; see too Jesus' implicit teaching in Mt. 7:11; Mk. 2:17; 7:23; Lk. 11:4; 19:10). While the biblical writers do not use the term 'original sin', Tertullian (c. 160/70–c. 215/20) and Augustine of Hippo (354-430) were correct to notice that from our birth we share in the reality of alienation. Furthermore, it is not just a potential for wrong-doing and sin, it is something we manifest.

Care is required. I am not suggesting that if a week-old baby

106

dies due to cot death, she will be rejected by the Lord. Nevertheless, she is of the human race, and her tragic and untimely death is a mark of Adam's progeny. The glory of Christ's death is its full sufficiency. The baby is saved and pardoned, not because of her innocence (she was incapable of wrong-doing), but through the merits and satisfaction of Christ's substitutionary death. Death underlines sin, not necessarily personal wrong-doing but corporate disobedience.

Return again to the parents of the young woman suffering from anorexia. Have they sinned? Yes. Has the sixteen-year-old sinned? Yes. Do these facts mean, therefore, that sin explains her illness? No, not strictly or in such a limited manner. Wisdom and sensitivity suggest that we ought not to draw a straight line between anorexia and personal sin. The whole family needs to know this: God is not punishing her or them for some past wrong-doing. Nevertheless, because we are all fallen creatures, human sinfulness, with its consequences of alienation and imperfection, is there. Tensions between parent and child arise because we are fallen parents and children. We place false or damaging expectations on each other and ourselves. Young girls are misled by glossy-magazine cover-pictures of today's waif-like models because our fallen culture places value on particular forms of female appearance. We are not apportioning blame here as much as highlighting the realities of alienation and imperfection.

The Bible teaches that all humans share in alienation from God and corresponding sinfulness. Alienation and sin are part of who we are even before we act in specific ways. Human alienation from God is not a neutral or passive state. It describes our being, until we are reconciled to God by Christ's death and our repentance and faith (see Jn. 1:1–13; Acts 17:16–34; Rom. 1:18–32).

We cannot understand humanity in both its wonderful uniqueness and its ruins until we see that our paramount problem is our refusal to worship and obey God. The alienation between God and humanity is staggering and catastrophic; it is no ordinary disharmony.

This raises a crucial problem. How could a supposedly sovereign God allow the fall to mar his original creation, leaving humanity wounded and alienated not only from him but from one another? Humanity may have fallen, but does not the blame rest ultimately with God? Surely he foreknew and permitted the antagonism of the serpent and the Garden rebellion?

When we read and study the whole of the Bible, we notice two important aspects of alienation and imperfection that can help us. First, God is still sovereign. There is not the slightest suggestion that God has resorted to some 'plan B' after the fall. In fact, the apostle Paul argues the opposite. 'And he made known to us the mystery of his will according to his good pleasure, which he purposed in Christ, to be put into effect when the times will have reached their fulfilment – to bring all things in heaven and on earth together under one head, even Christ' (Eph. 1:9–10). In an earlier verse he claimed that he and the other apostles were chosen 'in him [Christ] before the creation of the world to be holy and blameless in his sight . . .' (1:4).[11] Despite the fall, and the subsequent imperfection, God is sovereign. His will is accomplished.

Second, despite the fall God will glorify himself. God's intention and glory will, in the end, be enhanced. We may not fully comprehend what this means; in fact, we are incapable of complete comprehension. Still, the New Testament writers insist that in Christ there is hope and pardon. Christ is the second Adam who will bring humanity back to Eden in a new and fuller way than had Adam and Eve never sinned. The Bible tells us that the work of redemption and the glorification of God's people are not just for their benefit, but primarily for God's greater glory. The fall is not the final statement about God. Though the evidences of alienation and imperfection abound, the one true God has not failed.

We can see clearly now

We meet women and men who need help seeing things clearly and realistically. It should grieve us that people are hurt by our modern secular society and the vacuous promises of postmodernism, whose answers go only half way. Yet so things continue. In our schools, universities, artistic communities and business organizations as well as city slums, reality damages us. Clearly, many escape the crushing despair: personal affluence can buy personal peace. To be sure, humanity displays a wonderful ability to remain human in every good and truly lovely way. Nonetheless, contemporary men and women are at risk.

What do I mean? In his book *The Saturated Self: Dilemmas of Identity in Contemporary Life*, Kenneth J. Gergen expresses it well:

> As we enter the postmodern era, all previous beliefs about the self are placed in jeopardy, and with them the patterns of action they sustain. Postmodernism does not bring with it a new vocabulary for understanding ourselves, new traits or characteristics to be discovered or explored. Its impact is more apocalyptic than that: the very concept of personal essences is thrown into doubt. Selves as possessors of real and identifiable characteristics – such as rationality, emotion, inspiration, and will – are dismantled.

He then concludes,

> Under postmodern conditions, persons exist in a state of continuous construction and reconstruction; it is a world where anything goes that can be negotiated. Each reality of self gives way to reflexive questioning, irony, and ultimately the playful probing of yet another reality. The center fails to hold.[12]

What we are concerned about, then, is humanity as humans. Our self-understanding and, essentially, what makes us human are at risk. The implications are numerous, but certainly include an inability to deal with the realities of life.

In this chapter the central argument has been theological: the fall of humanity in the rebellion of Adam and Eve explains and clarifies our present predicament. Our contemporary personal, corporate and ecological problems are mirrored in the first three chapters of Genesis. But there is something further here. Genesis 1 – 3 not only mirrors realities of today's life; they offer a causal explanation. In essence, these chapters tell us *why things are the way they are*. We know that something today is not right. God's revelation tells us that today's *something* is the result of a time–space *something* which occurred in the Garden rebellion.

We begin to see more clearly as we understand the interface between our present world and this ancient text. What we need to know is knowable. The meaning, significance and purpose of creation are vital for us to know. This is part of reality. As to our humanity, it is life-giving to know of our significance and identity within creation and in relation to the creator God. We are not insignificant pieces of matter in a meaningless and random-chance universe. Likewise, however, we are not autonomous beings in our self-created and self-defined little world.

Correspondingly, it is disturbing and humbling to know the seriousness of the fall as rebellion against the one, true, creator God. The fall explains what we already know, but in terms we do not normally employ. Imperfection and alienation: these are realities. But here is the good news. How terribly important to know that these human experiences are not mere illusions! How assuring to learn that they are not the result of an impersonal determinism or the consequences of a cosmic battle between two demigods!

Here is a fundamental aspect of our theological framework which *begins* to lead us to Christian confidence. I stress '*begins* to lead us', for we need more; and our framework involves what we will examine in the following chapters. When we see the themes of alienation and imperfection in the Bible, in our society and our private lives, we are even more in awe of God's work in Christ (see Mt. 1:21; Lk. 1:76–79; 2:10–14; Acts 10:34–43; Rom. 3:21–26; Col. 2:13–14). However great and chilling God's alienation from humanity, there is hope. Despite the reality of imperfection, it does not have the last word. Even in Genesis 3 hope is present. Genesis 3:15 has traditionally been interpreted by Christians as a promise realized in the gospel. As we read the flow of biblical revelation, we see God's willingness to initiate a covenant relationship with Abraham and his descendants and, through them, all humanity. He takes the first step, in sovereign mercy and undeserved favour.

The one true God is loving and merciful. Men and women are not beyond the love of this God's love and compassion. Fallen modern men and women are still lovable. A holy and just God still loves fallen people. Profound pastoral and psychological implications exist here. To these we move next as we think about the person and work of Jesus Christ. We will discover that alienation and imperfection are not insuperable. In Christ there is a way back to Eden. To quote Milton:

Of man's first disobedience, and the fruit
Of that forbidden tree whose mortal taste
Brought death into the world, and all our woe,
With loss of Eden, till one greater Man
Restore us, and regain the blissful seat . . . [13]

Questions for reflection and discussion

1. Does it really matter that we accept an objective, real and historical fall? What alternative explanation describes what we see and experience around us? Do other explanations deal with the realities of our contemporary world?
2. Do you accept the important distinction between a 'religious' story and a worldview story?
3. How does a better understanding of Genesis 1 – 3 give us an insight into the gospel? How could this understanding help you meet your friend's objections: (a) 'If your God is so good, why is there so much evil and suffering in the world?' (b) 'Why did the Lord allow my dad to die in a car crash?'

5

The glory of Jesus Christ

The one we can confidently know

Ignorance is not bliss

Suppose I ask you to meet a friend of mine for me at the airport. I could tell you his name, but you need more. A physical description is necessary. His arrival time is also crucial. I cannot send you without clear knowledge, otherwise you would either miss my friend or pester every man you see. You need to know about the person, or confusion would develop. Who he is matters, and your ability to pick him out from others matters.

To be confused or mistaken about Jesus is more serious precisely because of who Jesus is. Of course, some people ask, 'Jesus who?' The vast majority of our contemporaries do not know what they can know about Jesus. So the questions arise. 'Is there accurate information about him?' 'Are the New Testament Gospels based on events in history, reliably conveyed?' 'Is Jesus of Nazareth unique compared to Buddha, Muhammad or Shirley MacLaine?' Supremely, 'Does knowing Jesus Christ ultimately matter?' What makes it all the more complicated is the difficulty contemporary people have in knowing where to begin to figure out Jesus. Some begin with particular presuppositions.

The Japan Festival of 1991 brought *Jesus Christ Superstar* back to London, this time in a Kabuki version. Yuichiro Yamaguchi, who played Jesus for ten years in Tokyo, said, 'At first I wanted to play Jesus like the Son of God. Now he is just a normal person to me. Maybe being Japanese I can see Jesus Christ as a pure human being more than Christian people can.'[1]

Recently, A. N. Wilson again brought the question 'Who was Jesus?' into the minds of popular readers.[2] He seeks to redefine, iconoclastically, the Jesus of Christian faith. Wilson quite honestly admits his own view.

112

I had to admit that I found it impossible to believe that a first-century Galilean holy man had at any time of his life believed himself to be the Second Person of the Trinity. It was such an inherently improbable thing for a monotheistic Jew to believe. Nor, having learnt how to read the New Testament critically, could I find the smallest evidence that Jesus had ever entertained such beliefs about himself; nor had he preached them.[3]

Wilson's questioning, or any other contemporary scepticism, matters. These doubts are important. Too much hangs in the balance, and if it is possible to know truths about Jesus Christ – whatever they may be – then we need to know. Our working definition of confidence stresses the centrality of Jesus Christ: *a consequence of my faith in Jesus Christ, brought about over time by the Holy Spirit, experienced in my heart and realized in my mind, that God's promises in the gospel are true and personally applicable to me a believer.*[4] As we have been arguing, Christian confidence depends upon the knowability of the one true God, supremely in the revelation in Jesus Christ. Later, in chapters 6 and 7, we will describe how Christian confidence is consequent upon faith in Jesus Christ. Throughout the rest of this book, considerable stress is laid on the appropriateness of Christian living in the light of the uniqueness of Jesus Christ. In short, everything depends upon who Jesus is.

Think of it this way. Can Christians know anything about Jesus that gives us confidence in our faith in him as Lord and Saviour? If we can, is this trustworthy? Here is a terribly crucial issue, and not just in the light of contemporary thinking. At the heart of the Christian life is Jesus. If a follower of Christ is confused about him, he or she will have problems. Praying, resolving guilt, coping with lifestyle issues or answering the challenges of those who reject the gospel, all hinge on who Jesus is.

Equally, a right knowledge of Jesus is necessary for those today who are *not* followers of Christ. If Christianity is nothing more than a developed distortion of one holy man's teaching (a man who never intended his followers to make claims about his exclusive saving uniqueness), then why should ányone bother? At best, let us Christians keep our enthusiasm to ourselves. If there is something knowable about Jesus, however, and if this information *truthfully* tells us that he is Lord of all existence and will eventually judge us all, then people need to hear and know. Their misapprehensions, ignorance and foolishness must be corrected. Everything is at stake. For the sake of *all* humanity a right view of Jesus must be given.

This is the task before us. Again, we are tracing out our theological framework; but, I must stress, as we look at the framework we will see how, by its very nature, our experiential problems relate to it. As we go through the material in this chapter, we should keep in mind the claim that all men and women are called to respond to Jesus Christ. This response is not conditional upon our culture or point in human history, although both influence us profoundly. We are summoned to know Jesus *specifically*: namely, as he relates to God's saving work among his people, Israel; to the reality of his incarnation, as the one true God made flesh; to the trustworthiness of the faithful biblical witness; to his being the supreme Lord and sufficient Saviour; and finally to the claim that he is one whom we may not ignore.

Our personal experiences, whether we are Christians or not, will impinge on these aspects of Jesus. Equally, what we have to say about the specifics of Jesus unavoidably meets our human experiences and situations. A contemporary person, with all that makes her or him contemporary, can know about Jesus Christ. Ignorance is not bliss. We may have questions, but we need not be in the dark.

The fulfilment of promises

We need to start with a special emphasis. When we talk about *Jesus* (the English translation of the Hebrew–Aramaic *Yēšua'* and the Greek *Iēsous*), we mean a particular Jesus. Today there is the New Age Jesus, the Jesus in western paintings, the Jesus in the Qur'an and the word 'Jesus' used as an expletive. When a person speaks of 'Jesus', we must ask, 'Which Jesus?' In our age, even among Christians, we need precision.

Specifically, we must point to the Jesus to whom the New Testament witnesses. Our discussion and consideration concerning Jesus begins with a specific and particular perspective: the New Testament reference. As we will suggest in this chapter, a failure to appreciate this witness will lead to serious problems.

To be sure, this approach differs from certain assumptions of our age. We claim the possibility of a trustworthy knowledge of Jesus: the Jesus who was born, lived, ministered, died, was raised from the dead, is now ruler of all, and who will return to be the judge of all. This claim is based on the New Testament witness, explanation and interpretation. There is a particular Jesus. In this section we stress Jesus as the fulfilment of God's promises to his people Israel.

The New Testament accounts of Jesus do not appear in a blatant 'Christian' context.[5] Jesus' teachings and actions interact with the Jewish Scriptures. The New Testament writers presume a relationship between the gospel and the Jewish Scriptures. The key aspect of this relationship is *fulfilment*.

We see this as we detect a thematic unity to the Jewish scriptures. There is a flow. From Genesis to Chronicles (the Jewish canonical order), or to Malachi (the Christian order), we see a multicoloured and multi-fabric tapestry, but an artwork with a total message, a message that exceeds the sum of its parts.[6]

We read how the creator and sovereign God intends to reverse the rebellion of Adam and Eve in Eden. We are presented with accounts of God's saving actions and covenant commitment to the Jews, and through them, all other nations. The ancient stories and theological reflections of those encounters with God form an unified and purposeful whole. The Old Testament moves towards a goal. Yet, to begin with, we are not sure what the goal is.

To Israel the one true God commits himself. His covenant with Abraham is both future (Gn. 17:1–14) and present (Gn. 17:15–22). In whom would this promise be fulfilled? Isaac is born to Abraham and Sarah, but there is a greater promise. A people will descend from Abraham, a nation with whom the Lord is in covenant relationship. Yet, with the subsequent generations, Jacob and his children, tension rises. How can the covenant be fulfilled if Jacob's progeny lives in Egypt (Gn. 50:22–26)?

Egypt is not the land of promise; generations later, it is the area of oppressive slavery. Moses is raised up, however, and the people are delivered, again stressing the covenant promise (Ex. 3:16–17). The covenant people receive the law and ordinances. These not only shape Israel's self-identity, they further the promises and hope of the covenant (see especially Ex. 19:1–6). God's people are to know him, serve him, worship him and live for him in specific ways. They are to be different, separate people.

As the Israelites enter the promised land, are the promises fulfilled? Is this the moment of consummation? The tragic and culpable failures described in the book of Judges reveal the incompleteness of the situation. Deliverers, judges, are necessary. Yet the deliverance is partial and temporary (Jdg. 21:25). Hope appears to rest in a forthcoming monarchy.

With the reign of David, expectations abound. The covenant is furthered, seemingly fulfilling earlier promises. There is a seed of Abraham on a throne. The promise to David, however, is greater than him alone. In his seed and in his dynasty there is hope (2 Sa. 7:1–29). There is also the temple.

Yet the history of the subsequent monarchies displays covenant infidelity and moral collapse. The temple itself becomes a centre for spiritual perfidy. There are periods of renewal and promise, but they are short-lived and nullified by successive leaders and the surrounding nations. Assyrian and later Babylonian domination bring the covenant into question (Is. 24:5; *cf.* Je. 31:31–34 and Ezk.16:59–63). The temple is destroyed.

Even the glorious return from exile (537 BC) and the second temple fall short of the covenant hope and promise. Faithfulness and true worship are present to an extent. There is even anticipation. But actualization is eclipsed by disappointment (Ne.13:14–31). The promises stand, with some aspects fulfilled, but only as shadows of things to come. Something or someone is hoped for and expected.

This is the backdrop to the jolting beginnings of the three synoptic Gospels (Matthew, Mark and Luke) and John's Gospel. These authors introduce the gospel with a subtle touch, but one that sends continuous shock-waves. All the covenant hopes and promises, including the reversal of the fall of Adam and Eve, are declared *arrived* and *fulfilled* in Jesus of Nazareth.

Notice how Mark begins his Gospel, with an emphasis not upon novelty but upon realization. 'It is written in Isaiah the prophet . . .' (1:2). The voice from heaven utters not new words but old words, '"You are my Son, whom I love; with you I am well pleased"' (Mk. 1:11; cf. Ps. 2:7 and Is. 42:1).[7] Jesus declares not so much a new age as an epoch of fulfilment with immediate implications, '"The time has come," he said. "The kingdom of God is near. Repent and believe the good news!"' (1:15).

Consider the accent on fulfilment in Matthew's Gospel. The

Gospel starts with a selective genealogy (1:1–17) with a specific intention, to show fulfilment. 'A record of the genealogy of Jesus Christ the son of David, the son of Abraham . . .' (1:1). The genealogy is a way of signalling continuity, furtherance for a reason. We start to see this reason as we consider Jesus' birth and ministry within the flow of God's dealings with Israel.

The first two chapters of Luke's Gospel are within a temple setting. While Luke shows how the good news spread from Jerusalem to the heart of the Roman Empire (apparent in his second volume, Acts), unmistakably the good news originated among faithful, expectant and pious Jews: Zechariah, Elizabeth, Mary, Joseph, Simeon, Anna and the young Jesus.

The fourth Gospel begins with a theological prologue emphasizing the Jewishness of the gospel (1:11). Continuity is apparent, but the accent is on someone greater as the fulfilment of Israel's hopes (1:15–17, 19–51). The first individuals we meet in John's Gospel are faithful Jews waiting and looking: John the Baptist, two disciples of John, Andrew and Peter, Philip and Nathanael. The stress throughout is on 'the Messiah'. John does not tell us straightaway how this term relates to Jesus; we must read the rest of his Gospel. Nonetheless, we are not to miss the continuity: there is no Christian gospel apart from Jewish hope and expectations.

Ultimately, the first Christians declared that the salvation of the human race offered in Jesus fulfils Judaism. Peter, in Acts 2, explains who Jesus is not by taking his audience forward into new insights but by taking them back to earlier prophetic promises. 'No, this is what was spoken by the prophet Joel . . .' (Acts 2:16). 'David said about him . . .' (Acts 2:25). His proclamation is principally an interpretation of the Pentecost event in the light of centuries-old prophecies. To understand Jesus we must look backwards to see ahead.

> Brothers, I can tell you confidently that the patriarch David died and was buried, and his tomb is here to this day. But he was a prophet and knew that God had promised him on oath that he would place one of his descendants on his throne. Seeing what was ahead, he spoke of the resurrection of the Christ, that he was not abandoned to the grave, nor did his body see decay. God has raised this Jesus to life, and we

are all witnesses of the fact. Exalted to the right hand of God, he has received from the Father the promised Holy Spirit and has poured out what you now see and hear. For David did not ascend to heaven, and yet he said,

> 'The Lord said to my Lord:
> "Sit at my right hand
> until I make your enemies
> a footstool for your feet."'

Therefore let all Israel be assured of this: God has made this Jesus, whom you crucified, both Lord and Christ (Acts 2:29–36).

Peter's apologetic (a positive explanation) stresses apostolic eyewitness, the outpoured Holy Spirit and his audience's own witness. The interpretive grid is the *fulfilment of earlier Scripture*. This is also a key to our understanding of Jesus.

The unique authenticity of the Old Testament writings is substantiated by the teaching, death and resurrection of Jesus of Nazareth. 'He [Jesus] said to them [the disciples], "This is what I told you while I was still with you: Everything must be fulfilled that is written about me in the Law of Moses, the Prophets and the Psalms." Then he opened their minds so they could understand the Scriptures' (Lk. 24:44-45). His gospel is also magnified as we look back to the previous work of God in the earlier biblical records. Promises made are seen to be promises fulfilled. Important implications follow.

But in what sense is Jesus unique?

While we may point to the fulfilment of Old Testament promises, however, this does not completely resolve some contemporary confusion about Jesus. Today an old battle grows fiercer. At issue is the uniqueness of Jesus Christ. It is not a battle peculiar to our day. Since the first century there has been confusion and debate on this issue. Yet never before has the church as a whole been less sure about the deity of Jesus, the Son of God. Present voices sound more convincing and plausible.

The New Age writer, John W. White, wrote, 'Christ, the Christos, the Messiah, is an eternal transpersonal condition of being to which *we must all someday come.* Jesus did not say that this higher state of consciousness realized in him was his alone for all time.'[8] The Dutch theologian, Edward Schillebeeckx, offered this puzzling, although not unique, observation:

> Theology, talk about God, is more than christology; in other words, while as Christians we can and may make Jesus the Christ the centre of history for ourselves, we are not at the same time in a position to argue that the historical revelation of salvation from God in Jesus Christ exhausts the question of God, nor do we need to. Although we cannot attain Jesus in his fullness unless at the same time we also take into account his unique relationship with God which has a special nature of its own, this does not of itself mean that Jesus' unique way of life is the only way to God.[9]

Both of these examples shift the question 'Who was Jesus?' on to a higher level. In one way, as we notice the fulfilment of Old Testament promises, we should begin to see how profoundly unique Jesus is. But, as the gospel spreads beyond Jewish settings, further questions arise. Was Jesus of Nazareth God incarnate? Is he the *only* way to the one true God, or is he one of many? Today there is a spectrum of wrong views.

Starting at one end, we find those influenced by Eastern religions and philosophies, run through New Age filters, who see Jesus as no more or less divine than all of us. Jesus is not unique according to this view. Moving towards the middle, there are those who argue that Jesus' teaching was misconstrued by later Christianity. Though he never claimed divinity, subsequent followers are guilty of an almost idolatrous view of Jesus. We think of differing sects such as the Mormons or Jehovah's Witnesses. There are also individuals within Christian circles who question Jesus' virgin birth, divinity and uniqueness. Beyond this are the followers of Islam, who will not accept the supremacy of Jesus, preferring their own prophet and messenger, Muhammad. At the far end of the spectrum are those who are agnostic. For them, even if God exists, the idea of the infinite and transcendent becoming limited and finite is unacceptable, or at best incomprehensible.

We can appreciate how the diversity of views might unsettle today's Christians. Not a few Christian university students are thrown by these conflicting interpretations. They try hard to display tolerance and cultural sensitivity to those of other faiths and those of no faith at all. At the same time, whether in lectures, assigned reading or in late-night discussions over coffee, it is hard to see a way through the maze of religious pluralism and theological relativism. How does a person respond to the statement, 'Well, I like to think of Jesus as . . .'?

It is not surprising that there are differing views about Jesus. In the Gospel accounts, Jesus' hearers misunderstood him. 'On the way he asked them, "Who do people say I am?" They replied, "Some say John the Baptist; others say Elijah; and still others, one of the prophets." "But what about you?" he asked. "Who do you say I am?"' (Mk. 8: 27–29 and parallels).[10] Similarly, the letters were often written in response to the problem of diverse understandings about Jesus.[11] Frequently, the writers link true teaching about Christ with the true gospel. There is a 'pattern' of tradition and apostolic teaching. There are essential and central truths about Jesus.

Yet some Christians today are easily confused and troubled by differing views about Jesus. One student asked me, 'You make it sound so straightforward, so why are there so many others who teach different things about Jesus?' It is an understandable question, though slightly naïve. The presence of diverse views does not mean an absence of truth. As the New Testament argues, some views are wrong. Modernity and postmodernism, of course, struggle with unequivocal claims. How can we say this, and can we be sure that what we say is right?[12]

There is, and has been, a specific and trustworthy orthodoxy about Jesus. In the face of various heresies, the ancient church rose to defend both the deity and the humanity of Christ.[13] At the Council of Nicea in 325 the deity of Christ was stressed against the challenge of Arius (d. 336). Arius denied the pre-existent, eternal divinity of Christ. He taught that the Son is a creature, and that there was a time when the Son did not exist. Arius was concerned to defend monotheism. He rejected the claim that the Father and the Son had the same substance. The word he used was *ousia*, which, today, we could express as the 'beingness' or 'whatness' of God. Arius denied that the Father and Son had the same *ousia* or beingness.

Arius' teaching (later called Arianism) challenged an already existing, if not fluid, orthodoxy. In a response led by Athanasius (*c.* 296–373), the ecumenical gathering at Nicea declared that Jesus Christ is 'the Son of God, begotten from the Father, only-begotten, that is, from the substance of the Father, God from God, light from light, true God from true God, begotten not made, of one substance with the Father . . .'[14]

At the Council of Constantinople in 381, the incarnation of Christ was defended against the influence of Apollinarius (*c.* 310– *c.* 390). Apollinarius accepted Nicene theology, but questioned the unity of the two natures in the one person. How can Jesus simultaneously be fully human and fully divine? Apollinarius argued that the divine Logos could in no way have fully united with the human. The divine Logos took over the human soul of Jesus and dwelt within his humanity. This human nature, therefore, was different from other men's. Christ was not a complete man. The Cappadocian theologians responded: Gregory of Nazianzus (330–389), Gregory of Nyssa (330–*c.* 395) and Basil the Great (*c.* 329–379). They insisted on the completeness of Christ's human nature. Christ was fully human and fully God.

Finally, the Council of Chalcedon in 451 taught the two undivided natures of Christ, opposing the claims of Nestorius (d. *c.* 451) and Eutyches (*c.* 378–454). Nestorius taught a duality of persons because there is a duality of natures, one human and one divine. Eutyches took the other extreme. He confused the two natures, mixing them up together. Chalcedon attacked both ideas. Chalcedon insisted that Jesus was fully divine in that he was *homoousios* (of the same nature) with the Father and, in an unmixed and unchanged manner, fully human in that he was *homoousios* (of the same nature) with humanity.

Subsequent western theology was shaped by these councils and the writings of Augustine of Hippo (354–430). Of course, many early heresies and differences of opinion continued. We might even reasonably ask if some contemporary Christologies owe their origin to these ancient debates. Nevertheless, while Christians have never intentionally placed the creeds and councils on a par with Scripture, the theology of Chalcedon has more or less expressed traditional western orthodox Christology up to the last 100 years. Jesus was both God the Son and fully human. These two natures were fully, completely, inseparably and mysteriously co-temporal in Jesus of Nazareth. Historic, orthodox, Christianity has affirmed this down through the centuries.

But we can hear the objections coming. Did these respective councils *create* doctrine that goes beyond Jesus' teaching? Is A. N. Wilson right to insist, 'If it were even half possible that an historical personage existed who said the words attributed to him in the Gospels, there could be no greater insult to his memory than to recite the creeds, invented in a Hellenized world which was, imaginatively speaking, light years away from both Jesus and from ourselves'?[15] This is the nub: is there a central body of teaching about the supreme uniqueness of Jesus Christ? Did the one, true, creator God become human?

To answer this, it makes sense to listen to Tom Wright's helpful cautionary note. 'What we should say, instead, is: "It all depends upon what you mean by 'God'."'[16] A first glance at the New Testament suggests that Jesus of Nazareth did *not* claim he was God, at least not in such a bald fashion. We must accept that Jesus did not walk around exclaiming, 'I am God, the second person of the Trinity.' His contemporaries would only have expressed their bewilderment. We must appreciate the Bible's absolute insistence upon monotheism (see Ex. 20:3 and Dt. 6:4). Jesus stressed this point of orthodoxy, to the extent that at times he drew a distinction between himself and God the Father (Mk. 10:18; Mt. 4:1–11; Jn. 5:19, 30, 36–37; 8:18; 14:1; 17:1–5; 20:17).

This differentiation is heightened by Jesus' use of particular Old Testament terms: Son of Man and Messiah. These point not so much to a co-equality with God as much as a significant role within Israel.[17] They are expressions whose meaning is derived within late Old Testament Judaism. When these terms are employed in the various Gospel accounts, however, an important picture emerges.[18] Jesus' actions and teachings suggest a provocative equality with the Lord God of Israel.

Jesus taught with a recognized, if not always appreciated, authority (Mt. 7:29; Lk.4:32). He claimed that his words would last for ever (Mk. 13:32; Lk. 21:33; Mt. 24:35; *cf.* Mt. 5:18). Yet the prophet Isaiah declared that only the Lord's Word is eternal (Is. 40:8). Jesus asserted an authority to forgive sins, but as the

Pharisees *rightly* understood, only God can forgive sins. Jesus appropriated the function of a future judge, which the Old Testament supremely associates with the Lord God (Mt. 25:31–46; Mk. 2:1-12; Jn. 5:19–27; *cf.* Ezk. 34:17ff; Dt. 32:36; Ps. 9:8; and Joel 3:12).[19]

Some argue that it is difficult to read the Gospels and make unassailable conclusions about Jesus' self-understanding. There is no autobiographical 'I' to the Gospels. We do, however, have the Gospel reports of his teaching. The four Gospels present the sayings of Jesus, adapted into written form. This material suggests that he taught in such a way that people believed him to be unique. More importantly, it appears from the way the material in the Gospels is presented that Jesus taught people to accept his uniqueness, but on his terms.

The apostolic preaching and teaching moved further, but in a specific and deliberate direction. They taught that Jesus was unique. In the dazzling light of the historic bodily resurrection and the risen Christ's personal teaching, the apostles were led to the only logical and essential conclusion. Radical though the statement may be (but consistent with a revealed monotheism), there is a tri-unity of Father, Son and Spirit. Jesus, whom they knew in the flesh and as risen from the dead, is Lord and Christ. The pre-existing Son of the Father became incarnate. The agent of creation walked the planet Earth at a special point in the flow of history, in a particular and confined geographic area and with fully human limitations.

The subsequent church councils articulated and clarified doctrine *implied but undeniable* within the New Testament apostolic witness. This was not the development of doctrine but the sensible conclusion drawn from divine revelation. As G. C. Berkouwer states, 'The limits of dogmatic reflection on Christology lie, not in a given historical decision of the church, but in exegesis or rather in Scripture itself.'[20]

What then do we know for sure?

Earlier this century the German theologian Rudolph Bultmann insisted, 'I do indeed think that we can know almost nothing concerning the life and personality of Jesus, since the early Christian sources show no interest in either, are moreover fragmentary and often legendary; and other sources about Jesus do not exist.'[21] However, since the post-war years, Bultmann's scepticism has been displaced by a 'conviction that certain things about Jesus may actually be known within the bounds of historical probability'.[22] A principal figure in this new approach to historical Jesus studies, E. P. Sanders, claimed, 'The dominant view today seems to be that we can know pretty well what Jesus was out to accomplish, that we can know a lot about what he said, and that those two things make sense within the world of first-century Judaism.'[23] Even A. N. Wilson acknowledges this degree of certainty about the historical Jesus.[24] In biblical scholarship, over the last several decades, interest has again turned towards a new 'quest' for the historical Jesus. Whereas, a hundred years ago, there was scepticism, now some scholars have reached a certainty: yes, there was a historical Jesus, who travelled and taught and was executed.[25] However, what these historical evidences *tell* us, however, is an altogether different question.

The crucial point is that the Gospels do *tell us what we need to know*. Just as we saw in chapter 3, regarding the knowability of God's truth through the written page, we can legitimately invite contemporary men and women to 'read' the Gospels. It is not wasted time or an impossible task. We are not groping in the dark. A late-twentieth-century person can intelligently read the four Gospels as literature that relates to historical reality. There is a trustworthy correlation between what happened in time–space events and what the Gospel writers tell us these events *mean*.

Readers have to be careful in the use of the word 'historical'. The word is fluid and problematic. Do we mean that the Gospels are 'objective' history like some of our present-day historical biographies (if even they are!)? Clearly not: there are gaps in our Gospel records; each Gospel has structured the sequence of events in a slightly different way; some records of the sayings of Jesus vary in vocabulary and syntax; and some events and sayings found in one or more of the Gospels are not found in one or more of the others.

Nevertheless, we can have confidence that the reported sayings of Jesus (although transposed from oral sayings to written form, from Aramaic to Greek to our own language, and from various manuscripts into an agreed compilation) are presented not only through the filter of religious conviction but with a commitment to 'earth' the Jesus of faith in the actions, events and history of Jesus of Nazareth. The interpretive framework of the Gospel writers does not nullify the trustworthy historical presentation.[26]

Consequently, the particular information we receive from the Gospels has to be measured and associated with the New Testament letters. The apostolic writings certainly further our information about the risen and exalted Jesus, but in no way contradict the Jesus we meet in the Gospels. There is a crucial symmetry. We need both, and both are given to us . . . for a reason!

OK, but so what?

At the close of the twentieth century we can know that the eternal Son of the one true God became fully human. He lived on earth in a particular historical and social context. Eyewitnesses saw him do miracles, heard his teaching and remembered for a reason. The pivotal point in history for his first followers, and one that commands our attention and surrender, is the bodily, time–space resurrection of Jesus of Nazareth from the dead. No-one actually saw this occurrence, but they encountered the risen Jesus physically, historically and spatially. They put their faith in him, but a 'him' they knew in history, whose sayings they recalled, whose actions they remembered and whose history they proclaimed.

In the Gospels we are given particular information, and interpretive portraits, about Jesus Christ. There are differences between the Gospels. The church, from the earliest days (see Lk. 1:1-2 for evidence of various traditions and sources) has acknowledged the plurality of Gospels.[27] We do not have one, monochrome account of Jesus. We have four perspectives, with both a unity and diversity. There is complementarity among the four Gospels.

The information we have, however, is particular. First, it is not exhaustive. John's Gospel tells us this, 'Jesus did many other miraculous signs in the presence of his disciples, which are not recorded in this book' (Jn. 20:30; 21:25). There are some things about Jesus of Nazareth we simply do not know. What we can read, however, is sufficient to lead us to a knowledgeable response to the good news of Jesus.

This leads to a second observation. The Gospels are principally theological; we might go as far as to say they are evangelistic (telling people what they need to know to be Christian) and pastoral (what they must believe and do to live as followers of Jesus) rather than biographical. Certainly, we read in the Gospels some information about what Jesus did and where he travelled. Nonetheless, their primary objective, evident from their own internal argument, is theological. They present us with a Jesus to whom we must respond, not a Jesus about whom we have only biographical information.

'But', someone cries out, 'all the so-called information comes in the form of stories from the past, a far-off and distant past. I live in the here and now, in the 1990s. Can't I just climb up into the mountains and experience the Jesus sensation up there? Why insist that I have to respond to the Jesus who walked around in the first century and spoke a language I don't know?'

The Gospel writers want us to respond to the risen Lord Jesus – in one permissible sense, the Jesus of the 1990s. But this Jesus is none other than the Jesus who walked on earth in history. Any distinction between the Jesus of faith and the Jesus of history has to be made carefully. The New Testament writers wrote on the basis of a conviction that the Jesus of faith is the risen Jesus – he who was once crucified. Their witness to the historical Jesus is shaped by their faith in the exalted Lord Jesus as the fulfilment of Israel's hope.

To draw too sharp a line between the Jesus of faith and the Jesus of history necessitates a radically altered understanding of what is history as well as faith. This would lead to a dilemma, and we are back again to what I described in earlier chapters as a 'contentless' faith. This idea of 'faith' is somehow based on the movement of our hearts and minds, but in ways detached from asking ourselves, 'Well, wait a minute. Why am I claiming this faith? Do I just accept the popular idea that we all choose whatever suits us? Why do I believe in Jesus?'

We believe we experience 'Jesus' by our faith. It is more than an intellectual thing, for we delight in the intimacy of prayer to Jesus, his Spirit lives in us. But what do we mean? Who do we mean? The Jesus of faith cut off from the time–space events of human existence, and most importantly from a crucifixion and resurrection, means we have a Jesus of faith cut off from real humanity. How can we know if Jesus the Saviour shares our humanity and

126

experience and was truly our substitute when he died on the cross?

To be sure, the New Testament invites us to 'know' Jesus, the risen Jesus who no longer resides in Israel. The apostles, likewise, proclaimed a risen and exalted Jesus; their preaching and writing pay little attention to stories about, and sayings of, the historical Jesus. Nevertheless, the apostles assumed, as do the Gospels, that the Jesus whom subsequent followers can know is none other than the Jesus of Nazareth they saw, heard and touched (Acts 2:22; 10:39; 1 Jn. 1:1-3; and 2 Pet. 1:16-18). Tom Wright makes the following point:

> If you tried to tell an average first-century Jew that God had redeemed his people, and invited him to believe this despite the fact that Israel was still under Roman rule, that the ancestral law was not being obeyed by most Jews, that the world as a whole was still full of arrogance and evil – he would say that you had simply not understood what you were talking about. What mattered at the end of the day was history. Something had to happen in the real world. This is why, as historians, we have to grapple with the question . . . what, historically, had occurred shortly after Jesus' death, to make first-century Jews say that the great redemption had indeed happened? A 'spiritual' redemption that left historical reality unaffected was a contradiction in terms. If the gospels, seen in terms of the pagan culture to which the church went in mission, are inescapably biographies, then, seen in terms of Jewish culture which gave them their theological depth, they are inescapably theological history.[28]

Picking up on Wright's ideas, we are stressing the importance of knowing the *particular* Jesus. Christian confidence depends so much on knowing, in relationship, the particular Jesus, the Jesus to whom the Bible witnesses and whom we can know personally.

While we have to work hard when we read Gospel narrative, parables and sayings, in order to appreciate their literary integrity, we may be sure that we are reading information trustworthy and certain. Ultimately, the Gospel accounts' aim is to persuade men and women to repentance and faith. By this distinguishing nature,

Gospel material differs from, say, a biography of Winston Churchill. There is a difference not only between the type of literature, but also between the aims of the writers. No biographer of Churchill claims their subject is Lord and Saviour. The Gospels do. We are not simply asked to respond to a literary figure. Rather, through this trustworthy literary witness we can meet *him*. In his wonderfully clear and eminently helpful book *Chris Chrisman Goes to College*, James Sire reminds us of this.

> Bob was illustrating a principle he couldn't yet articulate: reason's most important function in apologetics and evangelism today is to clear away the objections to Christian faith, so that a person becomes willing to look at the positive evidence that comes through clearly from revelation. And what comes through most convincingly is Jesus. Jesus himself is the best reason for believing in Jesus. The truth is seen only by those who come to the Gospels with open eyes, open ears, open minds and open hearts. Without this the Bible remains a closed book even when it is open before us. But we do not have to have perfect vision to begin to glimpse the majesty and mystery of Jesus. Often just a peek at him will so startle us that our eyes spring open, our ears perk up, our minds turn on and our hearts begin to melt.[29]

Here is the point, but a point involving us: how will we respond?

Supreme Lord and sufficient Saviour

Several years ago the British Museum mounted an exhibition entitled 'The Art of the Fake', showing a large collection of paintings, sculpture and other items that were frauds. These fakes were not obvious. They appeared priceless and beautiful. The exhibition showed not only how easy it is to be fooled by the fake, but how beautiful and artistic the fake can appear.

The analogy with Christian confidence in our age of change should be apparent. Suppose someone responds to the New Testament witness to Jesus for which we argued above. How may a Christian be confident that Jesus is the way, the truth and the life? Because of her new-found joy and peace? She may experience considerable joy and happiness in Jesus. Is confidence gained because the believer sees his life falling into place? He may indeed experience such well-being. But what if, after confessing Jesus as Lord, life becomes difficult and painful? In chapter 1 we identified some situations. Peace and a sense of well-being may disappear when family, friends or co-workers attack, or are uninterested. How can a new Christian be sure that Christianity is not a beautiful fake, not worth the price?

Moreover, may not a Christian discover that there are many others, with differing views about the world, who also appear happy and 'together'? Here is where the weight of modernity and postmodernity, described in chapter 2, is felt. In a multi-faith and pluralistic society we could wonder if Christianity truly is unique. Likewise, there are groups and sects, claiming to be Christian, which seek to modify biblical orthodoxy and promote a particular spirituality or lifestyle. A person could ask, 'Is faith in Jesus right? Is there something more?'

In the New Testament, there is no greater battle than for the right view of Christ. Consider the apostle Paul's letter to the Colossians.[30] Paul's concern in this letter is clearly displayed in 2:4, 8. 'I tell you this so that no-one may deceive you by fine-sounding arguments . . . See to it that no-one takes you captive through hollow and deceptive philosophy, which depends on human tradition and the basic principles of this world rather than on Christ.'

The believers in Colosse may well have been struggling with a battle over confidence, equivalent to ours today. Maybe they were hearing new teaching that differed from the gospel they had received from Epaphras. This certainly occurs today. What is clear is how this letter concentrates on a clear view of Jesus. Paul's response to theological and ethical confusion involves a central concern with a right understanding of Jesus. We can study this letter as an example of his teaching. His encouragement to his readers relates to the confidence today's Christians can experience. Three points stand out.

1. The Colossians' faith is a faith in Jesus alone

The distinguishing feature of the Colossians is their faith in Christ and their love for other believers (1:2, 4). It is this news about the

Colossians that excites the apostle. Through the gospel they heard from Epaphras (1:5–7), they came to know God's grace, found nowhere else than in the truth of the gospel and in the person of Jesus Christ.

In Christ, God's Son, these believers have been liberated from an evil realm and bought back to be members of Christ's kingdom (1:13–14). Christ is the one whom Paul proclaims (1:28). Christ is God's mystery (2:2). What concerns Paul is their faith in Christ: 'For though I am absent from you in body, I am present with you in spirit and delight to see how orderly you are and how firm your faith in Christ is (2:5)'.

What is faith in Christ? They had received Christ (2:6), and he is the one in whom they have a continuing experience (2:7); still, they are to live with confidence and true spirituality, to walk in him. In him they have been made complete or given fullness (2:10). They need not fall into the trap of thinking that they require a higher spirituality or religious experience. Their present fullness involves a circumcision, a burial through baptism, a resurrection (2:11). In Christ there is a cancelation of guilt (2:13-15). Therefore, in Christ, a person is truly free; he or she does not need the shadows of a spirituality that is deficient (2:16-23).

The key is faith in Christ alone. The Christian trusts and believes in Christ alone. There are no others, angels, gurus or spiritual forces. Epaphras told them of none other than Jesus. Paul, therefore, concentrates his argument by saying, in effect, 'A true Christian has faith in Jesus alone because it is Christ alone who is supreme Lord and sufficient Saviour.'

Questions may have been lurking among the Colossian believers. They were *not* unfaithful. But they were new in the faith and prone to wrong views of Christ. Paul's teaching about Christ could well have been in response to problematic thinking and questioning.

2. This faith in Jesus is right because Jesus is the supreme Lord

Paul refers the Colossians to God and to the whole of creation (1:15–17). In Jesus Christ is God made fully known. In him we see the goodness of God. He is not leading us to God; he is revealing God to us. It is not just what Jesus does, it is also who he is – the image of God.

Accordingly, Jesus is not part of creation. 'Firstborn' (*prōtotokos*) might suggest he too is only a created creature, were it not for the clear stress of verses 16 and 17. Jesus is supreme over all creation and existence. He is the agent of creation. All creation derives its being and essence from him. Creation even exists for him. He is not even one part of creation; he stands over and above the created order. He is no guru or spiritual force; he is the Lord of the universe.

Since Jesus is the image of God and supreme over all creation, Paul moves in verse 18 to silence any idea that Jesus is only a stepping-stone for God's people. He is not just a great teacher for the church. God's people derive their being and life in Jesus. The church is described not as an organization, but as the body of Christ. The church's hope of resurrection is based only on Christ's pioneering resurrection. Accordingly, can there be anyone higher than or supreme beyond Christ? No, argues Paul, and summarizes it all again in verses 19 and 20: 'For God was pleased to have all his fulness dwell in him, and through him to reconcile to himself all things, whether things on earth or things in heaven, by making peace through his blood, shed on the cross.' Yet an additional and glorious stress is made.

3. This faith in Jesus is right because Jesus is the sufficient Saviour

Because Jesus Christ is who he is before God and over all existence, he is fully and perfectly capable of resolving our greatest problem, alienation from God (1:21–22). Jesus alone is the sufficient Saviour. This is expanded in 2:11–15. Could an ordinary human being, even a very holy and spiritual man or woman, accomplish reconciliation? They too are only creatures, not the supreme Lord over all. No other human can be described as in 1:15–23. This is what Epaphras' gospel, which is Paul's gospel, told the Colossians. It is this gospel that is spreading throughout the world (1:6). It is in this gospel that we can find and experience true and legitimate confidence.

He whom we may not ignore

I suspect most readers would understand and accept the arguments of this chapter. In fact, most would say that nothing new was offered. On one hand, I would be nervous if something novel appears in these pages. On the other hand, I think there is more here than may meet the eye. In the continuing view of our theological framework, as we see more clearly who Jesus is, and on what basis we can *know* he is who he is, we have something to say about a confident life in an age of change.

Jesus is a particular Jesus. His particularities tell us a great deal about him. Likewise, what we can know about him relates particularly to who we are. We find that to be human means we are *already* in a relationship with him: he is the author of all existence, including ours. We have already hinted at his death on the cross as the way for us to know reconciliation and peace. (More will be said about this in the next chapter.) Yet this links up with the realities of the fall. The mess of human life, corporate and personal, somehow relates to the Jesus we can read about in the Gospels. All our experiential struggles with guilt, suffering, frustration and imperfection meet at an intersection with this particular Jesus.

As we said at the beginning of this chapter, everything depends upon who Jesus is. For today's Christian, living in an age of change, everything in our human experience derives its significance, its resolution, its transformation and its duration because of who Jesus is. To know that we can know him, talk to him in prayer, and experience his love and power is a real and true part of our possible Christian confidence.

At the same time, we need not limit all we have said to our own personal and private Christian lives. Because Jesus is who he is, we can be confident in speaking to our changing society. Do we appeal to Jesus because he can bring peace and order into a person's life? Do we encourage our friends to consider the claims of Christ because he can resolve the guilt feelings, pain or confusion of life? Do we invite society to respond to the gospel because Christianity will establish social harmony? Yes and no.

An appeal based *only* on these concerns is inadequate. To begin with, not every person we meet has immediate and obvious profound emotional, psychological or physical needs. Furthermore, in an age of subjective relativism it is not surprising to hear people say, 'I'm genuinely happy that you think you've found what you need in Jesus. As for me, my answers are elsewhere.' Of course, as we probe deeper some people admit to a general dissatisfaction and confusion that they did not initially reveal.

An evangelistic appeal that is solely pragmatic or therapeutic is incomplete; at best it is limited. Such gospel invitations can possibly cater to human selfishness and self-concern: 'What can I get out of this? What's on offer?' People think they are free to ignore the claims of Christ as they might disregard advertised self-help and self-awareness courses.

The New Testament takes a different, more comprehensive and, thus, richer approach. Undoubtedly, Jesus Christ wondrously relates to the wounded, abused, bewildered and broken of our contemporary world. There are situations when the initial relevance of the gospel is precisely this way. The striking picture in the New Testament, however, is of Jesus primarily as Lord and forthcoming judge.

Because Jesus Christ is Lord of all and will judge all, he is profoundly relevant to all. Humanity is already in relationship with Jesus. They are created by him and in him they are sustained in their existence. Here is the universal point of relevance and application. This is the logic of John 1:3–5 and Paul's apologetic at Athens in Acts 17:25–29. A person's humanity (his or her personality, rationality and physical being) is the inescapable evidence of a dependent relationship. Before faith and repentance, there is alienation and rebellion; nonetheless a relationship exists.

When his lordship and rule are presented, the good news of his atoning death and saving mercy is germane. For what is salvation if it is not at least a salvation from the coming just judgment? The Lord's love is truly healing and liberating; at the same time it comes in mercy and pardon. Divine love does not just meet a human need, responding to the void created by social fragmentation and disintegration. It restores and reconciles rebels and insurrectionists.

The New Testament writers slice through any argument that dismisses the gospel subjectively. Quite simply yet disturbingly, they argue that this Jesus is one whom no person in history may ignore. He is not irrelevant to anyone's present and future existence.

Yet here is good news. The same Jesus who is Lord and promised judge also is the Saviour. Precisely because he is supreme Lord and sufficient Saviour, his word of forgiveness, his compassionate care, his healing power (all of which may touch the very situational particulars of our lives) have enormous veracity and relevance. Jesus does speak to the isolation that men and women feel in our crowded cities. The Lord can lift up those wounded, whether they are hurt through chemical abuse, sexual abuse or contemporary lovelessness. He can make whole the contemporary person who bleeds psychologically, intellectually and spiritually, despite the efforts of so many current therapies.

But our confidence in this Jesus exists only because we see and experience the Jesus we can know in Scripture. Jesus is not a book, to be sure. But we may experientially know no Jesus other than the Jesus of apostolic witness. When we take the appeal made by the New Testament we have a fuller and more relevant gospel than that which is often offered. There is good news about a Saviour, whom no man, woman or child may ignore. In the next chapter we move to consider how this Jesus accomplished what is now good news for our age.

Questions for reflection and discussion

1. How would you respond to the statement: 'Jesus is whoever I want him to be, because he relates to me'? Why should someone living today consider Jesus?

2. Why is it important to see the Jesus of faith as also the Jesus of history? In what ways do postmodernist views on history lead to further confusion about the Jesus of Christian faith?

3. If every human is already in a relationship with Jesus (for he is their creator), what does this imply for our self-understanding? What does it also say to those who think the gospel has nothing to do with them?

6

The peace of salvation

We are counted free

The high price of peace

George Bernard Shaw wrote, 'Peace is not only better than war, but infinitely more arduous.'[1] Shaw is right. In international affairs, corporate enterprise or individual relationships, peace is preferable to conflict; but peace demands a high cost and commitment.

So too our relationship with God. To be at peace with God is to know and experience true love, acceptance and healing. Here is the essence of Christian confidence. Peace is only possible, however, because God himself undertook an arduous toil.

Recall the argument so far. Chapter 3 considered revelation as God's desire that men and women should know him and be in a good relationship with him. The extensive and radical implications of the fall, however, make a good relationship problematic (as we saw in chapter 4). Something arising out of God's initiative, consistent with his character and capable of meeting our human need, is demanded.

In the previous chapter, therefore, we examined the uniqueness and supremacy of Jesus Christ. The eternal Son of God became fully human to fulfil the glory of the holy and merciful God. His life, work, teaching, death and resurrection are the means by which God is fully known, the effects of the fall reversed and humanity reconciled to the glorious and forgiving God. But, Jesus accomplished this peace at a great and formidable cost.

'Peace' well expresses the fullness and importance of why God became man, as Anselm (*c.* 1033–1109) put it.[2] John the Baptist's father, Zechariah, praised God and prophesied about his son's future:

And you, my child, will be called a prophet of the Most High;
  for you will go on before the Lord to prepare the way for him,
to give his people the knowledge of salvation
  through the forgiveness of their sins,
because of the tender mercy of our God,
  by which the rising sun will come to us from heaven
to shine on those living in darkness
  and in the shadow of death,
to guide our feet into the path of peace.

(Lk. 1:76–79)

The risen Jesus appeared to his frightened disciples and said, 'Peace be with you!' (Jn. 20:19; see also Lk. 24:36).[3] This is more than a Jewish greeting. Most of the New Testament letters begin with a salutation, emphasizing a peace indissolubly united with God's grace and mercy.[4] The apostle Paul's assurance in Romans 5 is the sure peace a believer has through faith in Jesus Christ. 'Therefore, since we have been justified through faith, we have peace with God through our Lord Jesus Christ, through whom we have gained access by faith into this grace in which we now stand' (Rom. 5:1–2).

A contemporary believer can have peace with the one true God. Here is the bedrock of our Christian confidence. We will not consider abstract doctrine. Misunderstand this wonderful promise and hope of peace with our God, and we run the risk of excessive guilt, wavering uncertainty or inappropriate glibness – all of which can be the result of a poor theological framework. Here is where the experiential sides of our life are influenced by our doctrinal understanding. With a skewed or mistaken view of who God is, how he is known, why things in the world are so wrong, and who Jesus is, problems develop.

The personal dilemmas of chapter 1 are then unanswerable, or at least profoundly disturbing. Too many Christians struggle with a crisis of confidence. Undoubtedly, their personalities and temperaments contribute to their difficulties. The helpful counsellor, pastor or friend has to recognize these influences.

But throughout this book an essential complementary argument has been developing. We could try to build an on-going Christian life, but without an appreciation for the comprehensive and trustworthy truths of God's gospel promises in Christ we would be building on a poor foundation. As this book is arguing, however, we need not fall into this error. A better foundation is possible.

Perhaps the image of a foundation is insufficient, too static. Think instead of a friendship or love affair beset by some miscommunication, misunderstanding and doubt. Whether the relationship was with a close friend, spouse, parent or child, the tensions and frustrations would be unpleasant and, in most cases, unsuitable.

In a greater way, a Christian's relationship with her or his creator, redeemer and sustainer is intended to be life-giving and rich. There is peace; and, as Shaw said, this is preferable to war. This chapter examines how this peace has been accomplished and the price that was paid. We will consider how the death of Christ is associated with reconciliation. Furthermore we will see how this reconciliation is on-going through the work of the Holy Spirit in the experience of our Christian living. Peace is real, available and magnificent, and in this we can know true confidence. It was bought at an infinitely arduous cost, but the result is dazzlingly glorious.

Peace through death: the death of Christ

The First World War was a tragic waste of human life. Too many young men from too many countries perished. As the British poet, Wilfred Owen (1893–1918), expressed it in 'Anthem for Doomed Youth',

> What passing-bells for these who die as cattle?
> Only the monstrous anger of the guns.
> Only the stuttering rifles' rapid rattle
> Can patter out their hasty orisons.[5]

Wars take life. Death strikes and there is so much abhorrent waste.

At the heart of Christianity is the death of a young man.[6] Certainly, his resurrection speaks of life and hope, but why do the New Testament writers link his exaltation with his death? They claim that his lordship and kingship are predicated upon his willingness to die (Phil. 2:9-9). Why then did Jesus of Nazareth

137

have to die? Why is his death so important? The answers are fundamental to Christian confidence.[7]

Appreciate the irony. Death on a Roman cross was shameful.[8] The Roman statesman and orator, Cicero (106-43 BC), described crucifixion as 'a most cruel and disgusting punishment'.[9] The cross was offensive to the Jews (cf. Dt. 21:22ff.). The first-century Jewish historian, Josephus, referred to Roman crucifixion as a 'miserable procedure' and 'cruel treatment'.[10] Justin Martyr (c. 100–165) encountered the incredulity of Trypho, a Jewish thinker: 'Be assured', argued Trypho, 'that all our nation waits for the Christ. And we admit that all the Scriptures which you have quoted refer to him. But whether Christ should be so shamefully crucified, this we are in doubt.'[11] Even the apostles acknowledged the problematic implications of their message of Christ crucified (see Gal. 5:11, 'offence', *skandalon*; 1 Cor. 1:18, 'foolishness' or nonsense, *mōria*; 1 Cor. 1:23, 'stumbling-block', *skandalon*; and Heb. 12:2, 'shame' or offence, *aischynēs*).[12] But why did they continue to stress the cross despite its ignominy? Why did Jesus have to die?

Fundamentally, it was the will of God. Quite understandably, the modern mind recoils in horror and distaste at the proposition that God demanded the innocent sufferings of Jesus in order for him to be appeased and satisfied. Stated thus baldly, it has an discordant ring. It was, however, according to the *good, loving and gracious purpose of God*.

Death, expressed in the shedding of blood, was required. There was a divine necessity for satisfaction; death and satisfaction are inextricable in God's loving and merciful plan.[13] The New Testament writers weave the various emphases on Jesus' death around God's glory and love.

The different Greek words used concerning Christ's death speak of a multifaceted significance and accomplishment: ransom (Mk. 10:45, *lytron*; 1 Tim. 2:6, *antilytron*); redemption (Eph. 1:7, *apolytrōsin*); to buy out of slavery (Gal. 3:13, *exēgorasen*); example (1 Pet. 2:21, *hypogrammon*); to bear away sin (1 Pet. 2:24, *anēnenken; to take away, 1 Jn. 3:5, arē*); sacrifice of atonement or propitiation (Rom. 3:25, *hilastērion*; 1 Jn. 4:10, *hilasmos*, and in a verbal form Heb. 2:17, *hilaskesthai*); disarming the powers of evil (Col. 2:13–15 and 1 Jn. 3:8). Throughout history these different themes have been underlined. The death of Christ has been explained in the light of example, substitution and rescuing power. As we have noted, all are present in the New Testament. It is wise not to stress unduly one over against the other. There is a unity.

Nevertheless, to dismiss outright the idea of substitution and satisfaction is to raise more problems than it attempts to displace. Powerlessness and oppression are not our only problems; we face the moral dilemma of guilt. Apart from the substitutionary death of Jesus, the holy justice of God and the seriousness of human sin cannot be *justly* reconciled.

Why accentuate justice? It is because of the glory and majesty of God. If there were no justice, God would not be a God whom we can trust. We would live in a universe of indifference. Even on a human level we know that justice is a necessity. Without justice, societies fall into either anarchy or oppressive totalitarianism. Our awareness of this importance reflects God's character. He is the God of holy justice.

People today risk missing the ultimate issue: humanity's standing before the particular God. The God with whom we must deal is the pure, true, majestic, holy and just God. Our generation denies this constantly. In a slightly different, but germane, context, C. S. Lewis (1898–1963), the British scholar and writer of popular theological works, identified this denial:

> What would really satisfy us would be a God who said of anything we happened to like doing, 'What does it matter so long as they are contented?' We want, in fact, not so much a Father in Heaven as a grandfather in heaven – a senile benevolence who, as they say, 'liked to see young people enjoying themselves,' and whose plan for the universe was simply that it might be truly said at the end of each day, 'a good time was had by all.' Not many people, I admit, would formulate a theology in precisely those terms: but a conception not very different lurks at the back of many minds.[14]

The question is, how will the holy and just God pardon sinful rebellious men and women without ceasing to be consistent with his character? Before we come to faith, we may think this is irrelevant. Surely, God's business is to forgive and let live! The Bible, however, focuses on the greater issue of justice, what is right. Why *should* God forgive without dealing with the transgression of his law and standards? It is not simply a question of conforming to an external code; it is congruity with truth, the very character of God.

Sin is 'contrariness' to God's character, lawlessness with respect to his standards. This is why the Bible frequently speaks of the wrath of God against sin.[15] Sin is non-truth in an active, relational and moral sphere: the relationship of humanity with its creator. Accordingly, a right verdict is delivered by a holy God against all that is the opposite of his nature.

Sin has human consequences too. We cannot save ourselves, through our religious life, through our own moral goodness or through our search for God. We are dead and lost until we are given new life in Christ. The apostle Paul stressed that 'Jews and Gentiles alike are all under sin' (Rom. 3:9). There is no special religious group, even those of the old covenant. Paul strikes at the heart of what we may call 'religion'. He deals with the question of a Jew's unique position. Religion is not the answer, insists Paul. Men and women do not seek God, they prefer something else (Rom. 1:21–25).

As Jesus' teaching shocked his listeners (see Mt. 23:1–36; Lk. 7:36–50 and 11:37–54), so Paul's reasoning was offensive. The same resistance comes today. We do not like the idea, but our problem is not religion; it is our self-declared autonomy from our creator God. Sin is humanity's fundamental problem. In another sense, it is also God's problem: it is rebellion against him.

What is God's solution, one both just and loving? The substitutionary death of Jesus Christ. Christ died because, before God, we are estranged and at odds with him. Christ's death resolves the conflict, and for this supreme reason it was the Father's will that his Son should die. Romans 3:21 illustrates the point: 'But now a righteousness from God, apart from law, has been made known, to which the Law and Prophets testify.' 'But now' refers to a specific period in human history, the days of the gospel, the days of mercy offered through the death of Christ.

The death of Christ relates to God's justice. Equally, because God loves, he pardons. When we see the satisfied justice of God in the death of Christ, we see the overwhelming beauty of God's love. As Paul explains, 'God demonstrates [the Greek denotes a present continuous demonstration] his own love for us in this: While we were still sinners, Christ died for us' (Rom. 5:8; see also 1 Jn. 4:10).

In Christ's death God's justice is met (Rom. 3:25–26 and Gal. 3:10–13). Christ's willingness to take the punishment is justice joined to mercy and grace. In Christ Jesus the righteous standards of God are met and fully upheld. The Law is not broken; 'through the obedience of the one man the many will be made righteous' (Rom. 5:19). To quote Paul further, 'For what the law was powerless to do in that it was weakened by the sinful nature, God did by sending his own Son in the likeness of sinful man to be a sin offering [*peri harmatias*, concerning sin]. And so he condemned sin in sinful man, in order that the righteous requirements of the law might be fully met in us, who do not live according to the sinful nature but according to the Spirit' (Rom. 8:3–4).[16]

The death of Christ demonstrates and procures God's justice. No-one and nothing in the universe will be able to mock and scorn him, saying, 'You do not care for what's right and true.' Divine forgiveness will be clothed in the beautiful garments of love and mercy; likewise its beauty will not be impugned by a neglected or nullified justice. He will point to his Son, the crucified Saviour (Heb. 12:24; Rev. 5:9–10).

There will be a final day of accountability for the entire human race. There is a final judgment. Too much of the New Testament teaching and apostolic preaching concerns the reality of hell for us to dismiss the notion as an impossibility. Obviously, we can reject the idea because we do not acknowledge a just and legitimate divine judgment. But there is little room for this dismissal if we also want to take hold of the promises of forgiveness and pardon. The cross of Christ is loving justice: the innocent dying for the guilty. Equally the sacrificial death of Christ is the death of a Saviour. The apostle Paul expressed it this way: 'In the past God overlooked such ignorance, but now he commands all people everywhere to repent. For he has set a day when he will judge the world with justice by the man he has appointed. He has given proof of this to all men by raising him from the dead' (Acts 17:30–31). There actually is a terrible warning in the good news of Jesus Christ.

On the other hand, Paul assures us that when we repent and believe in the gospel, we are truly and justly pardoned. We need not fear the accusations of either our conscience or the enemy of our souls, Satan. When God pardons us in Christ, we are free indeed. How great a proclamation this is for all of us! For some, the past suggests too many errors and wasted moments in wrong living and an anti-God lifestyle. Others find their present battles almost overwhelming. Their guilt screams too loudly. Yet a louder, more dominant declaration resonates from heaven. On that day when we stand before the judgment throne of God, if we have been Christians now in this life, no-one will justly condemn us before God. God will not, Satan cannot, even our conscience may not. This is Paul's argument in Romans 8:31–35.

When we trust in Jesus Christ and become Christians, it is vital for us to know how sure and true the gospel is. From time to time we will battle with a guilty conscience. We will fail and struggle with disobedience. The tension between trusting God's promises and a tendency to think in terms of religion, 'Have I done enough?', never completely disappears.

We experience legitimate Christian confidence when we understand and appreciate that the eternal and consistent purposes of God involve the death of his Son. It is the original plan for rescuing men and women of every generation. There is no question of the gospel's power and authority: it is the one true God's expressed planned purpose. Peace comes by a righteousness through the death of the Saviour. There is no other way. We must not look for another.

Peace between friends: the security of pardon and acceptance

At the same time, we must look more closely at the unlimited dynamics of this peace. Consider the following three: peace from our past; peace in our present; and peace for our future. Each, and all together, promise well-being, described by pardon and acceptance.

1. Peace from our past

In 1535, the German theologian, Martin Luther (1483–1546), who was caught up in the tumultuous events of what became the European Protestant Reformation, produced a commentary on the apostle Paul's letter to the Galatians. For Luther, the issue in the letter, and indeed the whole of the Bible, was God's promise of peace and forgiveness to all who believe in Christ. A person is brought back into a right relationship with God by Christ's goodness, substitutionary death on the cross and victorious resurrection from the dead. Here is the heart of the gospel, insisted Luther. One central strand of the gospel, he claimed, is the doctrine of justification.

> If this doctrine be lost, then is also the doctrine of truth, life, and salvation, lost and gone. If this doctrine flourish, then all good things flourish; religion, the true service of God, the glory of God, the right knowledge of all things necessary for a Christian man to know.[17]

Justification is semantically associated with righteousness. Both imply an acceptance according to the standard of God's law given to Moses, more comprehensive than merely the Ten Commandments. Jesus met the full standards and requirements. In him there was no sin. Justification is not found in ourselves. We lack the important righteousness and the acceptability. We are justified as we trust in Christ. This is what the Reformers such as Martin Luther meant by justification by faith alone in Christ alone.[18] Faith is not rewarded, as if it merited God's attention. Rather, faith has as its object the person, work and mediation of Christ Jesus. We are justified *through* faith in Christ.

This is central to our Christian confidence. Justification is, in one sense, a declaration by God that a believer, because of Jesus, is free from the just condemnation that sin warrants. But we must avoid too great a stress on the legal or forensic image. Human analogies are limited. As G. Schrenk has written,

> The forensic element, of course, is only a figure, for we are not in the sphere of human justice, but are dealing with the divine Judge who is also unlimited King. We have thus to transpose the legal aspect into the divine key. An act of grace replaces ordinary legal procedure. But this grace, as the legal concept shows, is not capricious. It conforms to true right. The image of God as Judge is tenable inasmuch as human law does to some extent express imperishable divine norms. But it must be understood in terms of the divine act that strictly finds no human parallel.[19]

'An act of grace' is the important phrase. Justification by faith in Christ does not declare us holy and perfect; rather, God waives the just sentence against us. It has very little to do with good people or bad people. 'Grace operates in the face of blameworthiness.'[20] Consequently, justification is a statement of status, not character. On the other hand, reconciliation is never static but an ongoing dynamic in the believer's life, both now and after the resurrection to eternal life (Rom. 8:28-30).

On what does justification depend? On God's saving initiative, which is also just – the point made in the preceeding section. Justification involves Christ Jesus: his own goodness and righteousness seen in his ministry on earth, his death, resurrection and ascension as Lord. At the core of justification is not only a declaration but a historical work, in time and space, when Jesus died on the cross and was raised three days later (1 Cor. 1:30).

2. *Peace in our present*

We can now bring together some of the points just made. For justification comes when we personally trust in Christ and repent. A moment in our time and history matters. This is not to suggest that our peace with God is based solely on our human actions and response. God the Father, the Son and the Holy Spirit are the principal agents in our peace. Still, the Bible calls humans to repent and believe. Human response is important. We are not totally passive. We are recipients but not mindless and will-less beings. God works in us according to our human nature. Our sure confidence and hope do not rest on our own actions, feelings or thoughts. They are, however, the human *experiential* side of the divine–human encounter.[21]

I think of the woman caught in a tangle of confusion, poor self-esteem and fear. The reasons were complex. Too many years passed, during which what she knew intellectually about the one true God was not necessarily coordinating with her emotions. She called herself a Christian, and tried so hard to live a Christian life. But her life only disintegrated, culminating in a panic and terror.

Over the past months, however, I see a transformation. The caring Christian community with whom she has lived for the past year are helping her to see afresh the realities of the total, once-for-all, finished work of Christ. She has been reminded of this accomplishment. Her growing joy is like a tender shoot, springing up from the soil. She is seeing how utterly free and unconditional are the promises of the gospel. There is pardon and reconciliation (the peace we mentioned at the beginning of this chapter). The one true God can be trusted, despite the past and in the face of the future!

Simultaneously, she sees the vital importance of her response to the gospel, as a mark of her dignity as a human – a human made to worship the one true God. Christ is the sole and trustworthy sin-bearer. She must yield her all to him. There must be a time when 'she decides to decide'. With a growing confidence, she knows she has responded. She can look back and say, 'Well, I know when things made sense, and when I gratefully acknowledged Christ's death.' There is an important 'bottom line' in her life. On the basis of this she lives, not without problems and struggles, but with a distinct reality.

There is a reasonable and legitimate confidence for the person who repents and believes. This is the wonderful reality of our life if we have come to faith in Christ. We are accepted. A wonderful security can speak clearly and legitimately to our conscience. Think back to the problems presented in chapter 1. At the root of our problems with guilt is the issue of acceptance. We know God is holy and has standards. The clearer our appreciation of God's character and perfection, the more prone we are to insecurity. We feel insecure because of our inconsistencies, our flirtation with sin and the forces in our culture. For some of us, the insecurity is evident not only in our self-esteem but in our approach towards guidance. We can fear that God will not lead us *principally* due to our wrong-doing. Ultimately, a Christian's fear of falling away from Christ is answered not so much by looking inwards and running through a spiritual checklist but by Christ's death for his people. It is a once-for-all accomplished victory and declaration.

3. *Peace for our future*

There is further good news! A Christian is not just pardoned. Justification is not the only thread in God's salvation. At times Christians can isolate justification from the other implications of salvation. We are promised far more than a legal standing before God!

The New Testament refers to the staggering promise and reality of fellowship with God (1 Cor. 1:9; 1 Jn. 1:2), reconciliation (Col.

3:12); adoption (Rom. 8:14–17; Gal. 4:6; 1 Pet. 2:10; 1 Jn. 3:1) and re-creation (2 Cor. 5:17; Gal. 6:15; Eph. 2:4–6; Col. 3:9–11).

Above all, the New Testament points believers to the certainty of a future hope, a hope strong and sure (Rom. 8:18–21; Col. 1:5; 3:4; 1 Pet. 5:10; Jude 20–21). In fact, apostolic teaching gives *comparatively* greater weight to the believer's future reality and hope than to his or her present experience in Christ (Tit. 2:11–14; 3:7; 2 Tim. 4:1; 2 Pet. 1:11; 3:11–14; Rev. 1: 1–8 and throughout). Our generation is so now-oriented that we miss this assurance and confidence.

North American and northern European Christians appear almost blind to the future hope (*eschaton*). Most of us, most of the time, live a comparatively comfortable existence. It is mainly when we face illness, grief or tragedy that our vision is cleared: Christian living and hope are more comprehensive than present experiences in Christ. To a Corinthian church too concerned with present experiences, Paul insisted, 'If only for this life we have hope in Christ, we are to be pitied more than all men' (1 Cor. 15:19). If the Christian reality is only the here and now, fine (if life is very pleasant) but if the present is painful and disturbing, why bother with Christ? But, our hope impacts our present because of the future's great promise.

This hope is infinitely more than an escapist fantasy. Western believers rightly rejoice at particular promises: 'Praise be to the God and Father of our Lord Jesus Christ! In his great mercy he has given us new birth into a living hope through the resurrection of Jesus Christ from the dead, and into an inheritance that can never perish, spoil or fade . . .' (1 Pet. 1:3–4). Christian readers in parts of the two-thirds world, however, see what western Christians might miss – the link Peter makes between present hope and future reality: '. . . kept in heaven for you, who through faith are shielded by God's power until the coming of the salvation that is ready to be revealed in the last time. In this you greatly rejoice, though now for a little while you may have had to suffer grief in all kinds of trials' (1 Pet. 1:4–6).

The peace that believers have with God is fuller and more significant than many Christians appreciate. In Christ, there is a peace between friends, from the day we repent and believe to the coming day in the future. Moreover, this peace does not dismiss the tensions and issues of our present life in Christ. God's dynamic peace works in our present, even a present in which there are disturbing problems. The triumph of Christ's atoning death involves more than a single-moment accomplishment in a believer's life. There is an on-going, continuous, moment-by-moment affect. Our confidence is based on something far greater than often appreciated. This is seen in clearer focus as we consider a Christian's daily dilemma.

Peace in the journey: the promise of change

Given this glorious peace in Christ, we might think all would be well. Knowing we were once far off but now brought back into a right relationship with God ought to result in a radically new way of living. So why do we do the very things we know we should not? Why do we continuously battle with sin? The seventeenth-century English Puritan, John Owen, observed about sin:

> It is such an inmate that we can never be quit of its company; and so intimate unto us, that it puts forth itself, in every acting of the mind, will, or any other faculty of the soul. Though men would fain shake it off, yet when they would do good, this evil will be present with them.[22]

Consider for a moment a phenomenon we will see more and more in the coming years. A young man, with no Christian or church-going background, becomes a Christian. He fully understands and responds with his whole being to the good news of Jesus. He knows his need for a Saviour – in part, because he slept with many women, including prostitutes. In many ways he represents men and women similar to the Corinthian Christians to whom Paul wrote, and who Paul knew required counsel concerning their past pagan backgrounds.

This young man, a new Christian, falls in love with a woman. They both love the Lord, and seek to live biblical lives. Yet Christian sexual discipleship is new to them. Alone with each other, they struggle with their desires to go to bed with each other. One afternoon, they do. They are torn between the pull of their shared pleasure and their mutual guilty consciences. I cite this one heterosexual example, but as the gospel marvellously sheds light into our postmodern darkness we will encounter similar pastoral problems with young believers who are gay, users of cocaine, alcoholics, and addicted to pornography, and those who are bedazzled by high fashion, sophisticated electronics and spender-friendly credit cards.

In the real world, we fall short of what God wants us to be and do. We know there are forgiveness and love, but for some reason we fail. There are times when we quite consciously do things which displease God, hurt others and do not edify ourselves. This can raise an enormous question: 'Is our peace with God threatened by our wrong actions, choices and desires?'

A tension exists between two realities: the scars of our fallenness and the reality of our regeneration. The Bible and our experience confirm this tension.[23] Even though we are made new in Christ, we battle with choices, actions and thinking influenced by the world, Satan and our rebellious humanity.

This tension is hard to understand, though readily experienced. At times, the New Testament speaks of our complete renovation and re-creation.[24] In other places, the suggestion is that we are not yet what we are becoming.[25] We will be what we are in process of becoming only when we are raised again to new life, with new bodies like Christ's. Then all the promises and declarations will be completed and realized. Until that time, the normal Christian experience is a tension between the now and the becoming, the being and the not yet being. In this tension we struggle with obedience and disobedience.

It is not just potential, but actual. We err if we are concerned only with actual conscious sins without appreciating the problems of a weak conscience. Equally, we must realize that sins are manifestations, actualizations, expressions of a root problem (Gal. 5:16–26).

The problem is universal; it affects every aspect of our being – our mind, will, emotions, and sexuality. It explains why we have so many difficulties. If this tension is ignored or mistreated, we do so at our peril. At the same time, we must appreciate the hope and security of the gospel. We need to keep a sharp focus on the vital truth of God's solution. It is not a hopeless problem and situation. The frustration we identified in chapter 1 has an answer, though one we have to work out over the whole of our life.

Realism is required. Romans 7:14–25 is an important passage to examine. In its context Paul is writing about the role and effects of the Old Testament law. He is answering his own question, 'Is the law sin?' No; but he points out that there is a problem in himself as a Christian (and representative of all believers).[26] He finds he is powerless to obey the law, unable to escape a continuous tension. He identifies the tension in verse 15: 'I do not understand what I do. For what I want to do I do not do, but what I hate I do.' As C. E. B. Cranfield comments, 'The more he is renewed by God's Spirit, the more sensitive he becomes to the continuing power of sin over his life and the fact that even his very best activities are marred by the egotism still entrenched within him.'[27]

Paul's point comes within the context of the preceding argument in chapter 6. Because of our union with Christ, continuous sin is fundamentally and essentially contrary to our new nature (6:1-14). If one side is true (our reconciled and regenerate nature) how can the other side be true (our continuous battle with sin)? We might think the two are mutually exclusive. The answer is that we are free from the bondage of a legalistic scramble for perfection (see Rom. 7:6). It is not that we are sinless, but that sin's dominion is finished. There is still a battle, but a re-creation has occurred within us; a new will, a new more positive inclination. The prophecy of Ezekiel 36:24–32 is fulfilled in the Christian. Paul's argument, culminating with the cry of Romans 7:24, carries the believer to the work of Jesus Christ and the Holy Spirit in his or her life.

Through union with Christ, there is no condemnation as a result of this tension (8:1–2). Furthermore, the believer has been set free from legalism and death and made alive in the Spirit (8:4–16). There is a battle, but there is no despair. In the Christian life there is a progressive work of the Spirit in the full character of the believer. This is the internal work of the Holy Spirit. The Spirit is the agent of sanctification.

The Holy Spirit, the agent of our change

The Spirit points us to Christ. God the Holy Spirit works in the hearts and minds of believers to remind us that there is a Saviour. He works as we read Scripture, as we engage in prayer, as we break the communion bread and drink the wine with other believers, and as we attempt to redirect our lives in the ways of obedience. However mysterious and indescribable the work of the

Holy Spirit, his work is an active, dynamic and moment-by-moment reality. He is why our definition of confidence includes the important phrase *'brought about over time by the Holy Spirit'*.

The Spirit of truth reminds the Christian of the power of God's grace and the completed work of Christ on the cross. Through the Scriptures the Spirit addresses the faithful in a way that instructs, comforts and prompts. As the Spirit validates our adoption by grace into the family of God, we find ourselves *appropriately* secure. It is not simply our own idea; the Spirit of God confirms our legitimacy.

For example, consider the believer who finds that he is plagued with guilt feelings over certain unethical business practices he committed before he became a Christian. To the best of his knowledge and ability he has tried to make restitution and correction. It is in his past. Others have forgiven him; and he now knows that Jesus died for this sin. The past is over and done. Yet, as he sits in church on Sunday or when he speaks at a Christian business persons' meeting, he remembers the past. It can be helpful to recall the past, as a warning for the present. His memories, however, weigh him down. So inwardly he groans. He wonders if his repentance and faith are fraudulent. He is not confident.

The indwelling Spirit ministers to people like him. In his situation the Holy Spirit not only convicts, he also comforts. There is a redeemer, whose finished work on the cross is the basis for pardon, peace and hope. Through grace and the Spirit, he can *experience* the reality of justification. There is a *true fact* of his life: he is forgiven for the wrongdoing which he disturbingly recalls. He is pardoned for a lot more! Furthermore, in ways involving prayer, Scripture reading and an 'internal witness', the Spirit assures him that he has every legitimate right to see himself as one of God's children. This is Paul's promise in Romans 8:16. We can say there is a valid confidence produced by the Spirit.

Of course, this confidence is not static. Some believers understand the application of this hope to their past, but it is their present struggles which disturb them. Again, this is the problem for this businessman; we can think of countless others. Yet here too there is hope. The Holy Spirit also relates to holiness.[28] Through the Spirit, God progressively transforms our moral character to become more and more like Christ's (sanctification). The businessman is given strength to change his financial actions, to say no to particular values and to reject choices that are both immoral and illegal. More subtly, the Spirit gives him a framework of truth: his self-worth and significance are not based on his work performance or outward lifestyle.

The call to holiness in the New Testament assumes a present sanctification as well as a summons to further sanctification. We may not discern this at all times, but God promises the progressive work of the Spirit will create a new character in us. Our salvation is not merely a static declaration; it is also a real and positive transformation. Involved is the work of the indwelling Spirit.

The Spirit creates in us an important willingness. The Bible teaches both divine sovereignty and human activity. In terms of our progressive growth in sanctification, we are not moved by God as we move a chess piece. The businessman is not entirely passive in his growth. Whether it be financial dealings or sexual temptation or the way we speak to people or evaluate ourselves, we are not excused from responsible action. In most cases, there are specific choices which we either make or do not make. The Spirit empowers us in the duties of Christian living. Holiness is produced in us by God, yet with corresponding actions on our part. John Calvin put it this way: 'We are adopted on the ground that He should in turn have us as His obedient children. Although obedience does not make us His children, since the gift is gratuitous, yet it distinguishes children from foreigners.'[29]

Our willingness and our spiritual growth involve practical and specific obedience. In chapter 1 mention was made of Christian duties. Duties are always dependent upon grace. Here too is the work of the Spirit. Richard Baxter, another late-seventeenth-century English Puritan, described the Spirit as 'the spring to all your spiritual motions; as the wind to your sails: you can do nothing without it'.[30] The Spirit leads us in the battle with sin (Rom. 8:13; Gal. 5:16–26).

At the same time, it is not a matter of our discipline or willpower. Fighting sin is a gospel duty, not a work of the law. Again, the businessman is expected to make choices and to engage in specific efforts. We always need to remember this. We can fall into rigid legalism or else the pretence of freedom that leads to sin. While there is a duty of fighting sin, it is not moral renovation. This is a crucial point. However laudable and even essential certain changes in habits, practices, speech, thinking and feeling may be, victory over sin comes only through a divine re-creation.

Too many Christians stumble not only into the danger of laxity but a pit of a legalistic despair, trying to calm their over-scrupulous conscience. It will take our entire life to fight sin, but this will not come solely by willpower, self-discipline or rigorous introspection. It is always because of our union with Christ and the indwelling Spirit. Here is a key element in our Christian confidence. It shows us how interconnected are doctrinal truths and experiential realities.

'A strong, a perfect plea'

In *The Pilgrim's Progress* John Bunyan (1628–1688) offers a vivid picture. Christian arrives in the home of Interpreter. In this home he sees a fire burning against a wall, with a figure constantly throwing water in the attempt to quench the fire; nevertheless, the fire burns continuously. Christian asks Interpreter what this all means. Interpreter answers:

> This fire is the work of grace that is wrought in the heart: he that casts water upon it to extinguish and put it out is the devil; but, in that thou seest the fire notwithstanding burn higher and hotter, thou shalt also see the reason of that.

Then on the other side of the wall, Christian sees a man with a vessel of oil in his hand from which he continually, but secretly, pours oil. Who is this?

> This is Christ, who continually, with the oil of His grace, maintains the work already begun in the heart; by the means of which, notwithstanding what the devil can do, the souls of His people prove gracious still. And in that thou sawest the man stood behind the wall to maintain the fire; this is to teach thee, that it is hard for the tempted to see how this work of grace is maintained in the soul.[31]

Like Bunyan's Christian, our late-twentieth-century situation is not hopeless. We not only have a Lord who pardons and forgives, but a Lord who actually is changing us. Because this is God's intention for the whole of our being, we have no excuse for foolish pride or ignorant laxity (2 Pet. 1:2–11). There is a greater dependence on the immediate internal working of the Holy Spirit and a joyous clinging to Jesus Christ, our only intermediary and advocate.

Sin is no longer the ruling force or dynamic in a Christian's life. Sin has been dethroned by grace and the Spirit. The usurper, sin, has been removed by the rightful Lord. We are no longer defined as enemies to God and subject to his just judgment. The wonderful self-identity taught in the New Testament is the Christian's through faith in Christ.

We are rescued from the moral guilt of the fall and we are also freed from the habitual necessity of sinning. God has not just pardoned us, he is changing us. It is important to understand the work of Christ, the activity of grace and the ministry of the Spirit. In essence, we have to appreciate our struggle with indwelling sin within the glorious context of our justification by faith in Jesus Christ and our progressive sanctification by the Spirit and grace. A hymn by Charitie Lees Bancroft (1841-1923) powerfully expresses these truths.

> Before the throne of God above
>   I have a strong, a perfect plea;
> A great High Priest, whose name is Love,
>   Who ever lives and pleads for me.
>
> My name is graven on his hands,
>   My name is written on his heart;
> I know that while in heaven he stands
>   No tongue can bid me thence depart.
>
> When Satan tempts me to despair,
>   And tells me of the guilt within,
> Upward I look, and see him there
>   Who made an end of all my sin.
>
> Because the sinless Saviour died,
>   My sinful soul is counted free;

For God, the Just, is satisfied
  To look on him and pardon me.

Behold him there! the risen Lamb!
  My perfect, spotless Righteousness,
The great unchangeable I AM,
  The King of glory and of grace!

One with himself, I cannot die;
  My soul is purchased by His blood;
My life is hid with Christ on high,
  With Christ, my Saviour and my God.

There is a wonderful confidence. It touches the whole of our existence and reality. Through this confidence we are not escaping problems or deluding ourselves. The chief reason we may say this is that Jesus is who he is, and that he accomplished what he accomplished. The person and work of the Lord and Saviour Jesus Christ fit our human circumstances and problems. Moreover, he is the Son of the one true God, and the one in whom the Father finds pleasure. Jesus is the one to whom we point men and women.

His character and being are coordinate with our contemporaries' existence. The relevance is trans-cultural and trans-temporal. We speak here of more than a narrow, religious invitation. Instead, this biblical call is all embracing and thoroughly comprehensive. Think back to the four questions about any worldview which we raised in chapter 3:

1. Does this describe the world we already know?
2. Does this describe the us we already know?
3. Is this consistent with itself?
4. Is it liveable?[32]

In biblical Christianity, men and women are called by the one true and knowable God out of contemporary insanity into order and well-being. In the gospel we are summoned out of intellectual, psychological and spiritual tragedy. The solution is found in the Lord Jesus, the rescuer and emancipator. His death and resurrection offer peace: a peace which embraces the whole of human existence and re-establishes our humanity. There is liveable consistency in his pardon and through his indwelling Spirit. Of this we may truthfully be confident.

This confidence is personally known and experienced in our life only as we respond to what God offers us. This response is called faith. What is vital to appreciate is that this human response does not shift the weight of trustworthiness on to our spirituality or human condition. Faith is required, for it is truly fitting. But our confidence is grounded and established on who the Lord God is. He is our confidence, for it is his love, mercy and power to which all men and women are called to respond. He speaks to humanity, calls humanity and can restore and heal humanity. Of this we may be sure and confident. The ultimate and urgent question before us is: will we respond? There are good and valid reasons why we must. What our response involves is explained in the next chapter.

Questions for reflection and discussion

1. In this chapter, considerable attention is given to Christ's death and justice. Would it matter if there were no final or ultimate justice? Would this change the way we understand who God is? Would it change the way we see ourselves? Conversely, how does the cross of Christ, as an expression of divine justice, speak words of good news?

2. How would real forgiveness start to reshape a person's self-identity and self-esteem? How would hope influence a person's view of life?

3. How would you respond to the statement by a Christian, 'I know God forgives me, but I can't see how he loves me, because of the wrong things I continue to do'?

4. In what ways do words like *love* and *caring* take on new meanings when a person hears the story of Christ's death? In the light of so much happening in today's world, how would the gospel's story of a *suffering* and *self-giving* Saviour offer points of contact with those who do not call themselves Christian?

7

The nature of Christian faith

It is not up to us alone

Finding the measure

There is a right confidence and a wrong confidence. Discerning the difference is not easy. We see this in various areas of life. We need to be able to trust people with our money, health care, safety and national affairs. But some professionals mislead, cheat and take advantage of other people's trust. Parents want their child to be self-assured and secure, but problems arise when this develops into dangerous braggadocio. Business competence is important, yet this sometimes leads to insensitive arrogance. Confidence is a puzzling thing: desirable up to a measure and harmful beyond that measure. Yet what is the measure?

Finding this measure creates particular problems for Christians. First, how may we speak of confidence when our own lives are plagued with inconsistency? We do not experience life in tidy categories. In chapter 1 we looked at the various ways in which our thinking, choosing, feeling and acting can be inconsistent. Life's sadness, pain and frustration affect Christians. There should be a difference in the way Christians respond but, sometimes, this uniqueness is not apparent. Our experience occasionally leads us to sense a lack of confidence. Is it futile for today's Christians, often inconsistent and troubled, to tell our society, frequently sceptical, there is sure and certain truth? What is the measure of Christian confidence that enables us to relate to other people's lives and, likewise, to acknowledge our own inconsistencies?

Secondly, how do we speak of certainty and confidence in an age of uncertainty and scepticism? In chapter 2 we considered the fact that our society mistrusts rigid intellectual and moral certainty. Nevertheless, a follower of Jesus Christ lives with a conviction that Christianity is right and true. It is not one of the many religious options; it is universally true, for all individuals, in all cultures at all points in history. Christians cannot accept the relativistic thinking so prevalent today. Central to Christianity is a controversial exclusivity. Jesus only is Lord. Arrogance, insensitivity or an unwillingness to listen to non-Christians, however, are illegitimate. The believer prays and hopes she will be able to share the gospel with her friends, keeping them as friends! How does she do this without minimizing either her friends' fear of intolerance or Christ's claims?

The answer has to do with the truthfulness and rightness of *faith* in the one true God. Intriguingly, it is not that we must marshal all possible evidence that points, say, to a convergence between Christian faith and contemporary science. It is not that we are obliged to find fault with every other religious belief. Both have a qualified validity, but there is more. We can say deeply significant things about Christian faith as it relates to what is real and true about all of reality. This is neither an appeal to irrelevances nor a call to abandon a critical mind. Faith is something altogether different.

Because we are part of a contemporary Christian community confused about the nature of Christian faith, it is essential to spend time in this chapter defining the essence of faith. But we will do this with our eye on some of the particular postmodern challenges. Attention will focus on faith's validity, faith's characteristics and faith's difficulties. What will surprise the Christian reader, I suspect, is how *faith* closely relates to Christian confidence.

What exactly is the problem?

We try to live by faith in the one true God while living in our world. Yet our contemporaries often do not share our perspective. From their point of view we are most likely misguided or foolish. Is it possible they are right? Circumstantially, we made a profession of faith when we may have been utterly convinced and certain. Yet are conviction and certainty alone accurate verifiers? Psychologically, faith resonates in us. It seems right to us. But on what legitimate basis? Does faith even have to have a justification?

The Oxford zoologist, Dr Richard Dawkins, disagrees profoundly with biblical Christians. He works on the basis of a closed-universe system: no-one and nothing exists outside the universe; only randomly evolved matter exists. As an atheist, he presents a logical and consistent understanding of faith:

> As a Darwinian, something strikes me when I look at religion. Religion shows a pattern of heredity which I think is similar to genetic heredity. The vast majority of people have an allegiance to one particular religion. There are hundreds of different religious sects, and every person is loyal to just one of these. Out of all the sects in the world, we notice an uncanny coincidence: the overwhelming majority just happen to choose the one their parents belong to. Not the sect that has the best evidence in its favour, the best miracles, the best moral code, the best cathedral, the best stained-glass, the best music: when it comes to choosing from the smorgasbord of available religions, their potential virtues seem to count for nothing compared to the matter of heredity.[1]

Dawkins follows his line of argument consistent with his fundamental presupposition: there is no biblical God. But his argument is open to challenge.

First, his Darwinian presupposition about religion yields a problematic understanding about the sociology of religion. Yes, many people do follow their parents' influence. There are, however, considerable exceptions. His presupposition minimizes the phenomenon of religious 'conversion'. I personally know a Muslim who converted to Islam precisely because he was convinced intellectually. He maintains that Islam is truth.

Secondly, Dawkins' argument confuses categories – a question-able methodology. He lumps together genetic hereditary with 'a pattern of hereditary'. The first is valid; the second is not hereditary in any genetic sense but rather sociological and cultural. He is exercising a verbal sleight of hand, similar to saying: 'I see an apple, which is a fruit, in the kitchen. I see a loaf of bread in the same kitchen. Therefore, the loaf of bread is also a fruit.' He is right to ask why people are committed to their religion. Undoubtedly, many would offer nothing more than their cultural upbringing; in this way, Dr Dawkins rightly challenges

Christians. Others, of differing faiths, however, would claim well-considered justifications for their belief. Of course, the entire question of which differing belief (worldview) is truth is another matter – one we welcome (as suggested in chapter 3), yet seemingly dismissed by Dawkins.

To equate genetic chance with religious pluralism, therefore, seriously misunderstands the issue. We need not share in the error. Yet we might be inclined to wonder if he is right. Is faith just *us*? This is the problem, and it is a problem demonstrated in other ways too.

A homosexual friend recently told me he felt an intolerable tension. He felt unhappy in, to use his words, both a promiscuous gay scene and, at the other extreme, a judgmental Christian scene. No middle ground really existed, he argued. The real problem, however, he told me, is not so much his sexual struggles as his faith. The rightness or truthfulness of his faith is open to question in the light of his intense personal problems. In his view, Christianity is not working for him; therefore, Christianity must be suspect.

Years earlier, when he became a Christian, he hoped for a complete solution to his loneliness and frustrations. Christianity was attractive in the light of these particular needs. But now he senses that these needs are not only unfulfilled, but that they are compounded by a feeling of guilt and condemnation. He is left wondering if faith is nothing more than wishes and aspirations. To speak to him about the *truthfulness* of the gospel promises is to run smack into his experiential struggles.

How do we respond to those who start to accept Dawkins' conclusions or to those increasingly disillusioned with the seeming lack of return from their spiritual investment? With special care and concern we insist that Christian faith's credibility is measured not only by human response and activity; here we speak to Dawkins. Human experience, character and beingness agree with faith but only in subordinate reflection. The moon shines at night because the sun radiates light. We see the moon's 'light', but the moon only reflects the sun's rays. Likewise, the human phenomenon of faith is evident (Dawkins is quite right), yet it only reflects the gracious faithfulness of God. In short, we say to Dawkins, 'OK, you may be right. So let's consider whether the Christian worldview is true or not, and let's see if it matters.'

Similarly, we speak to frustrated and disappointed Christians (people like my homosexual friend) and stress that the truthfulness or untruthfulness of our faith cannot be strictly determined by whether all our human needs are met at any point in time. We are not minimizing these desires or needs. What we seek to do is gently to correct the impression that faith is a gimmick or technique. Christian confidence is not a confidence in a philosophical system, a method or a way to reach self-actualization. Christian confidence involves faith, in the senses that we shall now consider.

Faith is significant because of who God is

Faith involves our heart, mind and will (our feelings, thinking and choosing), but it is not adequately explained as a human phenomenon. Faith necessitates the other side of the equation, the object of faith. The significance of Christian faith is the God to whom we come. Psychology and psychiatry quite rightly place certain human behaviour, emotions and reasoning under the broad heading of 'religious faith'. Faith, however, is far more than a frame of mind or emotion. We do not have faith in faith itself. God gives Christian faith its meaning and significance.

Our faith is primarily significant because of the *specific and knowable* character, promises and being of the one true God, who is the God and Father of Jesus Christ. We could choose and respond to a false god or goddess, and people do. Idolatry still exists. John Stott is quite right:

> Idols are not limited to primitive societies; there are many sophisticated idols too. An idol is a god-substitute. Any person or thing that occupies the place which God should occupy is an idol. Covetousness is idolatry. Ideologies can be idolatries. So can fame, wealth and power, sex, food, alcohol and other drugs, parents, spouse, children and friends, work, recreation, television and possessions, even church, religion and Christian service.[2]

We might well modify our behaviour on the basis of our faith in a god. Friends of mine deeply involved in New Age spiritualities have renounced an over-indulgence in alcohol and marijuana. One friend told me that his new way of thinking redirects his lifestyle.

160

There is still the problem of truth: is the god or goddess worthy of our reverence and worship? In short, neither our sincerity nor our consistency establishes the truthfulness of our faith. Only the creator and redeemer God does so. The flow of Scripture reveals this important clarification.

The Gospel of John begins with this assurance, 'The Word became flesh and made his dwelling among us. We have see his glory, the glory of the One and Only, who came from the Father, full of grace and truth' (Jn. 1:14). Consequently, in the Gospels, faith is never isolated from the initiating character of God. When Jesus began his ministry, he explained it as God keeping his promise (Lk. 4:17). Faith in Jesus is a response to the triune God's faith-keeping activity, word and love.

The early apostolic preaching also illustrates the primacy of God's faithfulness rather than the human experience of any 'religious faith'. It is especially helpful to notice what the apostles stressed when speaking to non-Jews, pagans. Preaching to Cornelius and his household, Peter declares, 'I now realise how true it is that God does not show favouritism but accepts men from every nation who fear him and do what is right. You know the message God sent to the people of Israel, telling the good news of peace through Jesus Christ, who is Lord of all' (Acts 10:34–36). The human experience is not denied, but the focal point is the Lord's activity.

Paul strikes an important apologetic note as he tries to calm down a crowd in Lystra who wanted to worship him and Barnabas. 'Men, why are you doing this? We too are only men, human like you. We are bringing you good news, telling you to turn from these worthless things to the living God, who made heaven and earth and sea and everything in them. In the past, he let all nations go their own way. Yet he has not left himself without testimony: He has shown kindness by giving you rain from heaven and crops in their seasons; he provides you with plenty of food and fills your hearts with joy' (Acts 14:15–17). In other words, there is already an interface between the gospel and these people: their God-authored humanity and experience. He takes a similar approach when addressing the pagan idolatry of cosmopolitan Athens (Acts 17:24–33). Faith is always legitimate as it turns from what is non-God to the God who is – the God who already initiates.

What we are saying is this. There is a definitive context for our experience of God. We have faith in the God who invites us to return to him, to be reconciled to him and to know him through Jesus. The key expression is *him*. We are back to the point in our theological framework identified in chapter 3. Harold Netland provides a helpful summary, for we need the existential encounter with God – the God who gives us propositional revelation to meet him.

> Not only is it possible to have both, one cannot respond appropriately to God without first having some knowledge of God. The believer can only respond personally to God as Lord and Savior if he or she already knows something about what God is like and what he expects from humankind. And the more one knows about God the more one will be able to know God personally and respond appropriately to him. As Nash puts it, 'Personal encounter cannot take place in a cognitive vacuum.'[3]

In this sense, when our contemporaries question the legitimacy of faith in God our response must concentrate primarily on who God is. He is the one true God, whom men and women can know. He is already relevant to their human experience, in that their humanity is a direct consequence of God's intention. Faith fits the way we are, not in any limited religious category but in the whole of our humanity. It is not a question of heredity or cultural chance, but of congruity with truth.

Furthermore, to our discouraged Christian friend we counsel the rightness of faith not in terms of a key to self-fulfilment but in terms of who the one true God is. We rightly point out that this *particular* God accepts broken, insecure and confused people. He receives people as they are and who they are. There is restoration and recovery, but not as we often expect. My friend's homosexuality is not immediately resolved (whatever he perceives a resolution to be). Yet the truth of who this God is means that his faith rightly trusts *this* God not to reject him, not to dismiss him, and not to give up on him. Undoubtedly there is a tension in his experience. As to the question whether faith is worth it or not, the answer is ultimately on a level far beyond himself. There is something about this God.

THE NATURE OF CHRISTIAN FAITH

He is goodness, purity, love, mercy, justice, faithfulness, power, knowledge and wisdom. If he had any other moral character and personal beingness, faith in him would be inappropriate. He would be a god *minus God*. We could not trust him; he, she or it might be a god but would be non-God. Because he is precisely who he is, however, faith is legitimate.[4] He is trustworthy. Let us go further with this idea.

Faith is not using a database, but is a trust

In his short but helpful book on the Apostles' Creed, Alister McGrath states things clearly and to the point:

> Faith cannot be equated with knowing. It is not something cold and cerebral, enlightening the mind while leaving the heart untouched. Faith is the response of our whole persons to the person of God. It is a joyful reaction on our part to the overwhelming divine love we see revealed in Jesus Christ . . . Faith is saying 'Yes' to God. It is a *decision*, an *act of will* to trust God.[5]

Trust is the response to one who is trustworthy. And the point of God's revelation to his people is to develop their trust.

For example, in Exodus 33 and 34 Moses gains a deeper knowledge of the Lord. His earlier experiences in Egypt of the Lord's power and provision had been real and significant. Nonetheless, he asks the Lord, 'You have said, "I know you by name and you have found favour with me." If you are pleased with me, teach me your ways so I may know you and continue to find favour with you. Remember that this nation is your people' (Ex. 33:12–13). When God teaches Moses and the people his ways, it is so they will trust him more. Yet trust can be possible only when his people know who the Lord is.

So the Lord's gracious agreement to Moses' request expands Moses' knowledge. 'And the LORD said, "I will cause all my goodness to pass in front of you, and I will proclaim my name, the LORD, in your presence. I will have mercy on whom I will have mercy, and I will have compassion on whom I will have compassion"' (Ex. 33:19). When Moses hides behind a rock and hears the LORD proclaim his name, God's beingness is manifest in profoundly relational terms. Trust, obedient trust, is expected:

> The LORD, the LORD, the compassionate and gracious God, slow to anger, abounding in love and faithfulness, maintaining love to thousands, and forgiving wickedness, rebellion and sin. Yet he does not leave the guilty unpunished; he punishes the children and their children for the sin of the fathers to the third and fourth generation (Ex. 34:6–7).

The Lord's response to Moses is self-disclosure, not to impart information, but with the aim of developing a covenant relationship. Central to this covenant is trust. Trust describes the heart of faith.

Yet what if we sense we are not full of a confident trust? Does this mean we have insufficient faith? Scripture stresses the need for faith.[6] It is good and right when people have a living faith in the Lord, not in an idol or false god. But recall our first point: the legitimacy of our faith is because of who God is and what he promises. Our self-involvement is vitally important, but the *validity* of our trust rests more with the trustworthiness of the one whom we trust.

This assures us that faith cannot be quantified. It cannot be measured on a faith meter: above the red mark we are fine, below that mark we are in trouble; so we had better find out where we are today. It is true, Jesus referred to the power of faith the size of a mustard seed (Mt. 17:20; Lk. 17:6). On another occasion he pointed to a Roman officer's great faith (Mt. 8:10; Lk. 7:9). Jesus rebuked his chosen disciples for having little faith (Mt. 6:30; 8:26; 16:8; 17:20; Mk. 6:16; 16:14). But these passages have to do with doubt in the face of Jesus' already presented power and greatness. Scripture certainly urges us to grow in faith.[7] Our faith is not to stay as small as a mustard seed! Nevertheless, the quantity of faith is not the issue.

The heart of the matter is the *appropriateness* of human trust in Jesus of Nazareth (2 Tim. 1:8-12; Heb. 10:19-25). Given who Jesus is, Lord and Saviour, faith in him is legitimate. A counterfeit 'faith' in another is false. Jesus, because he is who he is, establishes the truthfulness of our Christian experience.

Besides, how could we measure our faith? By zealous activities? Through the intensity of our emotions? On the basis of our knowledge? These are indicative to a point, but that point is considerably elusive and misleading even once located.

Instead, confidence is discovered and experienced in God's unconditional acceptance of us in Christ Jesus. Doubt, anguish, fear and inconsistency are not praiseworthy. Yet however weak or small our faith, we trust in Christ Jesus. As we turn away from our idolatry and autonomy, submitting our will, behaviour and minds to the risen Jesus and his gospel promises, we are accepted by God.

If we respond to the gospel of Jesus Christ and trust in the Lord Jesus as our Saviour and obey his commands, we are doing what is true and universally valid. In fact, while we have not the slightest justification for boasting, it is not we who are wrong and misguided but our contemporaries who reject the gospel. They are not simply rejecting a religious way of life, they are refusing the God and creator of us all. Trust in him is entirely valid, given who he is. At the same time it is wholly proper, given who we are.

Faith fits our humanity

Faith in the creator God involves everything about us which makes us human. Increasingly in our postmodern culture this is a vital declaration. As we argued in chapters 3 and 4, biblical revelation tells us a great deal about humanity. It gives us a point of reference which is able to relate to different cultures. Yet today, our present culture is in grave danger of losing sight of who we are as men and women. It is not so much the result of violence or cruelty but a loss of living definition.

Consider the *image* of Michael Jackson. Is he a white Caucasian, or is he a black Afro-American? Is Michael Jackson male or female? Did he really marry Elvis Presley's daughter? Moreover, does the image bear any real relationship to the *person*? In a postmodern culture, however, categories such as black, white, male and female are insignificant. A person can change, mix and match or revert. Postmodernism has no point of reference other than the immediate. Again, Kenneth Gergen's observations offer insight on this:

> In the postmodern world there is no individual essence
> to which one remains true or committed. One's identity
> is continuously emergent, re-formed, and redirected as
> one moves through the sea of ever-changing relation-
> ships. In the case of 'Who am I?' it is a teeming world of
> possibilities.[8]

Will men and women be helped and liberated with such a
worldview? We must sadly argue, 'No.' I say, sadly, because
postmodernism's quest for freedom and liberation is not altogether wrong. Men and women experience a sense of captivity. But
captive to what? And what or who can release us?

Furthermore, in the stuff of human experience – pride, affection,
hatred, compassion, loneliness, intimacy, cruelty and tenderness –
what will give us a point of reference for our meaning and
significance? Meaning and significance matter because we exist,
and our existence is never arbitrary. This is the critical issue in
terms of our humanness. We can pretend that it does not matter
who or what we are, but as we make love with another person,
when we hold our new-born baby, when we wipe the forehead of
our dying parent, our humanity (and theirs) is unavoidable. An
emotional, social and psychological point of reference is critical.

The gospel senses the postmodernist miasma, and brings a
breath of fresh air. In this respect, becoming a Christian is like
breathing deeply again after years of chain-smoking. Additionally,
the gospel provides a point of reference which is profoundly
personal: the infinite and personal God. In his mercy he not only
explains our meaning and significance, he deals with the very real
captivity which imprisons us.

In every way, faith in this God agrees with our humanity.
Becoming a Christian is not beyond the created capability of any
human. We are never asked to do something non-human, like
asking a person to flap their arms in order to fly. It is not a question
of ability, but suitability. Think of travelling to a foreign country.
Our own country's currency (normally) will not buy a meal in a
foreign land. With the right currency, we can eat and pay our bill
with the suitable money.

Because of God's holiness plus the radical extent of the fall and
our own sin, we are not able to live at peace with God; still, it is
suitable for humans to live in a good relationship with the Lord.

We are created for this quality of relationship. Accordingly, faith is not totally alien to humans. It is what we are intended to exercise as God's creatures. Believing the gospel is not irrational, unhealthy or inhuman.

A Christian is a re-created human, restored to the way things are meant to be. Her humanity is never done away with; it is renewed. Faith involves the whole of her being, not just her intellect or some spiritual part of her personality. When, by grace, she turns back to her creator through Jesus the redeemer, she chooses good rather than evil. This is what her will was intended to do, but for sin. There is a repentance, a sorrow for sin, a desire to please God and a deep, heartfelt love for Christ. Her feelings are supposed to experience each of these. Furthermore, faith moves her from a trust in personal righteousness ('I've become religious and live a clean life that God will reward') to a reliance upon the merit and righteousness of Christ Jesus ('He alone is good enough to make up for my not being good enough'). This is what her rationality is for, as she rightly worships with her whole being. While her regeneration is a supernatural occurrence, it never ceases to be a fully human experience.

Faith does not excuse us from responsibility

Faith, therefore, reflects the dignity God bestows to humanity. We are responsible before God. True faith corresponds to this responsibility and points to our God-given dignity. While faith is a trust in God, because of who he is, faith never nullifies human responsibility. A good relationship never works by force or compulsion.

When a person hears and understands the gospel of Jesus Christ and comes to trust this news as the way to true life, a miracle takes place. The miracle is that, whereas previously the person lived for himself, now, as he redirects his life along the lines of Christ's commands, he lives a new life for another. On his own, this individual could not respond to the good news. Sin is too extensive and radical. His belief and trust result from God's grace and the sovereign work of the Holy Spirit. The person is renewed from above; there is a re-creation (see Jn. 1:13; 3:3–10).

Concurrently, he is far from passive. He responds through a myriad of actions, choices and feelings. In fact, he does so because he is commanded to change, choose and love. In his autobiography *Surprised By Joy,* C. S. Lewis expresses his experience this way:

> I say, 'I chose,' yet it did not really seem possible to do the opposite. On the other hand, I was aware of no motives. You could argue that I was not a free agent, but I am more inclined to think that this came nearer to being a perfectly free act than most I have ever done. Necessity may not be the opposite of freedom, and perhaps a man is most free when, instead of producing motives, he could only say, 'I am what I do.'[9]

Lewis discovered what every Christian experiences: gospel exhortations or summons are not 'pretend'. They are necessary.

Consequently, the gospel commands us to choose. The beginning of Mark's Gospel stresses God's covenant faithfulness and prophetic fulfilment. The fitting human response is repentance. John (the baptizer) preaches 'a baptism of repentance for the forgiveness of sins' (Mk. 1:4). Jesus affirms John's ministry and confirms the gospel summons: 'After John was put in prison, Jesus went into Galilee, proclaiming the good news of God. "The time has come," he said. "The kingdom of God is near. Repent and believe the good news!"' (Mk. 1:14–15). Mark prepares the reader to see the interconnection between good news, 'the time', the kingdom of God and repentance. When the Saviour of the world comes into the world, he graciously summons people to repentance and change. Choice matters.

Looking again at Paul's speech in Athens (Acts 17:16–34), it is evident that human responsibility is significant. Grace and mercy are apparent in the Lord's command; the expression, 'In the past God overlooked such ignorance' (17:30; *cf.* Rom. 3:25–26) is a work of sovereign kindness rather than shortsightedness. F. F. Bruce points out, 'But, culpable as their ignorance was, God in mercy had passed it over . . . In the present place it is suggested that God has overlooked men's earlier ignorance of Himself in view of the perfect revelation that has been given in the advent and work of Christ. But if their ignorance was culpable before, it is far less excusable now.'[10] In our day, some insist, 'Show us evidence that God loves us!' One bit of news comes as a shock: 'God loves us enough to summon us to change in the light of a coming final judgment.'

We do not simply sit in our bedrooms asking God to hit us with his power before we will believe. We are summoned to hear, read, understand and respond to God's Word. It is presumptuous for a person to demand, 'Well, I'll become a Christian when God does something impressive in my life.'

In my work with university students I often meet this objection. A German student told me she was interested in Christianity. Several Christian friends told her she should ask God to 'work in her heart' to believe. She was urged to be open to a variety of experiences. But she honestly felt nothing. She wanted to know if God would work in her life. In desperation, she came to me.

I informed her that God was already working in her life. She was already experiencing God: she and I were talking in English, looking into the Bible and thinking about her life in relationship to the biblical worldview. This is the ordinary work of God. It is the supernatural impinging upon the full humanity of a person, calling her to change the way she thinks, lives and worships. I insisted that our discussion was not 'intellectual' in contrast to the counsel of her friends. It was just as experiential, but, in fact, much fuller and more suitably human. Even God will not displace her personal responsibility and moral choosing.

This responsibility continues after we take the first step of faith. In his third volume on the letter to the Hebrews, commenting on Hebrews 6:10, John Owen declared, 'He is a most vain man who thinks otherwise, who hopes for any benefit by that faith which doth not work by love.'[11] Faith continues to involve our responsibility. What does this look like? It involves the whole of our being: intellect, will and emotions. We are not merely to agree with our minds to the gospel but to embrace it and respond to its summons (Jn. 3:16ff.; Rom. 10:9–13). Richard Baxter likened this to marriage: and faith ties 'the marriage knot'.[12] There must be a moral response. We have to demonstrate on a daily basis an attitude or disposition correct for those who know they are sinners but who place their confidence and hope in Christ Jesus.

To be wise, realistic, true, and thus confident, today's Christians have to see both sides of the coin: faith is a trust in another but never denies our personal responsibility. The clearer we see this the better we appreciate our assurance for the whole of our lives.

The author of 2 Peter underlines this twofold confidence (2 Pet. 1:3–4).

> His divine power has given us everything we need for life and godliness through our knowledge of him who called us by his own glory and goodness. Through these he has given us his very great and precious promises, so that through them you may participate in the divine nature and escape the corruption in the world caused by evil desires.

By what he has given we are to participate; the implications of this become all the more apparent and significant as we conclude with an examination of the call to endure in the way of faith. Here is the intersection of who God is and how we trust him by faith in our daily life. Here too is where we see the challenges to our faith, yet also the tremendous hope and confidence faith can give us.

Faith involves endurance

In the letter to the Hebrews, the author offers a statement on the essence of faith: 'Now faith is being sure of what we hope for and certain of what we do not see' (Heb. 11:1). Certainty and hopefulness are closely associated with faith. What might be missed, however, is how the author spells out this statement. The hope and certainty intrinsic to faith are constantly in juxtaposition to longsuffering and patient endurance.

John Calvin observed that 'we shall never arrive at the goal of salvation unless we are furnished with patience'.[13] Why do we need patience? Calvin continued:

> Eternal life is promised to us, but it is promised to the dead; we are told of the resurrection of the blessed, but meantime we are involved in corruption; we are declared to be just, and sin dwells within us; we hear that we are blessed, but meantime we are overwhelmed by untold miseries; we are promised an abundance of all good things, but we are often hungry and thirsty; God proclaims that He will come to us immediately, but seems deaf to our cries. What would happen to us if we

did not rely on our hope, and if our minds did not
emerge above the world out of the midst of darkness
through the shining Word of God and by His Spirit?[14]

To live by faith is to hope for what is not yet seen. It is to live in a
way unlike a life lived by sight alone. Faith in the Lord is
reasonable and the right way for every human. It is not alien to us.
Still, it sometimes feels as though it flies in the face of everyday life
and experience. Here is precisely where so many of us have our
problems.

We know that there are times when obeying God and loving
others practically and specifically are costly and arduous. We
believe that Christianity is true and right. As our life progresses,
however, the certainty occasionally wavers. Total exhaustion and
even burnout develop. Stress fatigue is a common complaint. We
really should not be surprised; but often we are, or we try to deny
this experience. Likewise, we experience various pulls and tugs
from our culture to think, choose and act in ways contrary to
Scripture's clear teachings. Three centuries ago, John Owen made
an astute, and timeless, observation:

> Faith and love are generally looked on as easy and
> common things; but it is by them who have it not. As
> they are the only springs of all obedience towards God,
> and usefulness towards men, so they meet with the
> greatest oppositions from within and without.[15]

Is this to diminish the sovereign work of grace and the Holy
Spirit? It is not a contradiction.

We are called to a Spirit-enabled endurance. Scripture associates
endurance, or steadfastness, with faith and faithfulness. The
significant New Testament noun is *hypomonē*, derived from the
verb *hypomenō*. They both relate to the idea of 'staying behind', 'to
stay alive', 'to expect', 'to endure', 'to wait' or 'to suffer.'[16] Seeing
things clearly is crucial; faith provides this insight.

It is enormously helpful to realize that some of the problems we
experience are not abnormal but precisely normal, in that they are
part and parcel of Christian endurance. Do we find ourselves
rejected and ridiculed for the gospel's sake? Jesus encouraged and
prepared his first followers by warning them, 'All men will hate

you because of me, but he who stands firm to the end will be saved' (Mk. 13:13; *cf.* Lk. 21:12–19) Are we experiencing a constant tension between our life in this age and our allegiance to the gospel? Paul and Barnabas 'strengthened and encouraged' believers in Lystra, Iconium and Antioch telling them such hardships and difficulties are *the normal Christian experience* (Acts 14:21–22). Do we feel emotionally exhausted in our church fellowship due to the deaths of some dear brothers and sisters in Christ? Paul told the Corinthians to stand firm and not fall into the error of thinking all is in vain (1 Cor. 15:58). How many church leaders and pastors need to appreciate the refreshing realism of Paul's advice to Timothy? 'But you, keep your head in all situations, endure hardship, do the work of an evangelist, discharge all the duties of your ministry' (2 Tim. 4:5). Why give this advice and instruction unless everyday Christian living necessitates endurance?

It is not just a matter of knowing and seeing things rightly. Supremely, we endure not out of our courage or gritted-teeth toughness, but in a confidence and faith in the character of God. Endurance never calls forth from us either a stiff upper lip or a smile on our face at all times. We accept the call to endurance because God embraces us in his covenant faithfulness. In the Old Testament, endurance is theologically grounded in the covenant relationship established between the Lord and his people.[17]

This promise is fulfilled in Christ. Warning of the difficulties facing Jerusalem, Jesus assured his followers, 'If the Lord had not cut short those days, no-one would survive. But for the sake of the elect, whom he has chosen, he has shortened them' (Mk. 13:20). Confidence is rooted in God's saving grace. Paul told the Colossians of a hope fixed in the gospel (Col. 1:5, 21–23). James encourages his readers to endure and persevere in the face of 'trials of many kinds' not simply because of the consequent growth in a believer's life, but because of four factors. First, God gives wisdom to those who ask (1:5–8); secondly, God has promised the crown of life to those who love him (1:12); thirdly, it is not God who tempts us to sin in these difficult times (1:13–15); and lastly, God has brought us into a new creation which he will bring to completion (1:16–18).

We endure, just as we believe, because the Lord is who he is. In the Revelation given to John on Patmos, there is an essential and indispensable link between Christian suffering and Jesus' faithfulness. John describes himself as 'your brother and companion in the suffering and kingdom and patient endurance that are ours in Jesus . . .' (Rev. 1:9; cf. 3:10; 14:12). In fact, Revelation is a vivid reminder that to know and experience the wonders of Jesus is *always* to know difficulties and troubles. The hope and confidence, however, is that we know Jesus: the Lamb upon the throne, the one who will destroy the Beast, he who will come again. We endure because of him.

This endurance is not a grumpy, treadmill existence. Words like hope, joy, encouragement and promise surround and undergird the call to endurance. And so we come back to the statement on faith offered in Hebrews 11:1, 'Now faith is being sure of what we hope for and certain of what we do not see.' This is not a text to use in any 'name and claim it' spirituality. Instead, it explains the confidence of faith in the midst of real life. This is one of the principal themes in the letter to the Hebrews. We have a hope and certainty in Jesus: the 'something better' promised to the heroes of chapter 11; the Saviour who endured the cross for the joy of obtaining salvation for his people (12:2) and the Lord who is 'the same yesterday and today and for ever' (13:8).

Why bother? Why keep on struggling and walking in faith? Because the Lord God is who he is and he meets those who honestly seek him. There is no other legitimate basis. As we begin our life in faith because God is who he is, so we continue in the life of faith because God is who he is.

Do we not begin to see the dangers inherent in some forms of contemporary Christian spirituality? My friend's struggle with homosexuality and his love for Jesus will never be helped by superficiality and triteness. He does not need to be told that his tension exists because he does not believe enough or trust enough. What he needs is a Christian community to walk beside him and remind him of the faithful and committed Saviour. He does not need a fellowship that rejoices in seven-day wonders: boasting of this man or this woman who was miraculously healed or transformed because at last enough faith was exercised. Instead, my friend needs the encouragement from others (both homosexual and heterosexual) who assure him that it is worth it, and possible, to find significance and freedom in long-haul obedience to Jesus.

For each of us faith necessitates costly endurance. What assures us is the truthfulness and rightness of faith. It is worth the endurance because the focus of faith is on the faithful Good Shepherd. Because he is who he is, we continue – not always victoriously – but confident that the life of faith is not up to us alone. There is the faithful other.

The truthfulness and rightness of faith

If *faith*, therefore, is essentially nothing more than a human experience, we are in trouble. How can we know whether it is right, and how could we tell whether it might lead us to foolishness? Why not just shrug it all off, with a 'Who really cares?' dismissal?

Yet the argument in this chapter is that faith is always a response to the creator and redeemer God, known supremely in the Lord Jesus Christ. He promises, invites and acts. We hear, respond and follow. Without this specific God's faithfulness, our faith is empty and powerless. Faith is nothing in and of itself. What matters is the God to whom faith responds. This has been the thrust of this chapter, and what must constantly be a point of reference in our theological framework. Crucial implications follow.

We may know other believers remarkably used by the Lord. He or she modelled a courageous commitment to and a steady confidence in God. We look at these people, examine our life, and groan with disappointment and frustration. We are not like them. This is true, but for reasons often missed. The differences may have more to do with temperament, situation and circumstances than with spiritual strength. The assuring truth is that their God is our God, their Saviour is our Saviour. Through the gospel, we have access to the same heavenly Father and the same throne of grace.[18] God's promises in Christ Jesus are dynamic, irrespective of person, place or history.

Equally, there is no valid reason for accepting the contemporary idea that faith in the Christian God is one of life's many options. This would be so only if God were some other sort of god. He is not. Moreover, this popular line of argument would be right if we were anything other than humans. We are not.

Faith that acknowledges and yields to the personal and infinite God, whose eternal Son is imminent judge and present Saviour, is fitting and right. Always (and we will have to insist on this over and over), faith is right because God is worthy to receive humans' love, reverence and loyalty.

> You are worthy, our Lord and God,
>   to receive glory and honour and power,
> for you created all things,
>   and by your will they were created
>   and have their being.
>
> (Rev. 4:11)

Furthermore, the supreme uniqueness and exclusive saving power of Christ crucified warrants human worship.

> Worthy is the Lamb, who was slain,
> to receive power and wealth and wisdom and strength
> and honour and glory and praise!
>
> (Rev. 5:12)

Our perspective often needs to be corrected. Both our experience and our knowledge are too frequently confused and distorted. Our emotions go in various directions. Our choices are hard to make or, once made, cause us problems. As when we try to focus a camera in a crowded city street, but with difficulty due to the press of the crowd, our view of the way things are is bumped out of focus. We are prone to see faith mainly from a human vantage point. This is understandable, but such a limited perspective will never help us; it will be an optical illusion.

Our help is from God. The Holy Spirit graciously redirects the believer back to the person and nature of God (Jn. 16:13–15; 1 Cor. 2:6–15). This is far more than intellectual realignment. It is a sovereign work of mercy, assuring us that faith is a trust in the God whose nature bears the weight and responsibility of our trust. The Anglican communion service has a prayer which helpfully reminds worshippers of this truth:

> We do not presume to come to this your table, merciful Lord, trusting in our own righteousness, but in your manifold and great mercies. We are not worthy so much as to gather up the crumbs under your table. But you

are the same Lord whose nature is always to have mercy . . . [19]

The focus of faith is on the God whom we trust: 'your manifold and great mercies' and 'whose nature is always to have mercy'. Faith is legitimate because of who the Lord is. Our faith is inconsistent; but the ongoing work of God in our experience reminds us of himself and his consistent commitment to us. This is fundamental to our understanding and experience of faith. It is essential to a right and proper Christian confidence. This we may know and experience.

Questions for reflection and discussion

1. Do you think people's conviction and certainty substantiate the truthfulness of their faith? Is it a matter of a person's sincerity and behaviour towards others?

2. In this chapter, John Stott is quoted in reference to contemporary forms of idolatry. What is wrong with idolatry? Isn't it OK, provided no harm is done to another person? Why do you suppose that one of the more popular organizations in most European universities today is the Pagan Society?

3. Why does faith in God have to relate to the way things are in the world, our relationships and in our human existence? Isn't faith meant to take us beyond the stuff of this world and beyond ourselves?

4. How would you answer someone who told you, 'I wish I had your faith, but I am not the religious type'?

8

The security of Christian faith

Confidence in one greater than ourselves

Back to the future

It is a glorious, sunny day. There is laughter, love and joy. Parents, family and friends join in the special celebration, a festivity mixed with solemnity and wonder. As the two special people exchange promises in the presence of many witnesses, their wedding day is a time for confirmation and beginnings. They publicly confirm their love and acceptance of each other. Profound promises extend their previous love into the altogether different realm of husband and wife. The man and the woman begin a new life together. They love each other, like one another and experience the tenderness of their relationship. They look forward to what lies ahead.

Yet do they know what lies in the future? Despite their solemn vows, the couple do not know the future. Children's names and personalities are not known. Future homes cannot be imagined. New friends, opportunities and adventures await. Similarly, challenges will arise. Illnesses will arrive. Stresses and strains will be experienced. Moments will come when their love will be tested. The man and woman will know other couples whose marriages will not endure, for various reasons. Will theirs? Is their relationship secure?

God's relationship with his people is frequently compared to a marriage bond.[1] The analogy is vivid and striking, no matter what culture we have in mind. But may we extend the same questions we have about modern marriage relationships into the believer's relationship with the Lord? Is this relationship secure? Will it endure what the future may bring?

The Bible presents many warnings, exhortations and salutary character examples which suggest that walking with God is fraught with the *apparent* possibility of 'falling away' or 'apostasy'.

The apostle Paul warns Timothy that many 'will fall away' (1 Tim. 4:1). He names individuals (1 Tim. 1:19–20; 2 Tim. 4:10). Sadly, we too know people who express considerable initial interest in the Christian faith, even profess that something special has taken place in their hearts, but later grow cold. Ultimately, we know our own hearts only too well. It would be easy to turn right away. We are not wrong to ask, 'Is a Christian's relationship with the Lord secure? Will it survive?'

We come to what has traditionally been called the doctrine of assurance.[2] 'How can I know I am a genuine Christian? Will I make it to the end to live with Christ for ever?' Any book on Christian confidence has to relate to these questions. As I stressed at the beginning of this book, however, two important points must be made.[3]

First, God gives us assurance, but not as a separate or self-contained doctrine. His assurance is part and parcel of the whole and integrated offer of his grace, mercy and redemption extended to us in the Lord Jesus. Thus the word 'confidence' is preferred. To repeat, I define confidence as *a consequence of my faith in Jesus Christ, brought about over time by the Holy Spirit, experienced in my heart and realized in my mind, that God's promises in the gospel are true and personally applicable to me a believer.*

Second, this implies that at the heart of assurance is the question of confidence. On one level we may well ask, 'Am I *really* a Christian, and will I continue as one?' Here is the obvious problem of assurance. But encompassing this problem is the issue of biblical Christianity as truth, as reality.

Today's Christian may not always be able to separate the two. There are particular circumstances and experiences where it is impossible to figure out whether our problem is related to assurance or confidence.' Still, this book's central thesis is that the truthfulness of God's gospel promises gives strength and justification to the believer's personal application. I can illustrate the problem in this way.

Five years ago Rani professed a faith in Jesus Christ. She comes from a Hindu family. While at university she met Christians, and they helpfully explained the gospel. At first, Rani was not interested. Over several months, however, her resistance decreased and her interest increased. At last she acknowledged Jesus as her rightful Lord, and gratefully looked to his death on the cross as her only hope of a peaceful relationship with her creator. All seemed well. She became an active member of a student group, and her Christian friends cherished her warm personality and enthusiasm.

For various reasons, however, Rani is deeply insecure. This leads her to intense introspection and, to an extent, depression. Wisely, some of her Christian friends encouraged her to find professional counselling for her depression. The psychiatrist recognized a number of complex and interrelated problems.

Central to Rani's struggle is a developing disillusionment with Christianity. It is not working for her, she tells me. Christ feels too far off from the particulars of her life. Moreover, when she reads the Bible it compounds her own sense of failure. Scripture commands consistency. She is a bundle of contradictions. Paul's letters speak of triumph. Her heart screams disappointment.

Is Rani's problem a matter of assurance, or something else? It is not altogether obvious, but it strikes me that it is a matter of confidence. She not only cringes at her own failures and fears, which lead her to conclude that the Lord does not care for her; she is also inclined to dismiss biblical Christianity as one horrid mistake. It has no truth, because (in her opinion) it does not make any practical difference in her broken condition. The promises of the gospel are vacuous. Yet even as she tells me all this, she is worried on another level. If she finally rejects Christianity, when in fact it may well be true, is there any hope for her after she dies?

I want to point out quickly that Rani is an exceptional person. Many other Christians do not battle in the depths as she does. Yet we can look at some of her questions as a model for the fundamental concern about a believer's security. In this present chapter themes developed in previous chapters are brought together. We will do this as we pay attention to some central biblical passages dealing with assurance, security and perseverance (that is, keeping on as a Christian) and an overall confidence. While an extensive exegetical study is beyond the scope of this book,[4] our examination of particular texts will help us to reach a reasonable solution to the difficult and important question of a Christian's security.

With Rani in mind, as well as others, we are concerned ultimately to see how legitimate confidence relates to the issue of a believer's assurance. To do so, let us ask the following related questions: 1. Why would today's Christian be anxious and lack confidence? 2. Is there any *real* reason for this anxiety? 3. If it is a real problem, what should today's Christian do?

Why would today's Christian be anxious and lack confidence?

Each of the preceding chapters of this book answers this question. We outlined some of the personal, experiential problems that a Christian encounters: guilt from the past and present, a sense of frustration and disappointment in Christian obedience, struggles with guidance, as well as the trials of pain and suffering. It is possible for some readers to experience a combination of these. Rani's situation is a more obvious example.

There are Christians today who are discouraged due to problems in their local church or denomination. As one scandal after another breaks out, it is natural for some believers to wonder if Christianity is no different from any other movement. If an elderly couple see their local church fellowship lose hold of clear biblical doctrines, then no matter how relevant the music and seeker-friendly the worship service, they could well wonder if the church will continue into the coming century.

Certainly a late-twentieth-century follower of Jesus is (and should be!) troubled on reading today's newspapers, watching television or listening to radio news reports. The sovereignty of God sounds great when someone is offered the job she hoped for, but a disturbing concept as she travels through suffering parts of Africa or India on her holidays. It should not surprise us that today's Christian could be anxious and lack confidence, because of the experiential problems before us.

We also argued that our society is undergoing a significant cultural shift. The experiential difficulties we pass through are frequently compounded by the philosophical and intellectual influences of postmodernism. Undoubtedly, someone suffering the trauma of a marriage breakdown or long-term unemployment may not immediately see postmodernity as part of the problem! Nevertheless, the cultural context in which these difficulties are experienced and wrestled with is one shaped by particular assumptions about love, honesty, life, truth, fairness and spirituality. Because we live in an age of *rapid* change, believing in a gospel which supposedly stands above change is difficult. Little wonder that some of us are anxious and not always confident!

But there is something more, and it brings us back to one of Rani's concerns. In the midst of her questioning is a fear of rejecting Christianity and then after death meeting the very Lord she rejected. It is tempting for some Christians to minimize her concern. She is bright, however, and has studied the Scriptures well enough to detect a false or superficial explanation. Rani knows that biblical Christianity refers to a final judgment.

We must be clear about this. As we mentioned in chapter 1 and chapter 6, there is a coming judgment. Rani is right; a Christian's security ultimately relates to this coming day. All men and women will face the just (as well as merciful) judgment seat of Christ. Mention was made earlier[5] about the future hope believers have; they await the final day of Christ's victory and glory. Nevertheless, this is a day of judgment, when some people (those who are Christ's) will enter an eternal inheritance of joy and blessing, and others (those who reject Christ in this present life) an eternal banishment in hell.[6]

It would be more comfortable to ignore or minimize this biblical teaching. In 1927, Bertrand Russell insisted, 'I do not myself feel that any person who is profoundly humane can believe in everlasting punishment.'[7] Certainly, there are many, even in the church, who downplay the idea of judgment and hell. While he rejects the idea of universalism, David L. Edwards nonetheless argues:

> According to Christianity God is both all-powerful (or sovereign) and all-loving. If he is all powerful, will he not exert his infinite power to the utmost to save all the perishing? If he is all-loving, will he not save any soul with a glimmer of belief that the rejection of Christ would deserve blame? I would rather be an atheist than believe in a God who accepts it as inevitable that hell (however conceived) is the inescapable destiny of many, or of any of his children, even when they are prepared to accept 'all the blame'.[8]

To be sure, the idea that God will send people to hell is not a comfortable proposition. Nevertheless, it is patently clear that the

New Testament writers taught this doctrine.[9] Jesus' teaching is singularly straightforward.[10] Yet, in the light of all we have considered in this book on Christian confidence, we can draw together a helpful response.

It is not a question of 'inevitability', as David Edwards fears. As argued in chapter 3, there is no decree outside God that determines or forces his decision and judgment. There is neither chance nor law behind God. The Lord's decision is totally and absolutely within himself and because of himself. God's judgment is both just and merciful. He judges because he is who he is, not because of some inevitable and constraining rule.

Equally, as we considered in chapter 7, the sovereign Lord does not eradicate human responsibility and choice. These are not only marks of human dignity and identity; they supremely point to the character of God. He is moral; therefore, his summons to men and women to repent and believe the gospel is moral. While he overemphasizes human liberty, Michael Green is correct about the reality of final accountability:

> The love of God does not send anyone to hell. The love of God, with arms extended on a cross, bars the way to hell. But if that love is ignored, rejected and finally refused, there comes a time when love can only weep while man pushes past into the self-chosen alienation which Christ went to the cross to avert. God sends nobody to hell. But it takes two to make a friendship. If man firmly and repeatedly refuses the proffered hand of God, God will honour and ratify that man's decision to live to himself and die by himself. God respects our free will even in the hell of our own choosing.[11]

Nevertheless, the problem of a Christian's security thus relates to the coming judgment. It is more than a moment-by-moment experiential dilemma. The problem may manifest itself in a person's emotions and psychology. Rani comes to mind, but so too the person frightened of dying or the businessman who is convinced that his young wife died in an automobile accident because God was judging him. These real and important problems are finally only temporary problems. There is something even greater, eternal, at stake for today's Christian.

Will he or she be saved on this day? Stated thus baldly, it seems a rather questionable concern. If she or he is a true Christian, will not the merits of Christ's death and present lordship save? Surely this is the gospel promise! Is this not what the previous chapters about Christian confidence conclude?

The operative phrase is 'true Christian'. God is not in question; Jesus' faithfulness is not the issue; the crucial problem is a believer's inconsistency, failure and continued attraction to sin. Would these, on that coming final day, reveal the 'believer' as a fraud and an imposter? Could he, even with the best intentions, actually delude himself into thinking he has a true love for the Lord, the gospel and fellow Christians? Is it possible to display outwardly all the signs of Christian spirituality yet inwardly have the heart and mind of a hypocrite?

As if this were not enough, Scripture makes it clear there are forces working against believers: Satan,[12] principalities and powers,[13] false teachers,[14] and the attraction of this world.[15] There is not the slightest suggestion that these threats are insignificant, even in the light of the Lord's greater power and authority. These warnings are real. Therefore, could a Christian fall away because of his or her enemies?

Yet none of these experiential questions about Christian security is significant if there is no judgment and no hell. Why should we worry? If there is no judgment, or if all will be saved despite their choice and lifestyle, the fear is irrational and illogical. But the gospel is quite clear: there is a coming judgment, 'This will take place on the day when God will judge men's secrets through Jesus Christ, as my gospel declares' (Rom. 2:16). So what does Christian confidence have to say about this?

Is there any *real* reason for this anxiety?

We might conclude that the warnings in Scripture are intended only to direct us to Christ's mercy and steadfast covenant commitment to his people. The warnings do not, in themselves, relate to any real possibility. Yet this is utter nonsense, given the context of biblical warnings. The warnings are real because the dangers are real. Why warn if there is no legitimate cause for warning? To do so would be the height of pastoral and psychological insensitivity. Rani and others, while tempted to accept the ideas of those who deny judgment, see this as no real option. It does not ring true. Too many parts of the New Testament would have to be adjusted to fit in with a dismissal of accountability and judgment.

Jesus' parable of the sower in Matthew 13:3–23 (*cf.* Mk. 4:1–9, 14–20; Lk. 8:4–15) comes within an actual, non-hypothetical, context. At issue was the way in which his hearers were 'hearing' the gospel of the kingdom. This parable is a commentary on Jesus' ministry (as the sower) and the ways in which (like differing soils) people responded to his ministry.

In this parable and its later explanation, there are some situations (soils) in which the gospel is rejected, or accepted only temporarily. Some people 'fall away' (*skandalizetai*, which can also mean 'take offence').[16] It is sobering to hear that a person (like this soil) could hear the word and at once receive it with joy, and still fall away (13:20). Apparently, a reception can take place, with joy and appreciation; yet hardness, indifference and rejection can occur.

To be sure, we are not told whether these people were 'true' Christians or not. Presumably, Jesus (and the Gospel writers themselves, as later editors) were not concerned with this theological distinction. Perhaps such distinctions too easily become escape clauses. Instead, Jesus' message, whether inside the community or out, is 'Be careful how you listen!'

Earlier in Matthew's Gospel, Jesus speaks of a day of judgment when false prophets and professors will be identified and, consequently, rejected (Mt. 7:15–23). Until this final day, the growth of the kingdom in the world will be like a field in which wheat grows alongside weeds; the final day, however, will truly separate and justly distinguish them (Mt. 13:24–30).[17]

Is Jesus suggesting that true believers could actually fall away and apostatize? In one sense, the teaching of Jesus is not altogether straightforward. There are words of encouragement and assurance.[18] A disciple need not live in panic and insecurity. Nevertheless, subsequent sayings of Jesus about discipleship underline its costliness and difficulties. Temptation is ever-present, persecution awaits. Consequently, it would be extraordinarily foolish to deny the reality of Jesus' warnings. 'If anyone is ashamed of me and my words in this adulterous and sinful generation, the Son of Man will be ashamed of him when he comes in his Father's glory with the holy angels' (Mk. 8:38 = Lk. 9:26–27; *cf.* Mt. 16:27). Jesus did not regard the dangers as hypothetical.

This teaching continues in other parts of the New Testament. It is worth considering some examples. The author of 1 Peter identifies believers' suffering under persecution as an advance sign of an inevitable final (eschatological) judgment. In other words, he anticipates the end of all history with the return of the Lord Jesus. 'However, if you suffer as a Christian, do not be ashamed, but praise God that you bear that name. For it is time for judgment to begin with the family of God; and if it begins with us, what will be the outcome for those who do not obey the gospel of God?' (1 Pet. 4:16–17).

The author is not suggesting that his readers' experience is *the* final judgment. But he draws a very close parallel; one indicates the other. Therefore, his ethical instruction and exhortation involve, among other things, a clear-headed awareness of accountability before God. Endurance and perseverance are closely interwoven with a future certainty (1 Pet.1:5, 7; 4:7, 13; 5:6, 10–11). Perhaps this future is eschatological; nonetheless, it affects the present experiences of the gathered believers.

We also see this quite clearly in the book of Revelation. It is possible to interpret Jesus' words of warning to the seven churches in chapters 2 and 3 as symbols of a final day of judgment; yet, given the more obvious final judgment of chapter 5 to 20:15, it seems best to view Jesus' sayings to these particular churches as specific, pre-eschatological, warnings against apostasy and spiritual failure.

Jesus' rebukes and encouragements to these churches are hardly theoretical, even if later readers may not understand every detailed reference (we cannot be sure who and what were the Nicolaitans in 2:6, the teachings of Balaam in 2:14 and Jezebel in 2:20). The church in Ephesus had lost its first love, though they endured hardships for Jesus' name (2:3, 4). Thyatira was troubled by misleading teaching and sexual immorality that were affecting 'my servants' (2:20). Apostasy is not specified here, but the call to a counter-position is issued; for only by holding on and overcoming are Jesus' promised rewards possible.

Two of the more notable New Testament passages we should consider are Hebrews 6:4-12 and 10:26-31. In both settings the experience referred to certainly involved central gospel elements:

enlightenment, the heavenly gift, the Holy Spirit, the goodness of the Word of God and the powers of the coming age. Though the author is confident that his readers are in a different category (6:9), there is no *clear* textual indication that those mentioned in 6:4-6 were counterfeit and hypocrites.

On the contrary, from all essential and outward indications, these people looked as though they were believers. At the very least, the author will not let his readers dismiss his earlier warnings because the individuals in chapter 6 were pretenders. It may be that the specific 'falling away' (NIV)[19] is the 'crucifying the Son of God all over again', and parallel to the idea of 'being brought back to repentance' (6:6). This public, full-blown, denial of Jesus (see 10:29) is entirely different from the 'sin which so easily entangles' (12:1). But the author suggests that cold-heartedness and negligence could well be precursors to apostasy. They are not the same, but the danger looks very real and actual; one could lead to another.

Yet the author is less interested in answering the question 'Can a Christian lose salvation?' than in warning his readers not to wander away from the gospel through discouragement and disillusionment. This distinction is far more than convenient semantics. We must appreciate the overall context of the letter. Hebrews 6:4–6 and 10:26–31 highlight the dangers of what may well have been an actual threat for his readers. True, he expresses his present confidence in these Christians (6:9; 10:32–39); he does not expressly doubt their continuance in the faith. Nevertheless, the letter is shot through with a pastor's anxious concern for these people. They run the very real danger of losing confidence and assurance.

The letter to the Hebrews is a dazzling source of hope, edification and encouragement; but these are counterpoised with repeated warnings. The assurance and encouragement stand for a reason: so that believers will not fall. If the words of hope and promise are not hypothetical, neither are the warnings. Each is dependent upon the other. The ultimate conclusion of the letter is double-edged; wonderful and positive confidence is found in the unique and sufficient work of Jesus, so there is no need to live a heedless and reckless spiritual life that would only result in tragedy.

We can now bring together our brief observations of these

various New Testament passages. The danger is not hypothetical but real. Those passages in the Bible that exhort, instruct, summon and correct believers

> underscore our responsibility in our perseverance. They tell us that it is only as we prayerfully endure to the end, hold fast to what we have, continue in Christ's word, and remain in Christ that we can enjoy the blessing of perseverance. And they also remind us that God, in preserving us, uses means. Those include the exhortations, threatenings, and promises of his word.[20]

Gospel warnings are a work of God's covenant mercy and grace. They are not insignificant or 'pretend'. We are not saying that believers need to be cajoled or browbeaten. Rather, faith responds not only in joy but in reverence, or what the Bible frequently calls 'fear'. This is never the fear or terror of an outsider, but the respect and obedience a child brings to his or her parent. We are not to take things for granted, with a haughty presumption or insolent arrogance. As G. C. Berkouwer argued:

> The doctrine of the perseverance of the saints can never become an *a priori* guarantee in the life of believers which would enable them to get along without admonitions and warnings . . . For the correct understanding of the correlation between faith and perseverance, it is precisely these admonitions that are significant, and they enable us to understand better the nature of perseverance.[21]

Scripture's admonitions warn us of the seriousness before us. We are not to give up meeting with others. Negligence is recklessness. We must watch and pray. Attraction to idolatry or immorality is a possibility unless we continue (through grace) in obedience and diligence. Gospel grace is given so that we might persevere in gospel duties. But there is a crucial qualification. And this brings us again to think of Rani, along with all of us.

Left to our own resources and strength we are in great peril of falling away and denying the gospel. We have neither the strength nor the integrity to keep walking the way of discipleship. The majority of Christians will not go through Rani's despair or experience the violent persecution recently experienced by believers in other parts of the world. Nonetheless, long-term Christian discipleship brings enough challenges to test the most resilient personality among us. The gospel hope, however, is that our perseverance and security are not based on our own self-effort and diligence. Our confidence rests in one greater than ourselves.

If it is a real problem, what should today's Christian do?

Given the reality of accountability, and the possible ways in which today's Christian could be anxious and lack confidence, what should be done? This is not at all an abstract or theoretical question. People who come into my office are rarely anxious about going to hell or state it so bluntly! Once again, Rani's situation is uncommon, as are my homosexual friend's struggles to obey biblical standards.

Yet underneath the behaviour and attitudes of so many Christians something is not quite right. As Christian people come into my office or speak with me in their homes or student accommodation about living Christianly in this generation, they do ask questions related to confidence, perseverance and security. All the impact of what we considered in chapters 1 and 2 is evident in what they say. What should people do today? There are at least three options; only one will really lead us, in our generation, to true Christian confidence.

Option 1

Rani could conclude that her Christian life would be maintained through greater discipline and effort. She reads these warnings in the Bible with a tender conscience, and determines to lead a life worthy of acceptance. She may even believe that although her life in Christ began by grace, its continuation is through the response and determination of her heart and will. She pays close, scrupulous attention to times of prayer, Bible reading and the occasions when she witnesses to her non-Christian friends. She is sensitively concerned not to accept a 'cheap grace', that is, the erroneous idea that the Christian life is easy and painless.

Can she be rightly criticized for this? Clearly, Christians today struggle with inconsistency and superficiality. We see it all around us, and we observe how little impact western Christians have on our society. Is it not because we are so lax and undisciplined? Who among us, therefore, would wish to caution an overly-tender believer from taking the commands of Christ more seriously?

In fact, every one of us should speak words of caution. Discipline and zeal are good and proper. We are to work hard, press on and strive. Laziness and moral laxity are serious hindrances. Yet there is a deep problem. Christian perseverance and confidence are not accomplished through human effort and self-discipline. Some may wish to say that there is a fine line here; nevertheless, on either side of the line are dangerous errors.

It may be that a Christian, in his or her love for the Lord and a zeal for holiness, is actually prompted by the psychological and emotional baggage of their past. Perfectionism and duty could well arise from a desire to please a parent figure. Rather than healthy love and respect, the response originates in fear and insecurity. A Christian can quite easily grieve over sin and aim for moral renovation, not so much out of a love for the Lord, but out of an inner desire for a feeling of well-being, security and 'cleanness'. This well-being, however, may be a carry-over from his or her childhood.

Some Christians might wish to draw a sharp disassociation between a believer's past life and present new life in Christ. Thankfully, there is a powerful transformation that is both now and progressive.[22] I, for one, do not seek to define a person's total identity solely in terms of his or her past. It is not only in deep psychotherapy, however, that past problems can be detected in a believer's life. As some believers talk with me about their life in Christ, certain aspects begin to ring false.[23]

They declare they are lazy and undisciplined in their relationship with the Lord. Yet their counter-measures look to be motivated by driven fear than by gratitude for the Lord's patience and sustaining love. Similarly, they ask deep theological questions about, say, free will and predestination. Insistently, they introduce these questions into almost every discussion. They explain that *this* is the number one problem in their life. But as they speak and wrestle with their questions, it seems that the real problem is fear that God is going to crush their personal desires and dreams. What is supremely at stake is confidence that the Lord genuinely accepts them, even though they struggle with their own self-acceptance. Behind all the rigorous acts of dedicated discipline or academic questioning are insecurity and lack of confidence. Yet they continue with increased labour, never dealing with essential problems.

Ultimately, this first option fails to understand the radical nature of God's grace and mercy in Jesus Christ. We are accepted as we are: broken, messed up, screwed up and flawed people. As we considered in chapter 5, this is a work of God's sovereign mercy and grace in Christ. But grace is not like a set of car-battery jump-leads: a quick jolt from someone else, and then it is up to us to keep running. Yet this first option has to reach such a conclusion.

Furthermore, it fails to understand, receive and experience the totally comprehensive, sufficient and unique toil of Christ on the cross. Jesus did not die just for our benefit. He died out of obedience to his Father. His Father's love sent Jesus into the world, and Jesus' accomplishment in the world is acceptable first and foremost to the Father. Even in our fear and pain we can become terribly human-centred, thinking of the cross in terms of human benefit. This one-dimensional perspective limits our seeing how satisfied the Father is. In the Lord's love, there is more than sweetness; there is just, true and perfect accomplishment.

Moreover, this approach is soul-destroying because it misunderstands the wonderful work of the Holy Spirit in a believer's life. This work is not theoretical or abstract; it is both objective and experiential. It is real and existential, because the Holy Spirit is not a force or dynamic; he is personal. An intense, driven effort to maintain our relationship with the Lord, apart from the moment-by-moment work of the Spirit, is misguided and problematic. It is, in effect, to shift things into an altogether different category, out of a personal relationship into a work of well-meaning but flawed self-achievement. The Lord who is our Saviour is not in a relationship with self-motivated individuals; he is in a covenant of grace with trusting, dependent and redeemed people.

Option 2

Another option is to hunt for evidence of God's work in our life and our progression in the Christian life. In other words, someone like Rani looks into her attitudes, behaviour and desires in order to look for the ways in which she conforms to what Christians *ought* to be. So she asks: 'Well, Christians are full of love and kindness. Am I?' Another day she reads in the Bible that faithful people are not ashamed of making the gospel known. She asks herself: 'OK, how do I act when I come back to my parents' home?' She is not the exception; many of us move in this direction.

We well appreciate that God is the author of our redemption. We want to respond to his call to holiness. In moments of insecurity, however, we look inwards to measure our spirituality. We examine ourselves to assess our well-being and life in Christ. We know that a Christian is a person who hears the gospel, understands it and responds by repentance and trust. He or she knows that Christ died to rescue his people. Only his saved people receive the Holy Spirit. Accordingly, we look inwards to see if our life has changed. We detect faith and trust in ourselves and so deduce that we must be one of those for whom Christ died and in whom the Spirit dwells. In this approach, a sense of confidence arrives initially by looking at ourselves and working our way, reflexively, to God's promises.

But is this an entirely satisfactory approach? Does introspection not give rise to particular problems? Is this really the way to help confused and concerned believers? Introspection is not necessarily bad. 'It is the duty of every one to give all diligence to make his calling and election sure,' claimed the seventeenth-century Westminster Confession of Faith.[24] The Larger Catechism (Q. 80), produced at the same time, referred to the Spirit enabling believers 'to discern in themselves those graces to which the promises of life are made'.[25]

The problem is that we can look inward and judge wrongly. We can be either excessively hard on ourselves or lenient with ourselves. In both cases we can easily lose sight of the one whom we trust and love – Jesus. We can trick ourselves. A further danger is one of comparison. 'I'm not perfect, but compared to the members of that church or that student group, I am not so bad.'

At one level, it is not wrong to examine ourselves to evaluate how we are walking with the Lord. It is not uncommon for someone to say, 'Tell me about your conversion.' In pastoral counselling, a believer is often asked, 'What changes do you notice God working in you?' It is sometimes encouraging to see how the Spirit is changing us. The question 'How is your devotional life?'

191

can remind us of the vital importance of regular times of prayer, Scripture reading and thanksgiving. In themselves, these are not bad questions. They can be helpful diagnostic tools. Nevertheless, we could too easily fall into both simplicity and superficiality. Neither will lead us to the legitimate Christian confidence that the Lord desires for us. What, then, should we do? This leads us to the third option, and the best of all.

Option 3

In his book *A Fresh Start*, John Chapman sums it up well:

> When we came to Christ our promises were far reaching and absolute. As we live out those promises the best we will do is approximate to them. When we fail we need to admit and apologise. God for His part will forgive. You don't, however, have to become a Christian again. There is God's word, there are God's actions and His promises. All are wonderful evidences to you that it did 'really take' for you.'[26]

If we look back at the texts considered earlier, and others, we find what Chapman is driving at in this quote. Jesus' instruction to his people commands our diligence and watchfulness.[27] How we hear and respond to the gospel, illustrated in the parable of the sower, is vital: 'He who has ears, let him hear' (Mt. 13:9; *cf.* Mk. 4:24–25; Mt. 7:24–27). We are to pay heed, and continue forward in the ways of discipleship. This is just as true for the man or woman who has been a Christian for years as for the new believer from a non-church background.

The apostle Paul, stressing justification by faith alone, equally called attention to our accountability. 'For we must all appear before the judgment seat of Christ, that each one may receive what is due to him for the things done while in the body, whether good or bad' (2 Cor. 5:10; *cf.* 2 Cor. 6:1–2). Believers need not live in despair and panic about their shortcomings, but they are to take obedience seriously. Instructing the Christians in Philippi, Paul instructed them to work out their own salvation 'with fear and trembling' (Phil. 2:12). He is referring not to individual Christians, but to the corporate call to imitate Christ's humility and servanthood. In short, they are to put into practice the implications of being encouraged through union 'with Christ' (Phil.2:1; 'if there is any encouragement in Christ', RSV). They are to live a life worthy of the gospel (1:27).

This effort, however, comes not through their own diligence and striving alone (which is really Option 1). Paul's confidence is in the Lord who is already at work in them (1:6; 2:13). His exhortations are rooted in the supreme efficacy of the gospel and grace. He prays they may be 'pure and blameless until the day of Christ' (1:10); and, while this involves their corporate and personal obedience, the chief means is the gospel: 'filled with the fruit of righteousness that comes through Jesus Christ – to the glory and praise of God' (1:11).[28] In the gospel is our hope and confidence, and, consequently, our security. Accordingly, Paul urges his readers to 'stand firm in one spirit, contending as one man for the faith of the gospel . . .' (1:27).

This is the New Testament call: cling to the gospel, defend the gospel and commend the gospel. In God's good news, declared and explained for us in the apostles' writings, we have the means of our hope and security. The apostolic gospel is 'the power of God for the salvation of everyone who believes' (Rom 1:16). This is why Jude urges his readers to 'contend for the faith that was once for all entrusted to the saints' (Jude 3). Despite all efforts of certain people to pervert apostolic teaching, then and even now, the Christian community is to rehearse, teach, study and proclaim the truth. Why?

The reason is that in the gospel *alone* men and women have hope and confidence. Jude instructs his people: 'But you, dear friends, build yourselves up in your most holy faith and pray in the Holy Spirit. Keep yourselves in God's love as you wait for the mercy of our Lord Jesus Christ to bring you to eternal life' (Jude 20–21; *cf.* 2 Pet. 1:3–11). We are to do something, involving our actions and commitment towards one another. Jude makes this point more strongly in verses 22–23.

Yet surrounding, supporting and enabling these exhortations are the gospel power and reality. Where else will we find and experience 'the mercy of our Lord Jesus Christ'? How do we help one another at the end of the twentieth century? We teach one another, feed one another and remind one another of the staggering gospel promise:

> To him who is able to keep you from falling and to present you before his glorious presence without fault and with great joy – to the only God our Saviour be glory, majesty, power and authority, through Jesus Christ our Lord, before all ages, now and for evermore! Amen (Jude 24–25).

Though we will often fail and stumble in our gospel obedience, an effort that shows our love for the Lord, there is someone on our side (Rom. 8:31ff.; 1 Jn. 2:1). Our fellowship with Christ is not a licence for pretension and ethical indifference (1 Jn. 1:16; 2:4). We are to live counter-cultural lives (1 Jn. 2:15) and to love each other deeply and practically (1 Jn. 3:18). This will mean that we work hard at keeping and maintaining apostolic truth, for only here is the gospel (1 Jn. 4:1–3). For where a people walk in the gospel light they experience the confirming work of the Holy Spirit (1 Jn. 3:24 – 4:13), know God's love (1 Jn. 4:17) and experience the protecting and keeping power of the Lord and Saviour (1 Jn. 5:18).

Late-twentieth-century Christians, whether in the East or in the West, need to hear both the warning and encouragement of the letter to the Hebrews. We too run the risk of drifting away (2:1) through doctrinal confusion, but even more through the influence of postmodernity's whispers. Some of us, having known the first joys and freedom in Christ, face the danger of giving up as our life in Christ stretches out for years. Obedience seems wearisome. Faithfulness feels like folly. Yet recall who it is who has rescued us and pardoned us (3:6). In the midst of terrific challenge and difficulty, as well as a stultifying routine, in Christ we can experience a courage and a hope (3:6, 12–14). Let us watch ourselves, lest a spiritual hardening take place (4:1, 11).

Ultimately, our comfort and security are found in the one who knows weak, sinful and dysfunctional men and women: Jesus. There is no higher or surer source of our Christian confidence. The confidence we find in him is multi-faceted. It is based on truth we can read about in Scripture. Equally, it is profoundly experiential and existential (4:14–16).

It is never an individualistic experience; mutual strengthening and assuring are available for each of us in those times when, on our own, we are emotionally exhausted and spiritually defeated. This is why we need other believers, and they need us. Our life in

Christ is corporate. Our experience of confidence always involves a corporate life together. Whether through the support and friendship of a Christian brother or sister, a small-group meeting in a home, or a larger gathering of believers featuring worship, prayer, Bible study and receiving the bread and wine of communion, confidence is never independent of other Christians. The high point of the letter to the Hebrews is the pinnacle from which we may view our contemporary life with true confidence.

> Therefore, brothers, since we have confidence to enter the Most Holy Place by the blood of Jesus, by a new and living way opened for us through the curtain, that is, his body, and since we have a great priest over the house of God, let us draw near to God with a sincere heart in full assurance of faith, having our hearts sprinkled to cleanse us from a guilty conscience and having our bodies washed with pure water. Let us hold unswervingly to the hope we profess, for he who promised is faithful. And let us consider how we may spur one another on towards love and good deeds. Let us not give up meeting together, as some are in the habit of doing, but let us encourage one another – and all the more as you see the Day approaching (Heb. 10:19–25).

A slow-coming but sure confidence

Although it was written hundreds of years ago it is still a timely reminder. The Westminster Confession of Faith declared, 'This infallible assurance doth not so belong to the essence of faith, but that a true believer may wait long, and conflict with many difficulties before he be partaker of it . . .'[29] We must be equally realistic at the close of the twentieth century. It is possible to possess justifying faith and yet still have to wait a long time and endure a long struggle before coming to personal assurance and confidence. In one sense, this really should not be the case, given the clarity and sufficiency of the apostolic gospel. In another sense, experientially, we are troubled.

We are troubled because we are finite humans. Our personalities differ, our situations in life vary, our Christian communities are not identical. We are disturbed because we live in a fallen world, and we are fallen too. Equally, we have an enemy of our souls. Why does it seems that God is 'slow' to answer our questions, resolve our doubts and settle us into the security of confidence? There are multiple answers, including the response, 'I don't know.' Os Guinness wisely reminds us: 'The problem of doubt is not ultimately a matter of God's faithfulness but of our faith, just as the answer does not ultimately depend on our faith but on God's faithfulness.'[30]

Nevertheless, the hope of confidence requires no 'new revelation', 'further blessing' or *inordinate* exercise of faith. Faith and obedience are required. Yet we are wise to remember that this hope is ours in the wonders of the new covenant and available to every believer, though it might take long to emerge. The gospel is first and foremost a message of grace and mercy. Confidence is supremely based on nothing else. As J. I. Packer expresses it:

> If God in love has made Christians His children, and if He is perfect as a Father, two things would seem to follow, in the nature of the case. First, the family relationship must be an abiding one, lasting for ever. Perfect parents do not cast off their children. Christians may act the prodigal, but God will not cease to act the prodigal's father. Second, God will go out of His way to make His children feel His love for them, and know their privilege and security as members of His family. Adopted children need assurance that they belong, and a perfect parent will not withhold it.[31]

The hope of confidence is, of course, associated with God's predestinating purpose and with election; yet confidence is not promised by a detailed look at predestination and election. Always the hope is gained by looking at Christ. 'O what a comfort is it to a poor Christian', wrote Richard Baxter so long ago, 'that in his greatest infirmities, and deepest sense of unworthiness, he hath the beloved of the Father to take his prayers and present them to God, and to plead his cause more effectually than he can do his own.'[32] We can still say the same in our age of change.

Christian confidence in our changing age is possible. This is so for people like Rani, facing profoundly difficult problems. So too for the majority of us, whose challenges may not be so drastic, but just constant. True Christian confidence, as it gives us security, is not a matter of self-delusion. It is because we can know what we must know. We can learn why things are not right with the world and with ourselves, and why we still long for resolution and hope. There is a trustworthy and realistic way of knowing and experiencing him who makes restoration and transformation possible and practicable. We can be legitimately confident because of him, the Lord who is also the Saviour, Jesus. In this changing age, it is remarkable, but true: he continues to speak and reach out, that we may know.

We began this chapter with a picture of a newly married couple. Will their marriage survive the trials and challenges of a life-long union? As an analogy, what about a Christian's relationship with the one true God? Will it last? With characteristic cogency, John Chapman gets it right: 'Being a Christian is fundamentally different from marriage in one very important aspect. There is no dissolving of this relationship. It is forever, thank goodness.'[33] Yes, indeed. We can be confident.

Questions for reflection and discussion

1. Is it a mark of faithlessness to feel a lack of confidence? How much do you think a lack of confidence is a sign of a person's temperament? Was Rani just prone to her problems, regardless of her religious convictions?

2. Does the occasional problem we have with the idea of final judgment and hell only serve to underline how harmful these doctrines are in a contemporary world? What would the removal of these doctrines, or the playing-down of these themes, do in terms of our gospel presentation? Would our gospel remain *apostolic*? Does it need to be?

3. Of the three options illustrated in this chapter, which do *you* see more commonly?

4. How would you respond to this statement: 'Becoming a Christian is only going to lead a person into guilt, fear and a superstitious belief in something after death'?

5. Is security foolish arrogance? Can a Christian be confident and still humble?

9

The life of confidence in
this age of change

Within the realm of possibility

But will it work?

If you were to pick up this book, glance at the Preface and then
turn to this, the last chapter, you might well ask, 'Let's see his
conclusions, what is he really saying about confidence?' I hope
you would not do this, and that you not doing this now! You
would miss not only the flow of the argument, but, to shift to
another metaphor, you would miss the structure of my presentation. Throughout this book we have progressively seen the
theological framework that alone will help us know and
experience Christian confidence in our changing age. This framework enables our understanding and experiencing confidence.

At every point in this book we have faced a dilemma. We could
have gone deep into specific pastoral problems facing today's
Christians. Likewise, we might have offered pastors or Christian
counsellors a series of guidelines which will help people become
confident Christians. The dilemma, with all the various and
specific problems facing people today, is that generalized theory is
not immediately attractive.

Yet a choice was made, as I mentioned in the Introduction. Of
first importance, we sought to see a theological framework that
would help us understand the comprehensive truthfulness of
God's gospel promises to men and women today. In short, we
were looking for a biblical theology of Christian confidence. We
never wanted to avoid questions or presuppositions or implications. We could not, for we know that both non-Christians and
Christians cannot accept any blinkered view. Too many questions
are around in today's postmodern world.

Clarity is the order of the day. That is why we identified, in
chapter 1, some experiential issues that confront today's believers.

Men and women encounter specific situations and problems. We have consistently urged biblical Christians to meet their experiential concerns with directness. If the truth God invites us to know is not also experientially fitting, then something is wrong: not only with us but, more important, with this so-called truth. Yet when we examine both our life experiences and God's Word, supremely in Jesus Christ, we see that there is an immediate interface.

To be sure, chapter 1 does not detail a complete list of experiential problems facing Christians in our age. What we were showing is how an experiential problem carries with it, or beneath it, certain philosophical and theological baggage. There is a symbiotic relationship between theology and experience. This is too easily misunderstood today, and explains why our changing age seems, at times, to outflank contemporary Christians.

Compounding our experience is the weight of our contemporary postmodern culture. We described this in chapter 2. If it is true that our experiences have philosophical and theological baggage, then we need to know what this baggage is, where we got it from, whether it is right for us to carry it, and, for some of us, why it feels so heavy and cumbersome. For so many Christians today, it is as if we are walking along a crowded train platform carrying our bags. Certain voices in the crowd laugh at our baggage, saying it is old-fashioned and hopelessly useless. One or two in the crowd tell us to get rid of our bags and carry their luggage. What, in fact, we long for as Christians is for someone to lend us a truly helpful hand, perhaps repacking our bags for us, so that we can board the train.

The theological framework that we began to identify in chapter 3 and then examined more fully in the subsequent chapters shows us how we can find help. With this help we can know and experience Christian confidence. I recognize that it is initially easier to express this claim than prove it. Nevertheless, in each chapter efforts have been made to show the necessity of a real convergence between the gospel and reality. Far too easily it looks as though the two are mutually exclusive. This book, however, argues that any such divergence or dissimilarity is contrived and contrary to the way things are. The truth is that today's life and biblical Christianity do intersect. There is convergence, the possibility of a life-giving intersection. But we need this theological framework to see the possibility.

Biblical Christianity proclaims that there is a God who can be known and that by knowing him we are set free from delusion and errors. C. S. Lewis cogently insisted, 'Now the trouble about trying to make yourself stupider than you really are is that you very often succeed.'[1] Our postmodern age too easily takes us, if we are not careful, away from truth. Arrogance is not the confidence described in this book; neither is open-mindedness supposed to be the stupidity to which Lewis referred. In the truth we can know about the one true God and his Son and Spirit, we can know the way things really are. We meet reality with a way of seeing which is not exhaustive or pain-free, but realistic and liveable. God gives us truth.

In this truth things meet. This convergence is both comforting and challenging. It comforts because biblical truth explains that often our feelings of fallenness, alienation, imperfection and dysfunction are true referents. Yes, we are right to call into question the pain, injustice and chaos around us. We learn that there is abnormality in the world, *because God tells us what is correct*. Furthermore, we are comforted when we hear and learn that there is a God who pardons, loves, restores and is constantly in control. It is refreshing and therapeutic to learn that God can be trusted.

Simultaneously, we are challenged. The gospel invites us to legitimate hope, but equally demands our repentance from sin and submission to Jesus' merciful rule. God calls us to change. We are summoned to accountability. This is why we had to consider the reality of eternal judgment in some of the earlier chapters. Our autonomy is illegitimate. The real delusion is not among those who believe in the one true God but among those who deny his existence and rightful rule. Seeing things clearly, in this case, carries disturbing implications. These implications and consequences are not theoretical but occur in real time. We discover that much of what we thought rightly described and defined our lives, in terms of value, significance and purpose, is flawed. Idolatry comes as an alarming diagnosis. None of us can say this is easy or a trivial matter. It touches us at the core of our being. This convergence is never simple or one-dimensional. Truth is not like that.

So, if you have just picked up this book, and read this chapter first, here is the point. At the beginning of the book, this definition of confidence was presented: *a consequence of my faith in Jesus*

Christ, brought about over time by the Holy Spirit, experienced in my heart and realized in my mind, that God's promises in the gospel are true and personally applicable to me as a believer. Now, however, as we come to the conclusion of our study, we must be bold enough to allow two final questions to stand. First, 'So what; will this confidence work?' This is not a flippant or inappropriate question. The second question has to be, 'How do I experience this confidence?'

These questions look too pragmatic at first glance. But there are reasons for allowing them. We must be frank enough to admit that Christian confidence is not immediately self-evident. Despite the evidence presented in each chapter, a reader could still have problems with seeing the confidence God offers him or her. Moreover, a believer could understand what we have presented but find it difficult to engage with these truths. Either something internal, or the external reality of our late-twentieth-century society, is overwhelming. Both, or a combination of these problems, warrant the question: 'Can this promised confidence really make a difference? And how can I find it?' With this twofold challenge we now complete our study of Christian confidence.

This confidence is a specific kind of certainty

I must begin with this statement to warn of a problem. The problem is both theological and experiential. If we are to see how this confidence will work in the life of today's Christian, let us beware of the problem of *certainty*. In chapter 2 we saw some of the ways in which postmodernism challenges certainty. Today's Christian will constantly bump, and at times crash, into this postmodern obstacle.

How certain is Christian certainty? Are we certain about Christianity only because, for the moment, things look clear and straightforward? Should we cover our bets, and keep one eye open to see if something better arrives? The real reason for asking these questions is the influence of our postmodern culture. Tentative conclusions are permissible, but certainty is questionable.

Yet in this book on Christian confidence, repeated stress is placed upon the person and beingness of the one true God. Because he is, and acts, we know. This is the distinction we must constantly underline. God is. He is the way we can be certain.

Think back to all we presented in chapter 3, on revelation. The fundamental point is that we are certain because God is who he is. In this way, we can reasonably say to ourselves and our culture that God, being who he is, actually gives me more certainty that he exists than anything or anyone else.

This sounds preposterous to many; and I have to say that it sounds difficult to many Christians. But the stress of our certainty is not on our *human capability* to know, but on the God who is. If we were considering only our human ability to know, or at least were giving it primary importance, then the picture would look different. In this case, we would have to agree with our culture and say, 'Yes, seeing is believing.'

Human knowledge (our epistemology), however, is only a subordinate reflection of the infinite God, in whose image we are made. We should never forget we are only finite creatures. By this very definition, anything we say about our ability to know anything is qualified. Yet when the one, true, infinite and personal God makes himself known it is, thus, possible to know. The entire picture is different now.

We must, of course, appreciate a vital fact. Our confidence and certainty are affected by our human sinfulness and pride. There are other issues too, which we shall present shortly. In this carefully qualified sense, at any moment in our experience it may seem that our certainty is tentative. True, our knowledge about the one true God will be tempered by our finiteness. As we grow in maturity we will grow more knowledgeable about the one true God. Yet we must not erroneously think that our moment-by-moment tentativeness means that certainty is impossible. We may now 'see but a poor reflection as in a mirror' (1 Cor. 13:12). But the mirror holds no distortion.

I make this first point, therefore, to warn of the problem of certainty. People often ask me if there is such a thing as 100% certainty that Christianity is true. I understand why they ask this, but there is a twofold problem here. First, can they say that 100% certainty is *normally* possible in other spheres of knowledge? Usually, they admit that knowledge about anything is limited.

Secondly, are we not possibly confusing categories? Enlightenment thinking demands some way of proving or substantiating a claim. Yet this is singularly suspect in relation to the existence of another being. My 'proof' (whatever I may offer) does not substantiate the existence of my wife. She exists, and I know this because she is; in her beingness, she speaks, acts and communicates. The fact that I can tell you these things about her, however, does not prove her existence. Nonetheless, this does not mean that I am tentative about her existence. How much more is it ridiculous to think that I, a finite creature, can prove, with 100% certainty, the existence of the infinite God! The categories are confused. God is not measurable or quantifiable. He is infinite. Still, in his infiniteness he is totally capable of communicating to us in a knowable and discernible manner. The sufficiency and certainty of this communication are substantiated by who he is.

So, what kind of certainty may we have? Is it tentative? No. It is sure and certain. Why then do we have problems, sometimes even wrong understanding? I offer some answers in the following sections of this chapter. But I fear that this important point is too easily lost in the experiential problems many of us have; by very nature of who we are our knowledge of God is not exhaustive, for we are finite and limited. We are creatures. Yet our humanity never precludes a real and legitimate certainty. It is not a case of 'seeing is believing'. Rather, because of who God is, believing is seeing. And of this we may be most certain, unquestionably certain. This certainty is totally sufficient for us who are creatures. In the fullness of God's revelation to us, in his Word and Son, we may be certain.

Nevertheless, what is it that calls this certainty into a degree of question? Consider the following.

Between the head and the heart

Think of a traffic jam on a major road. Cars cannot pass. There are tailbacks, stretching for miles. Traffic comes to a halt. Drivers feel frustrated, impatient and powerless. It is no good looking at alternative routes or examining a wristwatch when stuck in a bumper-to-bumper jam. Progress seems impossible.

Many Christians feel another constriction in their life. This one is between their head and their heart. A friend once explained, 'I feel as if the truths I know about God and myself cannot pass down into my heart and emotions.' The desire is not just for emotional thrills, although, to be perfectly honest, thrills would be a welcome change from the prevalent numbness. Rather there is a longing for integration, for things to coordinate. We can hear sermons, read books or listen to lyrics and *know* that truth is expressed, but *feel* nothing and *see* nothing in our life. There is a blockage somewhere.

The Christian confidence presented in this book offers an initial response. For the person struggling with this constriction between the head and the heart, there are practical steps to take.

1. Identify the problems

First, identify the issues and problems. They can be as varying and multiple as are individual Christians. The point is that without coming to some understanding of the specific questions and troublesome issues the constriction will continue. Just as we cannot determine the whereabouts of a blood clot in the body without examination and testing, neither can we adequately deal with this 'spiritual' clot without investigation. The aim is not to spend countless hours in deep introspection; the purpose is to be honest before God, ourselves and trusted friends. What this means specifically for the role of our Christian communities I explain shortly.

2. Removing this blockage often calls for hard work

Second, removing this restriction may well call for the hard work of studying, reading and thinking. Clearly, the call is not to excessive intellectualism. What is needed is corrected under-standing about who God is, the cross, the person and work of the Holy Spirit, the nature of our fallen world and the hope of the gospel. Often a person wrestling with a sense of blockage is working with faulty knowledge that may have been offered in certain Christian circles where there was poor and inadequate teaching, or where the individual never had the chance to ask questions without the fear of looking 'faithless'. Here too there are profound implications for the contribution of our gathered Christian communities, and, once again, I hold these in reserve for a moment.

3. Actively trust that the ultimate responsibility rests with the Lord

The third step, although it is really taken at every point, is to understand that this is the Lord's concern. There is no way that we can truly deal with this constriction on our own. It is ultimately a work of God's sovereign grace and intervention that accomplishes our desire. Indeed, he uses various means, but it chiefly rests with him. Can he be trusted to resolve this dilemma? Can we be confident that he cares?

Supremely, it is the Lord's responsibility to remove this constriction. This is not to diminish human responsibility at all. There may be an unwillingness in a person's mind and heart to respond to biblical truth. Perhaps this is compounded by various painful experiences in the past as well as the present. Furthermore, it could be that this blockage is a sign that true repentance has not occurred. Conversely, none of these causes may apply. What is universally applicable is the Lord's supreme responsibility to care and pastor his people.

This is why we have constantly stressed the primacy of God's character, covenant faithfulness and Christ's atoning sufficiency as we think about biblical faith. If God is not who he is revealed to be in the Bible and the Lord Jesus Christ, then the effort to receive and experience his promises is utterly pointless; Christianity is fraudulent. But if he *is* as he reveals himself to be, then he is the one who takes the saving initiative and undertakes the sustaining endeavour. God is not passive or indifferent to his people. Repeatedly in the Bible he proves and explains his gracious commitment to his people.

In our experience, we may have our years of frustration and pain. These are not denied or minimized. As we considered in chapter 3, however, biblical revelation tells us what can be known and trusted. Edith Schaeffer rightly argued, 'It depends upon what god you are calling on, as to whether anyone is listening, or has power to help, or is able to be with you.'[2] Through Jesus Christ, men and women today can call on the one true God who can powerfully relate to them, answer them and care for them.

God is faithful and constant, despite all *outward* indications such as those found in our immediate circumstances. The point is never to deny these pressing circumstances but to cling tenaciously to certain promises. The Lord Jesus is more committed to his people, both corporate and individual, than his people are dedicated to him. Consequently, we say to those of us who struggle with this constriction, 'On our own it is impossible to remove this problem; but together we can implore and then wait for our sovereign Good Shepherd to work in your heart and mind.' The expectation of the

Lord's supernatural but covenant care is what Paul has in mind when he writes:

> I keep asking that the God of our Lord Jesus Christ, the glorious Father, may give you the Spirit of wisdom and revelation, so that you may know him better. I pray also that the eyes of your heart may be enlightened in order that you may know the hope to which he has called you, the riches of his glorious inheritance in the saints, and his incomparably great power for us who believe. That power is like the working of his mighty strength, which he exerted in Christ when he raised him from the dead and seated him at his right hand in the heavenly realms, far above all rule and authority, power and dominion, and every title that can be given, not only in the present age but also in the one to come (Eph. 1:17–21).

The one with whom the burden of our confidence supremely rests is the Lord. It is not a case of sitting back and waiting for some mystical experience to occur.

Rather, we must make the most of the ordinary ways in which God meets his people: prayer, Bible reading, fellowship, service and worship. Yet these are not means to catch the attention of a distant God who is far too busy with the problems of the universe to be concerned with ordinary, late-twentieth-century men and women. Our confidence is both active and restful because, through faith, we are in a redeemed and restored relationship with a God of proven and constantly demonstrated faithfulness and concern. He also brings us into new relationships with others in Christian fellowship.

The role of the gathered community

Of course, some readers could exclaim, 'I want this confidence, I want to be this sure. But I feel so alone.' There are few sadder cries than this one. Furthermore, it is nothing short of a tragedy to hear this from the lips of a contemporary Christian. But it is common. Why?

Too frequently churches do not proclaim and teach biblical

truth. The reasons for this are manifold, and explaining this failure would take another book. We may say, regretfully, that the late-twentieth-century Christian church is not helping itself and the world. We are living in a postmodern generation, in which even church leaders and teachers lead people into foolishness, immorality and heresy. Is it any wonder that the world mocks with derision? Is it any surprise that many believers, young and old, struggle with confusion and uncertainty?

The prophet Isaiah employed a vivid image to describe the moral, intellectual and spiritual catastrophe of his people:

> So justice is far from us,
>   and righteousness does not reach us.
> We look for light, but all is darkness;
>   for brightness, but we walk in deep shadows.
> Like the blind we grope along the wall,
>   feeling our way like men without eyes.
> At midday we stumble as if it were twilight;
>   among the strong, we are like the dead.
>
> (Is. 59:9–10)

Is our problem any different? What, then, are we to do to help us all know and experience Christian confidence in this changing age? I hinted at the possibilities earlier in this chapter. This book cannot fully develop specific pastoral practices; but the following implications are unavoidable.

Those of us in leadership and with pastoral responsibility must wake up and, in some cases, repent. Christians will not have legitimate confidence while they remain in churches where biblical truth is not taught and current intellectual foolishness and ethical immorality are embraced. They may feel sure and act with sincerity, but they will be ignorant and sincerely wrong.

Equally, people cannot be helped if they are prevented from asking questions and thinking. This is not to suggest that every member should become an intellectual, or that biblical Christianity is only for well-educated, middle-class men and women. But how many of us are living fragmented lives? In other words, in our fellowship we are not equipped to worship the Lord in the *totality* of our existence. More often than we want to admit, our music, movies and television speak more loudly and more authoritatively than our Sunday sermons or mid-week Bible studies. Our generation is one in which the diminution of *comprehensive* biblical teaching over the past several decades has left most believers high and dry and dangerously vulnerable to postmodernism's ethics, values and lifestyle.

In my own work I meet university students from many countries. As our western civilization staggers to the end of the twentieth century, I increasingly ask, 'What will this present generation of Christian students contribute, model and pronounce in the decades ahead?' I ask, 'Who will be the leaders? Who will influence my children and grandchildren? Who will point the way to truth? Who will speak for God in the rapidly advancing second Dark Ages?'

These students love Jesus, hunger for supposedly good Bible teaching and want a closer walk with their Saviour. Yet some watch certain movies blind to the explicitly modern views of sexual and ethical morals they portray. These young men and women accept a totally secular view of their self-esteem and self-authentication. They follow the identical pragmatic thinking evident among many non-Christians when it comes to abortion, eugenics and euthanasia. Perhaps I am too harsh; maybe these students are no different from the rest of us.

The gathered community of believers is intended to help and equip people. Men and women are supposed to find in these gatherings acceptance and truth. They are meant to be embraced and included in a new way of living, a Christian counter-culture. No Christian will know and experience Christian confidence apart from such a community.

One principal means by which the Lord shows his care and support for us, after his indwelling Spirit and Word, is other people. This is why Jesus commands us to love one another. Ultimately, we love one another out of loving obedience to him. Nevertheless, we love one another, support one another and forgive one another so that each person may know *experientially* the truth she or he hears and reads about in the Scripture.

Increasingly, as our civilization reaches the end of this century, men and women and children are going to need to see and experience the demonstrated reality of biblical truths. As our society disintegrates at the level of family and personal relationships, the gathered communities of believers must present an alternative. If we fail in this already urgent task, more will lose Christian confidence.

What may we say to those who today struggle with a loss of confidence in the gospel, an uncertainty about the truth in Jesus Christ? Whether it be due to their intellectual problems, sexual struggles, psychological tensions or unidentified sense of numbness, let us urge them not to retreat into themselves. Let us invite them into our homes, to eat, laugh and talk. They require our encouragement to read sound books, listen to good tapes and, perhaps, spend time talking with other people who can handle their questions and problems.[3] It may be difficult to find a sound and helpful Christian gathering where the Bible is faithfully and sanely taught, prayer is encouraged and practised, the communion wine and bread is shared and the attempt to live Christianly in the whole of life is encouraged. Nonetheless, we work hard to support, listen to, care for and love these people. Here is one way for God's people to know and experience legitimate Christian confidence.

But is it worth the risk?

We need a strong and sure basis for choosing, thinking and acting according to God's Word. Two forces work against us. First, our culture presents a strong counter-pressure. Secondly, our own existential experiences tug at our psyches. While Christ's commands are not irrational or anti-human, obeying Christ frequently feels disturbing and bewildering, because of our society and ourselves. The issue is twofold. First, why *should* we do what we are called to do? Secondly, how *can* we do what we are called to do? The answer is: *for Jesus' sake*.

This expression conveys the primacy of Christ in all Christian living, or, better, discipleship. When believers hear the summons to live in a particular way sexually or financially, or in a way that touches their emotions, self-esteem and identity, they can truly respond only because of who Jesus is. We must not try to live Christianly out of a fearful legalism or a self-help moralism. Neither approach is true and, accordingly, neither will be fruitful.

For Jesus' sake emphasizes Jesus' lordship. Because he is who he is, he has every legitimate right to ask us to live his way. His commands are not arbitrary. He is not bound to any laws outside himself. There is no external moral code to which he points us. He defines and determines what is true, good and right. This expression, therefore, stresses the point of reference for all Christian living. It is Jesus who calls us to live specifically in this challenge. It is never Christianity, as a social phenomenon, which calls us to live in a certain way, it is Jesus as person, friend and Saviour. This is a crucial distinction.

For example, a young person learns that she is not to sleep with her boyfriend. Christians tell her this. Her society says the opposite. Assuming she has been sleeping with her boyfriend already, most likely her body (her physical sensations) tell her the opposite. It feels very legitimate. Nonetheless, she has become a Christian, or has been one for some time. Why should she follow biblical sexuality? Not because the Christian group to which she belongs advocates this practice. Sadly, many in this group will be inconsistent. If she has truly become a follower of Jesus she has not simply joined a sub-culture with a particular sexual practice. She is in a good relationship with Jesus Christ. Central implications follow.

The true, life-giving ethical point of reference is Jesus. In his Word, it is Jesus the Lord, the universe's sustainer, who speaks and commands. He has every right to instruct her as he does. It is not enough to say to her, 'Obeying Christ will keep you happy and safe and pure.' If this is our primary appeal, we are crassly utilitarian and not much better than the many available self-help books. Furthermore, it is not *always* true that obeying Christ will make her happier. Depending upon our understanding of 'happiness', she will experience some disturbing discomfort. She will have to say no to herself and to her boyfriend. Most of the time, this self-denial is hard.

Would she really want to do this for the sake of group conformity? 'I'll live like the other Christians to fit in.' True, much of our discipleship is shaped by group witness and agreement. Peer pressure is still operative in many Christian gatherings, and not only for the young Christian. It can be subtle as well as obvious. On one level there is nothing wrong with group conformity, depending upon the pattern to which it is conforming. Still, this basis is not strong enough. It will not hold the weight of our long-term struggles, sacrifice and momentary failures. What will?

Jesus will. We invite and exhort his people to obey him. Ethical rightness is never defined by an external moral code or a Christian community's practice. Jesus, himself, is the one to whom we refer. His rule is legitimate. There is no-one higher than the sovereign Trinity. Christ's lordship is the touchstone of truth and the essence of reality. Because he is who he is, and we are who we are, it is right and proper for him to instruct us how to live. It is true and appropriate for us to live as he commands. *For Jesus' sake*, therefore, expresses an ethic really right and truly authentic. Why should we live a disciples' life? *For Jesus' sake.*

For Jesus' sake also underlines the security of Christian ethics. Following Christ involves sacrifice and cost. Jesus made this abundantly clear. Why should a person take this step of sacrifice? Because Jesus is who he is. He is faithful, trustworthy, sympathetic, powerful, all-sufficient, merciful and gracious. Jesus Christ is the ever-active High Priest. His work as a go-between is a once-accomplished achievement which has present, moment-by-moment implications.

As we step out in obedience, will we be safe? Will our endeavours, self-sacrifice and cultural counter-resistance be in vain? These are meaningful questions. The Bible answers, 'Yes!' The risk, the difficulties and the cost are real, but Jesus can carry the weightiness of our self-surrender. Jesus is on the side of risk-takers. As when we tentatively step out on to ice, we might feel that following Christ in obedience will result in a crash and a plunge.

Yet Scripture teaches us that no-one who steps out in deliberate acts of responsive discipleship does so in vain. Even the call to self-sacrifice and self-abnegation has a fundamental corollary. 'Whoever finds his life will lose it, and whoever loses his life for my sake *will find it*' (Mt. 10:39; *cf.* Mt. 16:25; Mk. 8:35; Lk. 9:24; Jn. 12:25).

I cannot see why a person *should* live the Christian ethic, or more precisely practise discipleship, except for Jesus' sake. Why bother? Legalism and moralism are short-term illusions. Furthermore, it is seriously difficult for a person to live a life based on legalism and moralism. The social benefits of group conformity are temporary. Inherited family or church behavioural traditions are invalid if the guideline is ultimately either tradition or parents. Tradition and parents are true and life-giving only when they point to Jesus' teaching and to Jesus himself. And we cannot authentically know and experience one apart from the other.

I cannot understand *how* a person can live Christianly except for Jesus' sake. Who else can carry the totality of our self-sacrifice? No other creature is capable, in the fullest sense. Who other than Jesus has the right to command us and the legitimate words of mercy and pardon? Only Jesus brings us to the Christian's heavenly Father and enables us to receive the Holy Spirit.

Eyes overflowing with tears

Yet today's Christian could also declare, 'I am part of a gathered community that is very helpful, but I am frightened and uncertain about the world and society. If there is truth in the gospel, the world's evil and brokenness seem more dominant at the moment.' This is a significant problem, and it actually should be a problem for all of us. To walk with God in this generation inevitably brings difficulty.

To begin with, through God's gracious work of regeneration Christians not only view themselves differently but see and understand the world from a new perspective. In Christ, and according to Scripture, believers come to appreciate the world's beauty and humanity's potential.

Several years ago in London there was an exhibition of the work of the French impressionist Claude Monet. Walking through the gallery, I felt wonder and amazement at the creative genius of this man. Visitors were easily entranced by images and impressions of rural France, the tranquillity of Monet's garden and the peacefulness of the Seine. A fellow human being painted those works. He was a human being as we are now. We share a common reality. People do not have to be Christians to paint wonderful works of art. They need only be talented humans. The Bible explains this to us.

Nevertheless, from what we gather, Monet was not interested in biblical Christianity. Philosophically, his work and thinking attempted to move away from his Christian culture. He may have been right to reject some aspects of nineteenth-century French bourgeois Christianity. At the same time, he, as a creative genius, did not seek to worship the creator. A Christian walking through the gallery during that exhibition should have felt the tension expressed in the question, 'How can someone so talented reject the one who gave him this talent?' There is a sense of sadness and disappointment. Why do men and women live like this?

This question is always with God's people. We ask it not only about ourselves but about our culture. But talk about painters and creativity is one thing; thinking about the horrors of today's violent inhumanity and atrocious injustice is completely different.

The more we know truth, the way things are and the way things ought to be, it is inevitable that we will feel a heaviness. Psalm 73 expresses the tension each of us experiences from time to time,

> This is what the wicked are like –
>> always carefree, they increase in wealth.
> Surely in vain have I kept my heart pure;
>> in vain have I washed my hands in innocence.
> All day long I have been plagued;
>> I have been punished every morning.
>
> (Ps. 73:12–14)

The prophet Jeremiah frequently cried out to the Lord. The wrong-doing of his generation appalled him. His close intimacy with the Lord heightened his sense of discomfort.

> Since my people are crushed, I am crushed;
>> I mourn, and horror grips me.
> Is there no balm in Gilead?
>> Is there no physician there?
> Why then is there no healing
>> for the wound of my people?
> Oh, that my head were a spring of water
>> and my eyes a fountain of tears!
> I would weep day and night
>> for the slain of my people.
> Oh, that I had in the desert
>> a lodging place for travellers,
> so that I might my leave my people
>> and go away from them;
> for they are all adulterers,
>> a crowd of unfaithful people.
>
> (Je. 8:21 – 9:2)

Like Jeremiah, we cannot avoid the weight of our culture's offence. Francis Schaeffer declared: 'To think that one can give the Christian message and not have the world with its monolithic, post-Christian culture bear down on us is not to understand the fierceness of the battle in such a day as Jeremiah's or such a day as our own.'[4]

This burden is clearly related to Christian confidence. We grieve for many parts of the world where war occurs. It angers us to read and hear of people in our own country, the victims of evil and criminal violence. At times, we groan in prayer, 'How long, O Lord?' There are moments when we will rightly grow angry at the human waste, degradation and idolatry all around us. We know we do not live in paradise. Our present residence is east of Eden, in Vanity Fair. Most certainly, we grieve; but we do not despair.

Our confidence is in the one who rules in his present lordship. Of course, we ask why evil is allowed to continue and why human grief and suffering lash out at the human race. There is no denying the disturbing conundrum facing God's people. Yet the Bible speaks into our hearts and minds so that we do not despair or go insane. It would be so easy to do both at this point in human history.

But the Scriptures teach us that the Lord is sovereign.

> 'The LORD reigns,
>   let the nations tremble;
> he sits enthroned between the cherubim,
>   let the earth shake.
> Great is the LORD in Zion;
>   he is exalted over all the nations.
> Let them praise your great and awesome name –
>   he is holy.'

(Ps. 99:1–3)

He who is our Saviour and Shepherd is the one who controls and rules the natural elements (see Mk. 4:35-41 and parallels). Jesus is the death-destroyer (1 Cor. 15:53–58; Rev. 1:17–18; 2:7-11). Supremely, though the nations continue in their chaotic disintegration, we do not surrender, we do not sit in despair. We open our voices, our hearts and hands. Our confidence is in the Lamb who is on the throne (Rev. 5:1-14).

Christians are not called to be spiritually indifferent to the suffering of our world, the injustice of our economies, the violence perpetrated by various elements, the social breakdown of our communities and the abandonment of moral truth in our culture. We grieve and are angry too. We also acknowledge that we share in the culpability for these wrongs. Nevertheless, we do not despair, for we hope for a day when the Lamb will judge, and judge righteously. The deep longing we share with non-Christians for justice and restoration will be fulfilled. But they will come in the name of the Lamb; this is why we also plead with men and women to repent and wait in faith for this soon-to-return Lamb.

Contemporary Christians may feel bewilderment and pain as they watch television reports of atrocities in distant lands. We will recoil in horror at the crime and inhumanity we see in our own country. In the coming decades, unless things change, we may well sit in the ruins of our own Jerusalem. But while our eyes overflow with tears, nevertheless, because of Jesus, we may proclaim with the prophet Jeremiah an up-to-date confidence:

> Because of the LORD's great love we are not consumed,
>   for his compassions never fail.
> They are new every morning;
>   great is your faithfulness.
> I say to myself, 'The Lord is my portion;
>   therefore I will wait for him.'
>
> (La. 3:22–24)

Stepping through the door

John Calvin wrote, 'The knowledge of the godly is never so pure but that some bleariness troubles their eyes and obscurity hinders them.'[5] As mentioned in the Introduction to this book, Christians today suffer from this bleariness. In one sense we are not unique. If searching for confidence is normative, it is because blurred vision is common. At the same time, particular aspects of our contemporary age are new. But, the wonder is the ways in which God's timeless truths address the lack of confidence among his people at any age.

The final book in the New Testament is a vision to help all of us to see. In the Revelation given to John at Patmos, all God's redeemed people are meant to see the way things are and, moreover, the way things will be one day. This portion of Scripture unites many earlier themes. There is suffering countered by restoration and judgment. Re-creation is promised; hope's essence is established as reality. What every believer longs for and cries for is shown in picture language to be the way in which reality will be transformed.

> Then I saw a new heaven and a new earth, for the first heaven and the first earth had passed away, and there was no longer any sea. I saw the Holy City, the new Jerusalem, coming down out of heaven from God, prepared as a bride beautifully dressed for her husband. And I heard a loud voice from the throne saying, 'Now the dwelling of God is with men, and he will live with them. They will be his people, and God himself will be with them and be their God. He will wipe every tear from their eyes. There will be no more death or mourning or crying or pain, for the old order of things has passed away' (Rev. 21:1–4).

This is the focal point of our confidence. It is God's work, among God's people, in God's creation, in God's way. We are not on our own. History, in both its ugliness and its glory, is moving towards a final point. What we see and experience around us matters; it has significance. It is the circle in which we make choices, love, laugh, work, communicate and live. The 'now' of our life is the *only* time we have to respond to the gospel of Jesus Christ; it has the dignity of being the context that shapes our eternity.

Nevertheless, what is now will not last for ever. C. S. Lewis claimed that 'what modern Christians find it harder to remember is that the whole life of humanity in this world is also precarious, temporary, provisional'.[6] This is not pessimism or despair; it is the pathway not only to our hope, but to our home. In the world, Christians enjoy life, not withstanding its pains and evil. Simultaneously, we are homesick people. We willingly live and engage in the 'now' of history, but we want to come home. Our longing is for Jesus' return and the hope of the new creation.

To refer to C. S. Lewis again, one of his children's stories, *The*

Last Battle, concludes as the great lion, Aslan, leads the main characters into a new country of Narnia. It is no ordinary journey. Yet as the characters travel on this journey, they discover to their amazement that the new world into which they have come is really their home and country re-ordered. Their world is put back together in the way it was always meant to be.

In their amazement and delight, one of them, a unicorn, sums up what the others feel. 'I have come home at last! This is my real country! I belong here. This is the land I have been looking for all my life, though I never knew it till now. The reason why we loved the old Narnia is that it sometimes looked a little like this.'[7] Aslan the Lion, the Son of the Great Emperor, declares the end of the Shadow-Lands. The story concludes with a dazzling and triumphant restitution. But there is something greater and more significant.

> But the things that began to happen after that were so great and beautiful that I cannot write them. And for us this is the end of all the stories, and we can most truly say that they all lived happily ever after. But for them it was only the beginning of the real story. All their life in this world and all their adventures in Narnia had only been the cover and the title page: now at last they were beginning Chapter One of the Great Story, which no one on earth has read: which goes on for ever: in which every chapter is better than the one before.[8]

Lewis's fiction can serve as a metaphor for the true reality we can know as Christians. A hope and a destiny lie before us. Unlike so many current voices, the truths of God ring out with assurance. Men and women are not alone; they are not orphans in an empty and meaningless universe. There is meaning and purpose. Humanity possesses dignity, though we are at present bent on rebellion and autonomy. Hope and order are already introduced by the words of revelation given by the one true God. We need not live in ignorance. There are things we can and must know. There is a way of living. A rescuer has come. He has done his long-promised work on our behalf and for the Father's good pleasure. Modernity and postmodernity will continue to hurt and wound men and women, but they will not have the final word. On a day to come, every eye will see and behold the great accomplishment and victory. Then all that God's people have waited for through some of their most excruciating experiences will be theirs. On that day, we will come home, find rest, experience the Great Restoration. And before the throne of the Lamb, everything will be completely clear. We will see that what we are given by him to know *now* will enable us then to know completely, even as we are healed, loved and known completely. Of this we need not doubt, we can have confidence.

Questions for reflection and discussion

1. This book's claim is that without a true theological framework, we will not really be able to help each other to know and experience legitimate Christian confidence. Why is it, do you think, so many of us are reluctant to engage in thinking theologically? What could local Christian communities do to help us?

2. How would you respond to the Christian who says, 'But I don't feel anything any more from my Christianity. I wonder if the whole thing is painfully useless'?

3. Why is it important to appreciate, in Lewis's words, that 'the whole life of humanity in this world is also precarious, temporary, provisional'? How do we keep a proper vision of the present, and of our responsibilities in the present, while having an eye on the future?

Notes

Introduction

1. Diogenes Allen, *Christian Belief in a Postmodern World: The Full Wealth of Conviction* (Louisville, Kentucky: Westminster/John Knox Press, 1989), p. 1.
2. Some readers will recognize immediately that this definition echoes John Calvin's definition of faith in his *Institutes of the Christian Religion*, III.2.7 (the Library of Christian Classics edition, volumes XX and XXI, edited by John T. McNeill and translated by Ford Lewis Battles; Philadelphia: Westminster, 1960, vol. XX, p. 551). (All subsequent references are taken from this edition, and referred to as *Institutes*.)

   I recognize that this definition gives greater weight to an individual's relationship with God than to a corporate relationship. In no way do I wish to minimize the New Testament emphasis on the corporate body of Christ, for this is the predominate consideration in Scripture. To be sure, Christians raise questions about their corporate relationship with the Lord. But in our western experience, admittedly individualistic, I sense that this corporate identity is experienced and understood at a fundamentally personal level. Perhaps this is one of the problems a western Christian brings as he or she reads the Bible. Nevertheless, from my own pastoral experience, I think the search for confidence, as illustrated here, is more a personal problem than a corporate issue. This is not to deny a corporate or community responsibility towards an individual wrestling with the question of confidence. As I suggest in chapter 9, the community is one of the means through which God provides us with confidence.
3. Our English verb, 'to assure', is derived from the Latin *adsecurus*, implying security. In the biblical languages there is a variety of related words. One of the more frequent words in the New Testament is *parrēsia* (thirty-one times) and its verbal form *parrēsiazomai* (nine times), both suggesting outspokenness and directness in speech; in the majority of uses the word refers to persons, either in public or before men of high rank. For example see Mk. 8:32; Jn. 7:13; 7:26; 10:24; 16:25, 29; Acts 4:13; 4:31; 28:31;

13:46; 14:3; 1 Thes. 2:2. The word also refers to the apostles' confidence in the gospel they were charged to preach: see Acts 2:29; 9:27; 2 Cor. 3:12. It is worth noting that this word group also points to the believers' standing before God. In these cases there is an inextricable association with faith. See Eph. 3:12; 1 Tim. 3:13; Heb. 3:6; 4:16; 10:19; 10:35; 1 Jn. 2:28; 3:21; 4:17; 5:14.

The other important New Testament word is *bebaios* and its derivatives – translated more often as sure promise, hope, confidence or confirmation. See Rom. 4:16; 2 Cor. 1:7; Heb. 2:2; 3:14; 6:19; 9:17; 2 Pet. 1:10; 1:19; Mk. 16:20; Rom. 15:8; 1 Cor. 1:6; 1:8; 2 Cor. 1:21; Col. 2:7; Heb. 2:3; Phil. 1:7; Heb. 6:16.

See the article by H. Schönweiss on *bebaios* in vol. 1 of *The New International Dictionary of New Testament Theology*, ed. Colin Brown, 3 vols. (Grand Rapids, MI: Zondervan Publishing House, [2]1979), pp. 658–660 (hereafter referred to as *DNTT*). See also the article by A. Fuchs in *Exegetical Dictionary of the New Testament*, ed. Horst Balz and Gerhard Schneider (Grand Rapids, MI: Eerdmans, 1990), vol. 1, pp. 210–211 (hereafter referred to as *EDNT*).

4. Two helpful books which deal with doubt positively and constructively are Os Guinness, *Doubt: Faith in Two Minds* (Tring: Lion Publishing, 1979) and Alister McGrath, *Doubt: Handling It Honestly* (Leicester: Inter-Varsity Press, 1990).
5. John Calvin, *Institutes*, III.ii.17, p. 562.

1. The face in the mirror

1. Garrison Keillor, *Leaving Home* (New York: Viking, 1987), p. xv.
2. This is dealt with in chapters 6–8.
3. Richard F. Lovelace, *Dynamics of Spiritual Life: An Evangelical Theology of Renewal* (Downers Grove, IL: InterVarsity Press; Exeter: Paternoster, 1979), p. 101. Emphasis his.
4. The issue of the fall is dealt with more fully in chapter 4.
5. The issue of judgment is considered more fully in chapter 6, in relationship to the death of Christ, and in chapter 8, on the believer's assurance and perseverance.
6. John Owen, *The Nature, Power, Deceit and Prevalency of the Remainders of Indwelling Sin in Believers* (1668) in vol. 6 of *The Works of John Owen*, ed. William H. Goold, 16 vols. (Edinburgh and Carlisle: Banner of Truth, 1965), p. 201.
7. Dietrich Bonhoeffer, *The Cost of Discipleship* (New York: Macmillan, [2]1969), p. 68.
8. D. A. Carson, *How Long, O Lord?* (Leicester: Inter-Varsity Press; Grand Rapids: Baker Book House, 1990), p. 16.

9. Sogyal Rinpoche, *The Tibetan Book of Living and Dying* (San Francisco: HarperSanFrancisco; London: Rider, 1992), p. 375.

10. See C. S. Lewis, *The Problem of Pain* (London: Bles, 1940; New York: Macmillan, 1962). Other works of help are: John W. Wenham, *The Enigma of Evil* (Leicester: Inter-Varsity Press, 1985); Philip Yancey, *Where is God When it Hurts?* (Grand Rapids, MI: Zondervan, 1977); Jerry Bridges, *Trusting God Even When Life Hurts* (Amersham-on-the-Hill: Scripture Press, 1989), and D. A. Carson, *How Long, O Lord?* (Grand Rapids, MI: Baker Book House; Leicester: Inter-Varsity Press, 1990).

11. This idea is treated more fully in chapter 7.

12. By using these terms 'perfect' and 'secondary', I am not accepting such a distinction. I use them here only because within some Christian circles the terms are employed in everyday speech. The reader is encouraged to see the important study by Garry Friesen, *Decision Making and the Will of God* (Portland, OR: Multnomah, 1980), pp. 23–147. This is a stimulating and indispensable book. He provides a helpful critique of what he calls the 'traditional view' of guidance. My identification of the pit of Wrong Choice is a cartoon of certain extremes within the traditional view that Friesen helpfully challenges. Yet I think there is a potential problem with the application of Friesen's thesis. One could assume that God is not concerned with the *particulars* of an individual's life.

13. This is particularly the potential error I perceive in the book by Friesen, *Decision Making*, pp. 151ff. Friesen is quite right to liberate conservative evangelicals from the straitjacket of what I have called a deterministic view of guidance. There is freedom in the choice of the Christian. God is primarily concerned with the way in which we choose. Yet my criticism of Friesen concerns his far-too-tidy distinction between God's moral will and sovereign will, categories I rather suspect we impose upon Scripture. Equally I think he draws too convenient a distinction between our freedom to chose under God and the actual choice: both must somehow or other come within the very personal relationship we have as children of God. Where then does prayer enter?

14. Eugene H. Peterson, *A Long Obedience in the Same Direction: Discipleship in an Instant Society* (Downers Grove, IL: InterVarsity Press, 1980), pp. 11–12.

15. While reference is made to these passages, I do not suggest they warrant this kind of fear. I am only indicating where people might receive the idea of an unpardonable sin. Their interpretation may be way off the mark. See chapter 8 for a closer examination of this issue.

16. Martin Luther, *A Commentary on Saint Paul's Epistle to the Galatians* (Grand Rapids: Baker Book House, 1979), p. 505. Luther is commenting on Gal. 5:16. See also John Calvin, *Institutes* III.3.10, p. 602.
17. Following the definition given in the Introduction, p. 14.
18. John Bunyan, *The Pilgrim's Progress* (1678: Old Tappan, NJ: Fleming H. Revell, 1975), pp. 106–107.

2. The shifting sands

1. O. B. Hardison, Jr, *Disappearing Through the Skylight: Culture and Technology in the Twentieth Century* (New York and Harmondsworth: Penguin Books, 1989 and 1990), pp. xii-xiii.
2. For a general introduction to the flow of western thought, Colin Brown, *Philosophy and the Christian Faith* (Downers Grove, IL: InterVarsity Press, 1968) is helpful, 'reader-friendly' and based on thorough research. While at some points a bit too sweeping, Francis A. Schaeffer, *How Should We Then Live?* in *The Complete Works of Francis A. Schaeffer*, vol. 5 (Westchester, IL: Crossway Books, 1982) is a book well worth studying. Of special merit is Os Guinness, *The Dust of Death* (Downers Grove, IL: InterVarsity Press, [2]1979; Inter-Varsity Press, London, 1973).

   For those interested in pursuing the subjects more closely, especially postmodernism, see the following works: Walter Truett Anderson, *Reality Isn't What It Used To Be* (San Francisco: Harper, 1990); Barry Smart, *Postmodernity* (London and New York: Routledge, 1993); David Harvey, *The Condition of Postmodernity: An Enquiry into the Origins of Cultural Change* (Cambridge, MA, and Oxford: Blackwell, 1989); Thomas C. Oden, *After Modernity . . . What? Agenda for Theology* (Grand Rapids, MI: Zondervan, 1990); John Carroll, *Humanism: The Wreck of Western Culture* (London: Fontana, 1993); Matei Calinescu, *Five Faces of Modernity* (Durham, NC: Duke University Press, 1987); Kenneth J. Gergen, *The Saturated Self: Dilemmas of Self Identity in Contemporary Life* (San Francisco: HarperCollins, 1991); and, as mentioned in note 1 above, Hardison, *Disappearing Through the Skylight*.
3. David Harvey, *The Condition of Postmodernity: An Enquiry into the Origins of Cultural Change* (Cambridge, MA, and Oxford: Blackwell, 1989), p. 13.
4. John Carroll, *Humanism: The Wreck of Western Culture* (London: Fontana, 1993), p. 6.
5. Thomas C. Oden, *After Modernity . . . What? Agenda for Theology* (Grand Rapids, MI: Zondervan, 1990), pp. 45–51. On pp. 48–49

Oden presents a very helpful and concise diagrammatic summary. By his own admission, this is a thumbnail sketch; but it is singularly concise and helpful as an introduction. Another diagram is found in Harvey, *The Condition of Postmodernity*, p. 43. His chapter on 'Modernism and Modernity' (pp. 10–38) is very helpful, once some general themes and names are known. For a more detailed, and very specialist, analysis of modernity and modernism, see Matei Calinescu, *Five Faces of Modernity* (Durham, NC: Duke University Press, 1987), pp. 13–92.

6. Diogenes Allen, *Christian Belief in a Postmodern World: The Full Wealth of Conviction* (Louisville, KY: Westminster/John Knox Press, 1989), p. 3.

7. *Ibid.*, p. 3.

8. *Ibid.*, p. 3.

9. *Ibid.*, pp. 4–5.

10. *Ibid.*, p. 5.

11. Smart, *Postmodernity*, p. 88.

12. Smart, *Postmodernity*, p. 91.

13. See Calinescu, *Five Faces*, especially pp. 265–279.

14. Anderson, *Reality*, p. 75.

15. Looking back on the anti-modernist sixties could well be an important task facing those involved in apologetics and evangelism in the postmodernist nineties. Theodore Rozak's *The Making of a Counter-Culture* (New York: Doubleday, 1969) is a classic study. Os Guinness' *The Dust of Death* is a superb help for the Christian, reissued by Crossway Books (USA), 1994.

16. Harvey, *The Condition of Postmodernity*, p. 38.

17. Anderson, *Reality*, p. 44.

18. Nicholas J. Fox, *Postmodernism, Sociology and Health* (Buckingham, and Philadelphia, PA: Open University Press, 1993), p. 7.

19. See Harvey, *The Condition of Postmodernity*, pp. 44–45.

20. Harvey, *The Condition of Postmodernity*, p. 52.

21. Robert Venturi, *Complexity and Contradiction* (New York: Museum of Modern Art, 1977), p. 17, as quoted in Gergen, *The Saturated Self*, p. 115.

22. See Harvey, *The Condition of Postmodernity*, pp. 48–49.

23. Anderson, *Reality*, p. 79.

24. I regard Harvey, *The Condition of Postmodernity*, pp. 49–52, Anderson, *Reality*, pp. 79–102, and Gergen, *The Saturated Self*, pp. 81–110, as some of the clearest aids to understanding this vast field. The scholarly work that has stimulated my own attempts to respond is N. T. Wright, *The New Testament and the People of God* (London: SPCK, 1992), especially, pp. 47–80.

25. Peter L. Berger, *The Heretical Imperative: Contemporary Possibilities of Religious Affirmation* (Garden City, NY: Anchor Press, 1979), pp. xiff.

26. Lesslie Newbigin, *Foolishness to the Greeks: The Gospel and Western Culture* (London: SPCK, 1986; Grand Rapids, MI: Eerdmans, 1986), p. 14. See also Os Guinness, *The Gravedigger File* (Downers Grove, IL: InterVarsity Press, 1983), pp. 93–105.

27. Michel Foucault, *Power/Knowledge: Selected Interviews and Other Writings 1972–1977*, ed. C. Gordon (Brighton: Harvester Press, 1980), p. 133, quoted in Smart, *Postmodernity*, p. 82.

28. Anderson, *Reality*, p. xii.

29. Allan Bloom, *The Closing of The American Mind: How Higher Education has Failed Democracy and Impoverished the Souls of Today's Students* (Harmondsworth: Penguin Books, 1988), pp. 25–26.

30. For a helpful guide to religious and philosophical relativism see Harold A. Netland, *Dissonant Voices: Religious Pluralism and the Question of Truth* (Grand Rapids, MI: Eerdmans, Leicester: Apollos, 1991), especially pp. 166–180.

31. I am indebted to Dick Keyes of L'Abri Fellowship, who made this point in a public lecture entitled 'Pluralism, Relativism and Tolerance' at Cambridge University on 1 December 1990.

32. Harvey, *The Condition of Postmodernity*, p. 54.

33. Michael Medved, *Hollywood vs. America* (New York: HarperCollins, 1992), p. 225.

34. A. N. Wilson, *Jesus* (London: Sinclair-Stevenson, 1992), p. 240.

35. N. T. Wright, *Who Was Jesus?* (London: SPCK, 1992).

36. Wilson, *Jesus*, pp. 240–241.

37. Sogyal Rinpoche, *The Tibetan Book of Living and Dying* (San Francisco: HarperSanFrancisco; London: Rider, 1992), p. 13.

38. We should study both Jesus' words to Thomas in John 20:29 and the author's statement in 20:30–31. Likewise, note the author's stress on eyewitness objective authentication in John 20:6–9. Paul's claim in 1 Corinthians 15:1–8 assumes a category of knowledge involving historical events (while seen through the eyes of an interpretative 'filter') that very much determine the credibility of faith's claim.

39. Guinness, *The Gravedigger File*, p. 51.

40. Hans Küng, *On Being a Christian* (Eng. trans. Glasgow: Collins, 1974), pp. 26–27.

41. Two of the more helpful works are Russell Chandler, *Understanding The New Age* (Dallas, TX: Word, 1988), and Douglas R. Groothuis, *Unmasking the New Age* (Downers Grove, IL: InterVarsity Press, 1986; Leicester: Inter-Varsity Press, 1991).

42. Alister E. McGrath, *The Renewal of Anglicanism* (London: SPCK, 1993), p. 17. Dr McGrath's point is tantalizing, and it is regrettable that he does not elaborate. I suspect, for the reasons I present in this chapter, that he may be more optimistic than I.
43. Smart, *Postmodernity*, p. 89.
44. Paul Tournier, *The Whole Person in a Broken World* (Eng. trans. San Francisco: Harper and Row, 1964), p. 12.
45. Kevin Fedarko, 'MTV Rocks Europe', *Time* (International), 29 March 1993, p. 68.
46. Stephen W. Hawking, *A Brief History of Time: From the Big Bang to Black Holes* (London: Bantam, 1988), p. 171.
47. *Ibid.*, p. 174.

3. The majesty of revelation

1. See Introduction, p. 14.
2. Calvin makes this point quite plainly in his treatment of the witness of the Holy Spirit as the verifier of Scripture: 'The Word will not find acceptance in men's hearts before it is sealed by the inward testimony of the Spirit. The same Spirit, therefore, who has spoken through the mouths of the prophets must penetrate into our hearts to persuade us that they faithfully proclaimed what had been divinely commanded.' *Institutes* I.7, p. 79.
3. N. T. Wright, *The New Testament and the People of God* (London: SPCK, 1992), pp. 41–42.
4. Emil Brunner, *Dogmatics*, vol. 1: *The Christian Doctrine of God* (Eng. trans. London: Lutterworth, 1949), p. 14.
5. In this respect, James Sire is quite right to insist that 'epistemology can best be framed by starting with *ontology*. *What is* is prior to *what can be known*, for knowing itself implies the existence of a knower and something to be known.' *Discipleship of the Mind* (Downers Grove, IL: InterVarsity Press, 1990; Leicester: InterVarsity Press, 1990), note 9, p. 207, emphasis his.
6. This point is helpfully made by Paul Helm, *The Divine Revelation* (London: Marshall, Morgan and Scott, 1982), pp. 1–2.
7. J. I. Packer, *God Has Spoken* (London: Hodder and Stoughton, 1979), p. 46.
8. The question of the Bible and God's revelation is vast and complicated. The number of books and articles written on this topic is quite extensive. In this chapter I only sketch some of the essential arguments for a legitimate confidence in the Bible. Those wishing to study this issue more closely should consult the fuller, although slightly differing, approaches of the following: D. A.

Carson, *Exegetical Fallacies* (Grand Rapids, MI: Baker Book House, 1984); Peter Cotterell and Max Turner, *Linguistics and Biblical Interpretation* (Downers Grove, IL: InterVarsity Press, 1989); David L. Edwards and John Stott, *Essentials* (US title *Evangelical Essentials*): *A Liberal–Evangelical Dialogue* (London: Hodder and Stoughton, 1988; Downers Grove IL: InterVarsity Press, 1989), especially pp. 41–106; Gordon D. Fee and Douglas Stuart, *How to Read the Bible For All its Worth* (Grand Rapids, MI: Zondervan, 1982; London: Scripture Union, 1983); Graeme Goldsworthy, *According to Plan* (Leicester: Inter-Varsity Press; Homebush West, NSW: Lancer, 1991); Paul Helm, *The Divine Revelation* (London: Marshall, Morgan and Scott; Westchester, IL: Crossway Books, 1982); I. Howard Marshall (ed.), *New Testament Interpretation* (Grand Rapids, MI: Eerdmans; Exeter: Paternoster, 1977); Leon Morris, *I Believe in Revelation* (Grand Rapids, MI: Eerdmans; London: Hodder and Stoughton, 1976); J. I. Packer, *God Has Spoken* (London: Hodder and Stoughton, 1979); *idem, Freedom, Authority and Scripture* (Leicester: Inter-Varsity Press, 1982); R. C. Sproul, *Knowing Scripture* (Downers Grove, IL: InterVarsity Press, 1977); A. C. Thiselton, *The Two Horizons* (Exeter: Paternoster, 1980), and Wright, *The New Testament*.

9. William Wordsworth, *The Prelude or Growth of a Poet's Mind* (1805), book VI: lines 635–640, in M. H. Abrams, *et al.* (eds.), *The Norton Anthology of English Literature,* vol. 2 (New York: Norton, 1968), pp. 186–187.

10. Os Guinness, *The Dust of Death* (Downers Grove, IL: InterVarsity Press, [2]1979: Inter-Varsity Press, 1973), p. 226. Although this work is over twenty years old, its relevance is even more striking. Guinness' study of western culture as it emerged out of the sixties can give us an insight into the nineties' pantheism, attraction to eastern mysticism and, tragically, the re-emerging interest in LSD and other mind-orienting chemical experimentation.

11. The critical reader will observe here that I accept the notion that words are referential. Words take on their meanings and significance not in an arbitrary fashion. It is true that convention shapes language, and this should not be underestimated by even the conservative interpreter. At the same time, the essential humanness of language and symbols as communicating signs necessitates a greater degree of consistency and conformity than mere social convention. I argue that language may well have multiple levels, but there is a level that transcends social conformity.

12. The critical reader is encouraged to read Cotterell and Turner, *Linguistics,* pp. 11–76, and, although more challenging, Anthony

C. Thiselton, 'Semantics and New Testament Interpretation' in Marshall, (ed.), *New Testament Interpretation*, pp. 75–104. My opinion is that a popular, clear, readable and thorough work on the co-ordination between revelation and language has yet to be written.

13. See Cotterell and Turner, *Linguistics.*

14. Cotterell and Turner, *Linguistics*, p. 69.

15. Gordon D. Fee and Douglas Stuart, *How to Read the Bible For All its Worth* (Grand Rapids, MI: Zondervan, 1982; London: Scripture Union, 1983).

16. Anthony Bash, *Stepping Into Bible Study* (New Malden, Surrey; Colorado Springs, CO: NavPress, 1988).

17. I am especially indebted to Tom Wright's arguments in *The New Testament*, chapter 3, pp. 47–80. Those who wish to pursue this further are encouraged to read this material and the suggested literature in Wright's footnotes.

18. Calvin, *Institutes* I.1.1, p. 35.

19. Calvin, *Institutes* I.1.1; note 3, p. 36.

20. Wright, *The New Testament*, pp. 32–46.

21. To anticipate myself, let me stress that when I use the fashionable, postmodern word *story*, I do not deny the trustworthiness and accuracy of the narrative accounts in the Bible. These stories refer to *referents* that took place in real time and real space. I follow Tom Wright's suggestion that 'Stories are a basic constituent of human life; they are, in fact, one key element within the total construction of a worldview' (Wright, *The New Testament*, p. 38). He goes on, 'That is, when creational and covenantal monotheists tell their story, the most basic level of story for their worldview is *history*. To say that we can analyse stories successfully without reference to their possible public reference, and therefore that we cannot or should not make such a reference, is to commit the kind of epistemological mistake against which I have been arguing . . . It is to deny referent by emphasizing sense-data. If we fail to see the importance of the actual historical nature of some at least of the stories told by Jews of this period, we fail to grasp the significance, in form as well as content, of the stories themselves' (p. 78).

22. David L. Wolfe, *Epistemology: The Justification of Belief* (Downers Grove, IL: InterVarsity Press, 1982), p. 71.

23. The reader is best advised to see the whole of Netland's argument in *Dissonant Voices: Religious Pluralism and the Question of Truth* (Grand Rapids, MI: Eerdmans; Leicester: Apollos, 1991), but especially pp. 106–111 and 200.

24. James Sire, *The Universe Next Door* (Downers Grove, IL: InterVarsity Press, 1976; Leicester: Inter-Varsity Press, 1977), pp. 16–19. This highly recommended book has been up-dated in recent years in a new edition (1988).

25. See Netland's summation in *Dissonant Voices*, pp. 106–111.

4. The seriousness of the fall

1. Diary, *Independent*, 17 December 1991, p. 17.

2. M. Scott Peck, *The Road Less Traveled* (New York: Simon and Schuster, [2]1979), p. 44.

3. See chapter 2, p. 63.

4. Thomas L. Thompson, *The Origin Tradition of Ancient Israel: The Literary Formation of Genesis and Exodus 1 – 23, Journal for the Study of the Old Testament* Supplement Series 55 (Sheffield: JSOT Press, 1987), p. 202. In fairness to Dr Thompson, he makes a good case for trying to understand the text (in this case the stories) rather than allowing one's systematic framework to dominate. His challenge is fair. But what really are we to do *in response* to the text? The narratives are not neutral, but compelling and inviting. Furthermore, Gn. 1 – 3 does not stand in isolation from its canonical context. These ancient narratives are placed into a totality greater than its individual parts. This includes the New Testament's *theological* interpretative grid. I cannot agree with Thompson's argument that 'to read Genesis as theology is much more a product of Paul, Augustine, and Christian tradition's need, than of the narratives themselves' (p. 202). Why did not Thompson include Jesus, who made a theological interpretation of Gn. 2:25 in Mt. 19:4–7 (*cf.* Mk. 10:1–9)? On the precedent of the Old Testament, Paul and Jesus, it is legitimate to ask what these narratives tell us theologically – provided we listen to Thompson's plea to respect the narrative genre.

5. Francis Schaeffer, *Genesis in Space and Time*, in *The Complete Works of Francis A. Schaeffer* (Westchester, IL: Crossway Books, 1982), vol. 2, pp. 3–4.

6. See the interesting argument of Gerhard von Rad, *Genesis* (Eng. trans. Philadelphia: Westminster, 1972), pp. 31–43. Von Rad prefers the term *saga*. This category is not at all unhistorical. I would not, however, follow von Rad completely. He places the weight of historical authentication on Israel's experience with God. He seems to play down the propositional aspect of these narratives.

7. See C. E. B. Cranfield, *The Epistle to the Romans*, vol. 1 (Edinburgh:

T. and T. Clark, [2]1980), pp. 413–417. See also, with its remarkable, almost late-twentieth-century ring, John Calvin, *Commentary on Romans* (Eng. trans. Grand Rapids, MI: Eerdmans, [2]1980; Edinburgh: Oliver and Boyd, 1960), pp. 172–174. For an interesting and slightly different perspective see Martin Luther, *Lectures on Romans* in Hilton C. Oswald (ed.), *Luther's Works*, vol. 25 (St. Louis, MO: Concordia, 1972), pp. 362–363. Luther argues that creation is now subjected to 'vanity'. He means that humanity sees undue worth in, and seeks undue gratification from, the created order. Vanity is a perverted enjoyment.

8. Derek Kidner, *Genesis* (London: Tyndale Press; Downers Grove, IL: InterVarsity Press, 1967), p. 34.

9. As an interesting digression, Kidner, *Genesis*, p. 36, posits the theory that polygamy was a distortion of God's plan. Society placed greater emphasis on the woman's role in procreation. As Kidner points out, this is not the original idea, expressed in Gn. 2:24. Subsequent accounts of patriarchal polygamy and domination must challenge us in the way we read Old Testament narrative. The narratives may lack either an editorial disapproval or a divine disapproval. This silence does not at all suggest condoning or approval. When we examine the narratives in *their total context*, we see that what passed as sexual/relational practice was contrary to God's plan. Often the stories conclude with this verdict. Ultimately, Jesus' words clarify the matter; see Mt. 19:5; Mk. 10:7, 8. See also 1 Cor. 6:16; Eph. 5:31.

10. Quoting Category 301.81, *Diagnostic and Statistical Manual of Mental Disorders* (American Psychiatric Association, 1980). Peter C. Moore, *Disarming the Secular Gods* (Downers Grove, IL: Inter-Varsity Press; Leicester: Inter-Varsity Press, 1989), p. 82.

11. I interpret Eph. 1:3–12 as an important description of the Jewish apostles (including Paul) rather than of the universal church. All Christians share in the benefits described in verses 3–12, but Paul is describing his unique position as 'we, who were the first to hope in Christ'. Verse 13 marks the decisive transition from the apostolic group to the Ephesian believers: 'And you also were included in Christ when you heard the word of truth, the gospel of your salvation.'

12. Kenneth J. Gergen, *The Saturated Self: Dilemmas of Self Identity in Contemporary Life* (San Francisco: HarperCollins, 1991), p. 7.

13. John Milton, *Paradise Lost*, book I:1–5 in M. H. Abrams *et al.* (eds.), *The Norton Anthology of English Literature*, vol. 1 (New York: Norton, 1968), p. 1037.

5. The glory of Jesus Christ

1. Kenneth Rea, 'In Tokyo Rose a Superstar', *The Times*, September 21 1991, p. 7.
2. Wilson, *Jesus* (London: Sinclair-Stevenson, 1992). A very helpful response to this book is N. T. Wright, *Who Was Jesus?* (London: SPCK, 1992).
3. Wilson, *Jesus*, p. xvi.
4. Introduction, p. 14.
5. I do not deny the Gospel writers' own influence and the influence of the 'Christian' communities for whom they wrote. Both are significant influences upon the Gospel material and its arrangement. Nonetheless, I am arguing that the original settings for Jesus' sayings and teaching were Jewish. The Gospel writers appear, for the most part, to underline this Jewish context, even if their material is no longer presented, in every case, in its original setting. They may not have known the original setting, but they maintain a Jewish theological and social background.
6. A good and basic introduction to the present argument is Graeme Goldsworthy, *According to Plan* (Leicester: Inter-Varsity Press; Homebush West, NSW: Lancer, 1991).
7. C. E. B. Cranfield comments on Mk.1:6: 'The voice does not proclaim Jesus' newly established status of sonship consequent upon his installation as Messiah; rather it confirms his already existing filial consciousness. In response to his self-dedication to the mission of the Servant, made in his submission to baptism, he is given a confirmation of his own consciousness of being the Son of God, that is at the same time a confirmation of his Servant-vocation.' *The Gospel According to St Mark* (Cambridge: Cambridge University Press, [2]1977), p. 55.
8. John W. White, 'Jesus and the Idea of a New Age', *The Quest*, Summer 1989, p. 14, emphasis his. Quoted in Douglas Groothuis, *Revealing the New Age Jesus* (Downers Grove, IL: InterVarsity Press; Leicester: Inter-Varsity Press, 1990), p. 16. In no way should John W. White be confused with the Christian psychiatrist, pastor and writer, John White.
9. Edward Schillebeeckx, *Jesus in Our Western Culture* (Eng. trans. London: SCM, 1987), p. 2.
10. Mk. 8:27–29 and parallels; see also Mt. 9:1–8; 11:20–24; 13:53–58; 21:23–27; Lk. 7:18–23; 11:14–28; Jn. 1:10–13; 5:16–47; 6:60–71; 7:25–52; 12:37–49; 20:24–29.
11. See the particulars of the following passages: Eph. 4:20–21; Phil.3:17 – 4:1; Col. 1:15 – 2:23; 1 Tim. 1:15–17; 3:16; 4:9–10; 6:3–

5; 2 Tim 1:13–14; 2:8–13; Tit. 2:1–15; 3:3–11; 2 Pet. 1:12–21; 1 Jn. 4:1–6; 4:13 – 5:21; 2 Jn. 7–11; Jude: 3–4, 20.

12. See the superb study of this whole issue, especially in relation to contemporary religious pluralism, in Harold A. Netland, *Religious Pluralism and the Question of Truth* (Grand Rapids, MI: Eerdmans; Leicester: Apollos, 1991), pp. 235–277. In his footnotes, Netland mentions the essential works for further, detailed reading.

13. See J. N. D. Kelly, *Early Christian Doctrines* (London: A. and C. Black, [5]1977), pp. 223–343. A somewhat easier work to follow is Justo L. González, *A History of Christian Thought*, vol. 1 (Nashville, TN: Abingdon, [2]1979), pp. 234–395.

14. Kelly, *Early Christian Doctrines*, p. 232.

15. Wilson, *Jesus*, p. 255.

16. Wright, *Who Was Jesus?*, p. 51.

17. See Norman Anderson, *The Teaching of Jesus* (Downers Grove, IL: InterVarsity Press, 1983), pp. 151–160; C. K. Barrett, *Jesus and the Gospel Tradition* (London: SPCK, 1967; Philadelphia: Fortress, 1968), pp. 20–34; Günther Bornkamm, *Jesus of Nazareth* (Eng. trans. London: Hodder and Stoughton, [2]1973), Appendix III, pp. 227–232.

18. For Gospel Christology see Larry Chouinard, 'Gospel Christology: A Study of Methodology', *Journal for the Study of the New Testament* 30 (1987), pp. 21–37.

19. For a helpful presentation of this material see Michael Green, 'Jesus in the New Testament', *The Truth of God Incarnate*, ed. Michael Green (Grand Rapids, MI: Eerdmans, 1977), pp. 17–57.

20. G. C. Berkouwer, *The Person of Christ* (Grand Rapids, MI: Eerdmans, 1954; London: Inter-Varsity Press, 1974), p. 96.

21. Rudolph Bultmann, *Jesus and the Word* (Eng. trans. New York: Charles Scribner's Sons, 1934), p. 8.

22. Robert L. Webb, *John the Baptizer and Prophet: a Socio-Historical Study, Journal for the Study of the New Testament* Supplement Series 62 (Sheffield: JSOT Press, 1991), p. 20.

23. E. P. Sanders, *Jesus and Judaism* (Philadelphia: Fortress, 1985), p. 2 quoted in Webb, *John*, p. 20.

24. Wilson, *Jesus*, pp. xvi-xvii. Wilson follows Sanders, and especially Geza Vermes, *Jesus the Jew* (Philadelphia: Fortress, 1973), a seminal study of Jesus in his Jewish context which arrives at particular conclusions about Jesus: it is, however, extremely reductionistic and not in accordance with the gospel.

25. Those wishing to explore this issue further should consult Wright, *Who Was Jesus?* chapter 1, for a helpful survey and bibliography of scholarship over the last 100 years. See also I. Howard Marshall, *I*

Believe in the Historical Jesus (London: Hodder and Stoughton; Grand Rapids, MI: Eerdmans, 1977).

26. This subject is both complicated and highly technical, but the interested reader should consult Joel B. Green, *How To Read the Gospels and Acts* (Downers Grove, IL: InterVarsity Press; Leicester: Inter-Varsity Press, 1987), pp. 69–80; for a more detailed study see Craig Blomberg, *The Historical Reliability of the Gospels* (Downers Grove, IL: InterVarsity Press, Leicester: Inter-Varsity Press, 1987).

27. Bruce M. Metzger, *The Canon of the New Testament* (Oxford: Clarendon Press, ²1989), pp. 262–264. See F. F. Bruce, *The New Testament Documents: Are They Reliable?* (Leicester: Inter-Varsity Press; Grand Rapids, MI: Eerdmans, ⁵1960), pp. 29–61, for a detailed comparison between the Gospels.

28. Wright, *Who Was Jesus?*, p. 96.

29. James W. Sire, *Chris Chrisman Goes To College* (Downers Grove, IL: InterVarsity Press, 1993), pp. 142–143.

30. Detailed arguments may be found in Peter T. O'Brien's volume on *Colossians and Philemon* in the Word Biblical Commentary, vol. 44 (Waco, TX: Word, 1982), pp. xli-xlix, and Murray J. Harris, *Exegetical Guide to the Greek New Testament: Colossians and Philemon* (Grand Rapids, MI: Eerdmans, 1991), pp. 3–4. See also Donald Guthrie, *New Testament Introduction* (Downers Grove, IL: Inter-Varsity Press; Leicester: Inter-Varsity Press, 1990), pp. 572–577.

6. The peace of salvation

1. George Bernard Shaw, *Heartbreak House* (1920), Preface.

2. Anselm was Archbishop of Canterbury from 1093 until his death in 1109. Reference is made here to his work *Cur Deus Homo*.

3. It is true, however, that Jesus warned about a 'false' sense of peace. See Mt. 10:34; Lk. 12:51.

4. See the following examples: Rom. 1:7; 1 Cor. 1:3; 2 Cor. 1:2; Gal. 1:3; Eph. 1:2; Phil. 1:2; Col. 1:2; 1 Thes. 1:1; 2 Thes. 1:2; 1 Tim. 1:2; 2 Tim 1:2; Tit. 1:4; Phm. 3; 1 Pet. 1:2; 2 Pet. 1:2; 2 Jn. 1:3; Jude 2; and Rev. 1:4. The relevant Greek word is *eirēnē*. It closely parallels the Hebrew *šālôm*. See the article by H. Beck and C. Brown in *DNTT*, vol. 2 pp. 776–783. In the New Testament it is very much linked with salvation and the messianic fulfilment in Jesus' ministry. Blessing, healing and restoration are associated and interrelated benefits. For a helpful treatment see also the article by V. Hasler in *EDNT*, vol. 1, pp. 394–397.

5. Wilfred Owen, 'Anthem for Doomed Youth' in M. H. Abrams

(ed.), *The Norton Anthology of English Literature*, vol. 2 (New York: Norton, ²1968), p. 1856.

6. Many would prefer to stress the life of Jesus, and his teaching. In this chapter I certainly do not seek to minimize the significance of the life of Jesus Christ. But I do argue that the crucial importance of Jesus' earthly life and ministry is seen in his death. This is the New Testament writers' primary, although not sole, focus. Leon Morris's point is well made: 'But our examination of the evidence leads us to think that the view that "the blood" directs our attention primarily to "the life" is erroneous, and that, in point of fact, the Scriptures of both Old and New Testaments stress the death when they make use of this expression . . . the impression left by those biblical passages which refer to the blood of Christ is that they are pointing us to the death of the Lord considered as the means whereby sin is dealt with, not merely the means whereby man may be inspired to deal with it.' *The Apostolic Preaching of the Cross* (London: Tyndale Press, 1955), pp. 276–277.

7. Much of the argument developed in this section can be evaluated in the clear light of the following fuller works: Michael Green, *The Empty Cross of Jesus* (London: Hodder and Stoughton, 1984); John Stott, *The Cross of Christ* (Leicester: Inter-Varsity Press; Downers Grove; IL: InterVarsity Press, 1986); Leon Morris, *The Apostolic Preaching*; and *idem*, *The Cross in the New Testament* (Exeter: Paternoster, 1967).

8. See the article on *stauros* by E. Brandenburger in *DNTT*, vol. 1, pp. 391–403. For a Roman view on crucifixion see Stott, *The Cross of Christ*, p. 24.

9. Cicero, *Against Veres*, II.v.64, para. 165, quoted in Stott, *The Cross of Christ*, p. 24.

10. Josephus, *Jewish Wars*, V.11.1 in *The Works of Josephus*, trans. William Whiston (Lynn, MA: Hendrickson, 1980), p. 565.

11. Justin, *Dialogue with Trypho*, 89, quoted in Michael Green, *Evangelism in the Early Church* (London: Hodder and Stoughton; Grand Rapids, MI: Eerdmans, 1970), p. 31.

12. See Green, *Evangelism in the Early Church*, pp. 30–31.

13. See, for example, Mk. 8:31; 9:12; Lk. 24:45–46; Jn. 3:16; Acts 2:23; 3:18; 1 Cor. 15:3.

14. C. S. Lewis, *The Problem of Pain* (London: Bles, 1940; New York: Macmillan, 1943), p. 40.

15. See Dt. 9:8; Ps. 21:9; 85:3; 90:11; Is. 9:19; 26:20; Je. 3:5; 7:29; Ezk. 22:20–31; Hab. 3:2; Mt. 3:7; Jn. 3:36; Rom. 1:18; 3:5; Eph. 2:3; 1 Thes. 1:10; Rev. 6:16–17.

16. The Greek in this verse does not explicitly say 'sin offering' as the

NIV suggests. It is better to translate the phrase as 'concerning sin' (*peri hamartias*). I follow Cranfield, *The Epistle to the Romans*, vol. 1 (Edinburgh: T. and T. Clark, ²1980), p. 382, and C. K. Barrett, *A Commentary on the Epistle to the Romans* (London: Adam and Charles Black, ²1962), p. 156. Still, the implication is clear: Christ's self-giving to die was for sin and the establishment of righteous forgiveness.

17. Martin Luther, *A Commentary on St Paul's Epistle to the Galatians* (Grand Rapids: Baker Book House, 1975), p. xxiii.

18. See the superb practical work by Alister McGrath, *Roots that Refresh: A Celebration of Reformation Spirituality* (London: Hodder and Stoughton, 1991), pp. 170–176.

19. G. Schrenk, '*dikaiosynē*' in Gerhard Kittel and Gerhard Friedrich (eds.), *Theological Dictionary of the New Testament*. Abridged in one volume by Geoffrey W. Bromiley (Grand Rapids: Eerdmans, 1985), pp. 173–174. Hereafter referred to as *TDNT*.

20. Goldsworthy, *Gospel and Kingdom*, p. 55.

21. This is explained further in chapter 7.

22. John Owen, *Doctrine of the Saints' Perseverance Explained and Confirmed* (1654), in Thomas Russell (ed.), *The Works of John Owen, DD,* 20 vols. (London: Richard Baynes, 1826-), vol. 6, p. 156.

23. See 2 Cor. 5:16–21; Gal. 5:16–26; Heb. 6:1–6; 10:26ff.; 1 Jn. 1:5, 8–10; 2:3–4, 9–10; 3:19–24.

24. See Rom. 6:1–14; 2 Cor. 5:17; Col. 2:10–12, 20.

25. See 1 Cor. 15:51; 2 Cor. 3:18; Phil. 3:12, 21; 1 Jn. 3:2–3.

26. Here I follow Barrett, *Romans*, pp. 151–152, and Cranfield, *Romans*, vol. 1, p. 341.

27. *Romans*, Cranfield, vol. 1, p. 342.

28. See the following: Jn. 3:6, 8; 16:8–11; Acts 2:38, 39; 10:44; 11:15–18; Rom. 7:6; 8:1–17; 15:16; 1 Cor. 6:18–20; 2 Cor. 3:3–18; Gal. 3:2; 5:16–26; Eph. 4:30; 1 Thes. 1:5; 4:3–4; 2 Thes. 2:13; Tit. 3:5; 1 Pet. 1:2. See also Ps. 51:11; Ezk. 36:26–27; 37:14; Joel 2:28–29.

29. Calvin, *Commentary on 1 Peter*, p. 244, commentating on 1 Pet. 1:14.

30. Richard Baxter, *A Christian Directory* (1673), in *The Practical Works of the Rev. Richard Baxter*, ed. William Orme, 23 vols. (London: James Duncan, 1830-), vol. 2, p. 197.

31. Bunyan, *Pilgrim's Progress*, pp. 33–34.

32. See p. 86.

7. The nature of Christian faith

1. Richard Dawkins, 'A Scientist's Case against God', *Independent*, 20 April 1992, p. 17, an edited version of a speech at the Edinburgh

International Science Festival on 15 April 1992.

2. John R. W. Stott, *The Message of Acts* (Leicester: Inter-Varsity Press; Downers Grove, IL: InterVarsity Press, 1990), p. 291.

3. Harold A. Netland, *Dissonant Voices: Religious Puralism and the Question of Truth* (Grand Rapids, MI: Eerdmans; Leicester: Apollos, 1991), pp. 126–127. In this quote Netland is referring to Ronald Nash, *The Word of God and the Mind of Man* (Grand Rapids, MI: Zondervan, 1982), pp. 46ff.

4. See 1 Cor. 1:9; 10:13; 1 Thes. 5:24; Heb. 10:23; 1 Jn. 1:9.

5. Alister McGrath, *Affirming Your Faith* (US title *I Believe*): *Exploring the Apostles' Creed* (Leicester: Inter-Varsity Press; Grand Rapids, MI: Zondervan, 1991), p. 19, italics his.

6. See Rom. 1:17; 3:22; 4:13–19; 5:2; Gal. 2:16; Heb. 4:2; 11:1ff.; 1 Pet. 1:5; 1 Jn. 5:4; Jude 20; Rev. 2:13.

7. See Lk. 18:8; Rom. 1:17; 1 Cor. 16:13; Phil. 1:25; Col. 1:23; 1 Thes. 3:10; 2 Thes. 1:3.

8. Kenneth J. Gergen, *The Saturated Self: Dilemmas of Self Identity in Contemporary Life* (San Francisco: HarperCollins, 1991), p. 139.

9. C. S. Lewis, *Surprised by Joy* (London and Glasgow: Collins, 1955), p. 179.

10. F. F. Bruce, *The Book of the Acts* (London: Marshall, Morgan and Scott, 1965), p. 361.

11. John Owen, *Hebrews*, vol. 3, p. 97.

12. Richard Baxter, *Aphorisms of Justification* (London, 1649), p. 264.

13. Calvin, *Commentary on Hebrews* (Eng. trans. Grand Rapids, MI: Eerdmans, ^{2}1976; Edinburgh: Oliver and Boyd, 1963), p. 157, commenting on Hebrews 11:1.

14. *Ibid.*, pp. 157–158.

15. Owen, *Hebrews*, p. 108, commenting on Hebrews 6:10.

16. F. Hauk's article in *TDNT*, pp. 582–584. See also *EDNT*, vol. 3, pp. 405–406.

17. See Pss. 52:9; 130:5–8; Mic. 7:7; Hab. 3:17–19.

18. See Acts 10:9–23; Eph. 2:11–22; Heb. 11:39–40.

19. *The Alternative Service Book* (1980), p. 128.

8. The security of Christian faith

1. See Is. 54:5; Je. 3:14, 20; Ho. 2:2–23; 2 Cor. 11:2; Eph. 5:25–33; Rev. 21:2.

2. On a popular level see H. A. Ironside, *Full Assurance* (Chicago, IL: Moody Press, 1937); R. T. Kendall, *Once Saved, Always Saved* (London: Hodder and Stoughton, 1983); Martyn Lloyd-Jones, *Saved in Eternity* (Westchester, IL: Crossway Books, 1988); *idem*,

Safe in the World (Westchester, IL: Crossway Books, 1988); *idem,*
Sanctified Through the Truth (Westchester, IL: Crossway Books,
1989).

For more serious study, consult the differing views of D. A.
Carson, *Divine Sovereignty and Human Responsibility* (London:
Marshall, Morgan and Scott; Atlanta: John Knox, 1981); Anthony
A. Hoekema, *Saved by Grace* (Grand Rapids, MI: Eerdmans, 1989);
I. Howard Marshall, *Kept by the Power of God* (London: Epworth,
1969) and Clark H. Pinnock (ed.), *The Grace of God, The Will of Man*
(Grand Rapids, MI: Academie Books, Zondervan, 1989).

3. See Introduction, p. 14.
4. Marshall, *Kept by the Power of God*, provides the most thorough
   exegetical study, even though some of his conclusions are
   debatable. Other than this work, for exegetical studies in
   preference to systematic studies, the reader is advised to consult
   various commentaries.
5. See chapter 6.
6. See the article by O. Böcher in *EDNT*, vol. 1, pp. 239–240.
7. Bertrand Russell, *Why I Am Not a Christian* (London: Unwin
   Paperbacks, 1979), p. 22.
8. David L. Edwards and John Stott, *Essentials* (US title *Evangelical
   Essentials*): *A Liberal–Evangelical Dialogue* (London: Hodder and
   Stoughton, 1988; Downers Grove, IL: InterVarsity Press, 1989), p.
   295.
9. For an interesting and helpful explanation of how the reality of
   hell and judgment influenced early apostolic preaching and
   evangelism see Michael Green, *Evangelism in the Early Church*
   (London: Hodder and Stoughton; Grand Rapids, MI; Eerdmans,
   1970), pp. 248–255. Green is quite right to point out that this is not
   the single motive, but it is a vitally central concern.
10. See Marshall, *Kept by the Power of God*, pp. 34–82.
11. Michael Green, *The Empty Cross of Jesus* (London: Hodder and
    Stoughton, 1984), p. 76.
12. See 1 Ch. 21:1; Jb. 1:12; Mk. 4:15; Lk. 13:16; 1 Cor. 7:5; 2 Cor. 11:14;
    1 Thes. 2:18; Rev. 2:9.
13. See 2 Cor. 4:4; Eph. 2:2; 6:12.
14. See Col. 2:8; 1 Tim. 4:1–16; Tit. 1:10 – 2:2; 2 Pet. 2:1–22.
15. See Mt. 13:7, 22; 1 Jn. 1:15–17; 5:21.
16. Leon Morris, *The Gospel According to Matthew* (Grand Rapids, MI:
    Eerdmans; Leicester: Inter-Varsity Press, 1992), p. 346.
17. See David Hill, *The Gospel of Matthew*, New Century Bible
    (London: Oliphants/Marshall, Morgan and Scott, 1972), p. 232.
18. See Mk. 13:20; Lk. 12:32; 22:31–32; Jn. 6:35–59; 13:8; 15:16; 17:12.

19. The RSV has 'apostasy'; Gk. *parapesontas*, to fall beside, to go astray, to fall away.
20. Hoekema, *Saved by Grace*, p. 246.
21. G. C. Berkouwer, *Faith and Perseverance* (Eng. trans. Grand Rapids, MI: Eerdmans, 1958), pp. 110–111, quoted in Hoekema, *Saved by Grace*, p. 247.
22. See Rom. 12:1–2; 2 Cor. 5:17; Eph. 4:22–24; Col. 3:1–4.
23. For closer attention to this issue, see the interesting work by Joanna and Alister McGrath, *The Dilemma of Self-Esteem: The Cross and Christian Confidence* (Wheaton, IL, and Cambridge, England: Crossway Books, 1992). For a slightly different approach, see also Paul Tournier, *The Strong and The Weak* (Eng. trans. Philadelphia: Westminster, n.d.; London: SCM Press, 1963).
24. Westminster Confession of Faith, XVIII.iii, in Philip Schaff, *The Creeds of the Evangelical Protestant Churches* (London: Hodder and Stoughton, 1877), pp. 638–639.
25. Quoted in T. F. Torrance, *The School of Faith: The Catechisms of the Reformed Church* (London: James Clarke, 1959), p. 201.
26. John Chapman, *A Fresh Start* (Sydney and London: St Matthias Press, 1983), p. 176.
27. See Mk. 13:33–37; 9:42–50; Mt. 25:1–30 and Lk. 12:35–48.
28. For a helpful, practical and sound study of this prayer see D. A. Carson, *A Call to Spiritual Reformation* (Grand Rapids, MI: Baker Book House; Leicester: Inter-Varsity Press, 1992), pp. 123–143, especially p. 134.
29. Westminster Confession, XVIII.iii in Schaff, *Creeds*, pp. 638–639.
30. Os Guinness, *Doubt: Faith in Two Minds* (Tring: Lion Publishing, 1979), p. 235.
31. J. I. Packer, *Knowing God* (London: Hodder and Stoughton; Downers Grove: InterVarsity Press, 1973), p. 204.
32. Baxter, *A Treatise of Conversion* (1657), in *The Practical Works of the Rev. Richard Baxter*, ed. William Orme, 23 vols. (London: James Duncan, 1830–), vol. 7, p. 207.
33. Chapman, *A Fresh Start*, p. 176.

9. The life of confidence in this age of change

1. C. S. Lewis, *The Magician's Nephew* (London: The Bodley Head, 1955), p. 124.
2. Edith Schaeffer, *The Life of Prayer* (Wheaton, IL: Crossway Books, 1992), p. 9.
3. The material and resources are available, but often only if a person knows ahead of time. It is always helpful to ask other Christians

for their recommendations. As a very practical suggestion, I often encourage people to contact L'Abri Fellowship, the ministry started by Francis and Edith Schaeffer. This work has residential and study branches in Europe and the USA. Tapes on a wide variety of subjects are available on loan and for purchase. Further information can be obtained from L'Abri Fellowship, The Manor House, Greatham, Hants. GU33 6HF, England, or 1465 12th Avenue NE, Rochester, Minnesota 55904, USA.

4. Schaeffer, *Death in the City*, in *The Complete Works of Francis A. Schaeffer*, vol. 4 (Westchester, IL: Crossway Books, 1982), p. 244.

5. Calvin, *Commentary on Ephesians* (Eng. trans. Grand Rapids, MI: Eerdmans, [2]1980; Edinburgh: Oliver and Boyd, 1965), p. 134.

6. C. S. Lewis, 'The World's Last Night' in *The World's Last Night and Other Essays* (New York: Harcourt, Brace and Jovanovich, 1960), p. 110.

7. C. S. Lewis, *The Last Battle* (New York: Collier Books, 1976; London: Bodley Head, 1956), p. 171.

8. *Ibid.*, pp. 183–184.